THE ILLUMINATION
ON ABANDONING SELF-DIRECTION

*Crown of the Faith, Abu'l Fadl
Ahmad bin Muhammad bin Abdul Karim
bin Ata'illah Al-Sakandari*

Foreword by Abu Bakr Sirajuddin Cook

Dhikr. Publications
First Published August, 2022
Sydney

Title: The Illumination on Abandoning
Self-Direction, Al Tanwir fi Isqat Al-Tadbir.

Author: Ahmad bin Muhammad bin Abdul Karim
bin Ata'illah Al-Sakandari

Editor, Foreword by: Abu Bakr Sirajuddin Cook

Translation: Omer Siddique

ISBN Print: 978-0-6450379-4-4
ISBN Ebook: 978-0-6450379-5-1

Other Titles by Dhikr.

Sayidah A'isha: Wife to the Prophet, Mother to A Nation. A Short Biography. Dr Muhammad Said Ramadan Al-Bouti

The Reviver of the Second Millenium: Imam Al-Rabbani. Shaykh Osman Nuri Topbas

dhikr.com.au

When the heedless man wakes up in the morning, he considers what he will do. While the intelligent one looks to what Allah will do with him.

- Kitab al-Hikam (Aphorisms)
Ibn Ata'illah Al-Sakandari

Map of Contents

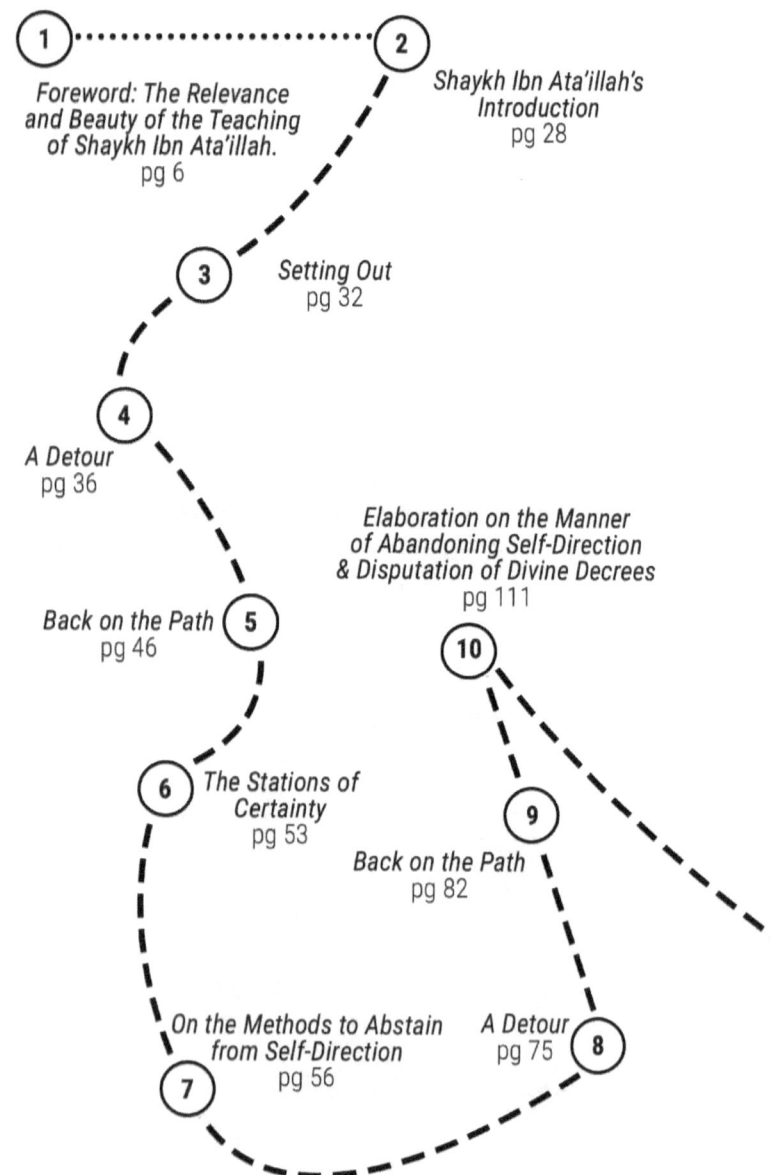

1. Foreword: The Relevance and Beauty of the Teaching of Shaykh Ibn Ata'illah.
pg 6

2. Shaykh Ibn Ata'illah's Introduction
pg 28

3. Setting Out
pg 32

4. A Detour
pg 36

5. Back on the Path
pg 46

6. The Stations of Certainty
pg 53

7. On the Methods to Abstain from Self-Direction
pg 56

8. A Detour
pg 75

9. Back on the Path
pg 82

10. Elaboration on the Manner of Abandoning Self-Direction & Disputation of Divine Decrees
pg 111

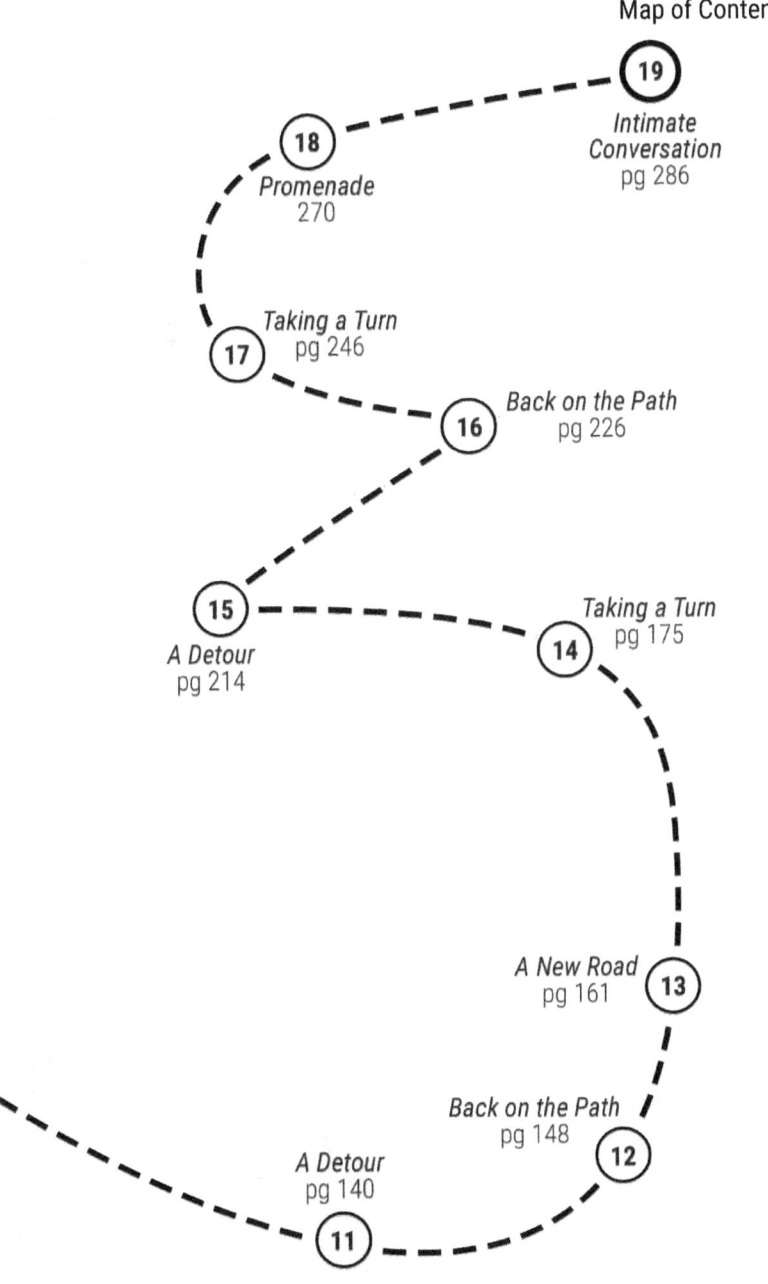

1. Foreword: The Relevance and the Beauty of the Teaching of Shaykh Ibn Ata'illah

Over the past 700 years the teachings of Shaykh Ibn Ata'illah have been repeatedly studied, commented on, reiterated, and have spread to the point where they are available across the globe, having been translated into almost every major language. This chapter is divided into three sections in an attempt to convey something of Ibn Ata'illah's life, works, and teaching. In doing so, it will be seen that despite being written so long ago the teaching of this Shaykh has lost nothing of its beauty or relevance for those seekers who happen to open any of the books of Ibn Ata'illah today.

His Life

Taj ad-Din Abu'l-Fadl Ahmad b. Muhammad b. 'Abd al-Karim b. 'Ata' Allah al-Iskandari al-Judhami ash-Shadhili, known simply as Ibn Ata'illah, was born in Alexandria, Egypt, somewhere around the middle of the 7th AH/13th CE century in Alexandria.[1] He was born into a "distinguished family of Malikite religious scholars", of whom his grandfather was "either the founder or the

---
1   Danner (1973: 1) and (1978: 13), Danner (1996: 2).

reviver of a dynasty of scholars known as the Banu Ibn 'Ata'illah."[2] Ibn Ata'illah "received a traditional Islamic education ... under some of the best and most illustrious teachers of Alexandria."[3] He looked to be following in his grandfather's footsteps "as an accomplished scholar in Maliki jurisprudence", gaining "certain renown even though he was quite young."[4] Even though his father was a disciple of Abu'l Hassan ash-Shadhili, the founder of the Shadhiliyya, Ibn Ata'illah was initially opposed to Sufism because "his fellow students had warned him that anyone who delved into Sufism would never master the Law."[5] Thus, his early life was dominated by his commitment to becoming, and being recognised by others as, a renowned jurist (*faqih*).

Ibn Ata'illah's initial opposition to Sufism manifested itself in arguments with the students of Abu'l 'Abbas al-Mursi[6], the successor to Abu'l Hasan ash-Shadhili.[7] This was

2 Danner (1978: 19).
3 Danner (1996: 2).
4 Danner (1973: 9).
5 Danner (1973: 9). Danner (1996: 3 – 4) writes that Ibn Ata'illah was "rather hostile to Sufism much like his grandfather ... but not for any definite reason".
6 On this figure see Ibn Ata'illah's *Lata'if al-Minan*, Dunlop (1945), and Botros (1976).
7 Cornell (1998: 147) challenges the successorship of Abu'l Abbas al-Mursi writing that the primary purpose of Ibn Ata'illah's *lata'if al-Minan*, against the commonly held view that it captures the teachings of the founder and first successor of the Shadhiliyya, was "to legitimize the leadership of Abu'l-'Abbas al-Mursi ... and, by extension, his successor, Ibn 'Ata'illah". While this comment is not upheld within other sources, it is understandable given comments that it was "through the circulation of Ibn Ata'illah's works the Shadhili Way began to spread in the Maghrib, which had rejected the master [i.e. Abu'l Hassan ash-Shadhili]" (Trimingham 1998: 50) and that Cornell's work examines a branch of the Shadhiliyya derived from the Tunisian, not Egyptian, linage. While this may make his comments understandable, this does not make either

until 674 AH/1276 CE when Ibn Ata'illah attended a public lecture given by Abu'l 'Abbas al-Mursi. From then on all objections towards Sufism were removed and Ibn Ata'illah became one of the most serious and promising students of Abu'l Abbas al-Mursi.[8] Evidence for this can be seen from his "development into a Sufi master capable of guiding and teaching others took place within the lifetime of his shaykh, i.e. well within the twelve-year period before [Abu'l Abbas' death in] 686 AH/1288 CE."[9] This change of heart came as a result of Abu'l Abbas' knowledge of *fiqh*, which forced Ibn Ata'illah to reassess the aforementioned judgement of his fellow students. Ibn Ata'illah was committed to both Sufism and religious law, becoming a distinguished teacher of both subjects, teaching at "both the Azhar Mosque and the Mansuriyyah Madrasah in Cairo"[10] while simultaneously "devoted to his duties as a *shaykh* in the Shadhili order ... [being] considered the foremost spokesperson for Sufism in the Mamluk capital."[11] Thus, during his life, Ibn Ata'illah was recognised as both *faqih* and *faqir*, being renowned for his knowledge of both the exoteric (*ilm az-zahir*) and esoteric (*ilm al-batin*) aspects of Islamic doctrine. Ibn Ata'illah became one of the successors of his teacher upon the latter's death.[12] Ibn Ata'illah died in Cairo "at around sixty years of age in the middle of Jumanda II 709 AH/November 1309 CE."[13]

Trimingham or Cornell correct. Furthermore, Cornell's argument ignores the fact that Abu'l Abbas al-Mursi "upon his death bequeathed the order to two men" (Durkee 2005: 57).

8   Danner (1973: 9) and (1978: 24), and Danner (1996: 4).
9   Danner (1996: 7).
10   Danner (1996: 6).
11   Danner (1973: 10).
12   Durkee (2005: 57).
13   Danner (1996: 9).

His Works

Ibn Ata'illah's works are the first compositions on the Shadhili method, without which little would be known of the first three leaders of the Shadhiliyya order, Abu'l Hassan ash-Shadhili, Abu'l Abbas al-Mursi, and Ibn Ata'illah himself.[14] Moreover, it was the dissemination of his works, especially the *Kitab al-Hikam*, which helped popularise the Shadhiliyya. Ibn Ata'illah's works also provide insight into the practice of Sufism. Regarding his works, Ibn Abbad of Ronda (d. 792 AH/1390 CE) wrote, in response to an aspirant, "the book which you have by Ibn Ata'illah, the *Kitab at-Tanwir*, comprises all that the books on Sufism, whether detailed or condensed, contain including both detailed explanations and concise expressions."[15] While Ahmad Zarruq (d. 899 AH/1494 CE) said that "the *Hikam* are to Sufism what the eyes are to the body."[16] More recently, Ibn Ata'illah's works have been used to "glimpse the ideas that were preached to the ordinary people"[17] in Mamluk Egypt and have been considered sufficient to stand as the sole representative of Sufism.[18] From this it is evident

---

14 This is not to deny the value of al-Sabbagh's (1993) *Durrat al-asrar* as a source of information on Abu'l Hassan, despite the fact that it was composed some time after the biographical *Lata'if al-minan*. However, Cornell's (1998: 147) pejorative view that the *Lata'if al-minan* "is mitigated by the fact that it was written as an apologia for the Egyptian branch of the Shadhiliyya" cannot be accepted for, among other reasons, no such apologia would be necessary (See note 7). For another early biography of Abu'l Hassan see Honerkamp (2005).
15 In Danner (1996: 16).
16 In Renard (1986: 44).
17 Shoshan (1993: 14).
18 Jackson (2005: 194 – 197).

that both historically and contemporarily the works of Ibn Ata'illah are held in high regard.

The importance of Ibn Ata'illah's works is not solely historical. They are of historical importance as his works provide the earliest documents on the earliest Shadhiliyya Shaykhs and the teaching methods they employed. Nevertheless, these works are of relevance for contemporary readers as they deal with key aspects of the Sufi teaching such as the primacy of Allah (*tawhid*), methods of invocation (*dhikr*), the relinquishing of self-choice (*tadbir*), the necessity of a Shaykh and the importance of their company, amongst others.

Ibn Ata'illah's works include:

Kitab al-Hikam (The Book of Wisdom): This is perhaps the most widely know of his works. It is generally considered his earliest known composition. Consisting primarily of aphorisms, this work has often been the source of much contemplation which have inspired numerous commentaries. The *kitab al-hikam* is seen as a masterful summary of the lessons necessary for travelling the Sufi path.[19]

Kitab al-Lata'if al-Minan fi manaqib Abi l-'Abbas al-Mursi wa Shaykhihi Abi l Hasan (The Subtle Blessings in the Saintly Lives of Abu l-'Abbas al-Mursi and His Master Abu l-Hassan): This biographical work records some of the sayings and litanies (*ahzab*) Shadhiliyya Shaykhs. All subsequent works on Abu l-Hassan al-Shadhili and Abu l-'Abbas al-Mursi refer, to varying degrees, to the *Lata'if* and is an essential source for information on this period

---

19   For a translation of this work see Danner (1973) and (1978).

of development of the Shadhiliyya order. This work is also somewhat autobiographical, without which very little could be said about the life of Ibn Ata'illah himself.[20]

Miftah al-falah wa misbah al-anwah (The Key of Success and the Lamps of Spirits): While not the first to discuss the topic of Sufi invocation (*dhikr*), this work is the first to deal solely with this topic. Ibn Ata'illah draws on the Qur'an and Hadiths, as well as earlier Sufis, to illustrate the necessity of invocation in attaining spiritual felicity. This work deals with both the general and technical aspects of invocation, covering such topics as its salvific necessity, the aliments that can be cured through the use of specific Divine names, as well as some of the etiquette (*adab*) that one should uphold within Sufi circles.[21]

Kitab al-Tanwir fi isqat al-Tadbir (The Illumination on Abandoning Self-Direction): The book before you. As the title suggests, this work deals with the elimination of self-direction. Ibn Ata'illah details how the elimination of self-direction (*isqat al-tadbir*) is necessary for the affirmation of Allah's Unicity (*tawhid*). In doing so, it is illustrated how this virtue elicits a plethora of virtues associated with the Sufi path, including, though not limited to, patience, sincerity, hope, fear, and love. This work abounds with the sayings of the first two Shadiliyya Shaykhs and as such is another important source for understanding their teaching. As quoted above, it has been considered one of the most important works in traversing the Sufi path.

Al-Qasd al-mujarrad fi ma'rifat al-Ism al-Mufrad (The Pure Goal Concerning Knowledge of the Unique Name):

---

20   For a translation of this work see Roberts (2005).
21   For a translation of this work see Danner (1996).

This work discusses various aspects of the Supreme Name, Allah. While all of his works are steeped in a metaphysics of Unicity (*tawhid*), this work draws out the ontological implications of this doctrine. In doing so, the relation of the Supreme Name, Allah, to the other Divine Names is discussed.[22]

Taj al-arus al-hawi li-tahdhib an-nufus (The Bride's Crown Containing the Discipline of Souls): Previously thought to be a composite work, this work is now considered to contain the sermons (*khutbah*) delivered by Ibn Ata'illah to both students and non-student alike. It is deemed to contain the essential principles of Sufism, though stripped of the technical language and controversial topics found in other Sufi works, presented in a manner palatable for a general audience.[23]

Unwan at-tawfiq fi adab at-tariq (The Sign of Success Concerning the Discipline of the Path): This short work is a commentary on a Qasida of Abu Madyan.[24] Through his commentary, Ibn Ata'illah highlights the importance of the relationship between a Shaykh and their student (*murid*). In doing so there is a discussion of a) the importance of keeping company with individuals who are more spiritually advanced than oneself, b) the etiquette (*adab*) of keeping such company, and c) the importance of such etiquette.[25]

Whilst Ibn Ata'illah is known to have written other works, only their titles are available.

---

22 For a translation of this work see Williams (2018).
23 For a translation of this work see Jackson (2012).
24 The Arabic and a translation of this *Qasida* can be found in Cornell (1996: 162 – 165).
25 For a translation of this work see al-Tarjumana (2005).

His Teachings

An entry point into the teachings of Ibn Ata'illah is to consider how he encourages his readers to understand the world around them. For Ibn Ata'illah one of the reasons for reconsidering the events in the natural world is the means through which an individual has the potential for spiritual development. Perception is an important tool as it is not the natural world, in and of itself, that changes rather it is the individual's response to and understanding of these stimuli that alters. The basis for such reconfiguring one's perception can be found in the Qur'an, which states "in time We shall make them fully understand Our messages [through what they perceive] in the utmost horizons [of the universe] and within themselves" (41: 53). Through his works, Ibn Ata'illah's readers are encouraged to develop a hermeneutic method which involves identifying and deciphering the signs. The imperative for developing such a method comes directly from the Qur'an in verses such as "We have indeed made the signs clear unto you, if you would only use your reason" (3: 118) and that "on the earth there are signs [of God's existence, visible] to all who are endowed with inner certainty, just as [there are signs thereof] within your own selves" (51: 20 – 21).[26] These signs (*ayat*), for Ibn Ata'illah, are existent so that the Oneness of Allah (*tawhid*) can be understood and affirmed through multiplicity. While they are evident upon the earth and within the individual, and concentrated within the Qur'an, they are difficult to decipher for those who do not a) use reason and b) have

---

26   Just as the Qur'an is made up of verses or signs (*ayat*), these verses indicate that so too is creation. This is one reason for it being called the "Book of Nature" in various traditions.

inner certainty (*yakin*).

Ibn Ata'illah's works attempt to aid the reader in developing their perception such that they can decipher these signs. The importance of this is that such signs are the communication between Creator and creation and it is through an understanding of them that an individual can gain insight into how they can affirm Allah's unicity (*tawhid*), what could be said to be *the* central purpose of Islam and Islamic practice. Ibn Ata'illah can be seen to deploy a method that will here be called soteriological semiotics. It is an understanding of the signs within creation so that the individual can further understand their relationship with Allah. Due to Allah's all-inclusive Oneness, His communication to creation through creation exists irrespective of an individual's awareness of it. As a result spiritual development is linked not to a change in the quantity of an individual's perception but to the quality of their perception. This is an aspect of what is meant when Sufi texts encourage the reader to focus on the meaning and not the form. An example of this can be seen in the following statement of Abu'l Abbas who stated,

There are four times in which the slave will find himself, of which there is no fifth: blessing, affliction, obedience, and disobedience. In each of these times, there is an aspect of slave-hood which the Truth requires of you by virtue of His Lordship. If it is a time of obedience, your path is to bear witness to God's grace, since it is He who has guided you into this obedience and has made it possible for you. If it is a time of disobedience, your path is to seek God's forgiveness and repent. If it is a time of blessing, your path is to give thanks, which means for your heart to rejoice in God. If it is a time of affliction, you path is to be content with

God's decree and to endure patiently.[27]

These four epistemic states delimit the possible states of the contingently existent with regard to Allah. It is important to note that these four states are not necessarily connected to the individual's soteriological development, in as far as the transition through them does not necessitate progress nor does their occurrence indicate any particular development within the individual. Rather these can be considered as four doors at the centre of Ibn Ata'illah's soteriological semiotics which demarcate the possible conditions confronting the individual and their four keys, for once a condition has been correctly diagnosed the appropriate key can be utilised, thus opening the way to pass onto another epistemic state. The importance of self-knowledge for the individual's soteriological development is here evident in that it allows for a) a correct diagnosis and b) the knowledge of which key to utilise. Thus it is evident that once the sign is deciphered the possibility for further spiritual development arises. Yet, while Ibn Ata'illah's soteriological semiotics involves the development of the ability to correctly decipher the signs, he also places great emphasis on keeping company with those "endowed with inner certainty" (*yakin*) so that the novice can be certain about their deciphering of the signs (*ayat*).

Within Ibn Ata'illah's works reason and certainty, while having a complimentary function, differ by degrees. While, he commends the use of reason,[28] it is seen as a stepping stone to the development of certainty (*yakin*). While the use of reason can produce sound proofs, and for

---

27 *Lata'if al-Minan*, p. 251.
28 For an example of this see his analysis the logical necessity of the existence of one, and only one, God in the *Miftah al-falah*.

this reason are a useful aid in establishing certainty, they are completely noetic, and thus of limited use. Whereas, certainty (*yakin*) arises as a result of enacting a deep seated conviction and it is this embodiment of a proof that highlights their qualitative difference. Ibn Ata'illah touches on this difference by explaining that "all certainty entails faith, though not all faith entails certainty" as "the difference between them is that while faith might be attended by heedlessness, such is not the case with certainty."[29] Certainty is epistemologically greater than proofs because it carries an unshakable and unrefusable resolve unlike evidence or proofs. He writes that "Shaykh Abu'l Hasan (may God be pleased with him) said, 'we view God with the perceptive powers of faith and certainty, which has freed us from the need for evidence and proof.'"[30] While this in no way discards the use of reason, this quote is important because it highlights that reason is seen to be only a preliminary stage, the proofs from which the individual is later free to hold or discard upon the advent of certainty (*yakin*).

As an individual increases in certainty (*yakin*) their self-direction (*tadbir*) decreases. The increase on certainty (*yakin*) allows the individual to understand what Allah requires of them and why Allah has placed them in that particular state in any given moment. Rather than choosing a course of action that will seemingly benefit them, the individual begins to be certain of the course of action that will affirm Allah's Unicity (*tawhid*). In deferring to Allah the individual begins to abide in the station of slave-hood (*'ubudiyyah*). Regarding this, Ibn Ata'illah states that "the most majestic station a slave can attain is

---

29 *Lata'if al-Minan*, p. 47.
30 *Lata'if al-Minan*, p. 53.

(complete) slave-hood to Allah."[31] The exulted position within which this station is held can be seen in Qur'anic verses such as "Limitless in His glory is He who transported His slave by night..." (17: 1), "and in what We bestowed from on high upon Our slave" (8: 41), and "whenever a slave of God stands up in prayer to Him" (72: 19). It is the intimacy and connection between Allah and His slave that is the focus for Ibn Ata'illah, whether the slave stands to commune with, receives bestowal from, or is moved by Allah rather than choosing their own direction (*tadbir*). For an individual to develop this intimate connection with Allah, according to Ibn Ata'illah, it is imperative to "know that the spirit of slave-hood and its secret is only abandoning one's choice and opposition against Allah's decrees."[32] The reason for this is that "self-choice" and "self-direction" treats the individual as an independent, rather than contingent, entity, thus contradicting Allah's Unicity (*tawhid*). In order to "abandon self-choice" Ibn Ata'illah divides this task into two distinct aspects, writing "external submission is to act following Allah's commands" and "inner submission is the absence of opposition to His decrees."[33] Outer compliance, which includes religious rites, involves the abandoning of self-choice in preference for deferring to the Prophetic example, whereas inner compliance, involving "the absence of conflict and opposition" to Allah, is abandoning self-choice in preference for Allah's choice. In both cases slave-hood can be seen to detach the individual from preoccupation with worldly concerns so that they are free to devote their attention to Allah.

Self-direction and self-reliance are intimately

---

31 *Kitab at-Tanwir*.
32 *Kitab at-Tanwir*.
33 *Kitab at-Tanwir*.

connected, and for this reason are equally contrary to Allah's Unicity (*tawhid*). Ibn Ata'illah quotes Abu'l Hassan as having said, "*choose not to choose*,"[34] which, in light of Allah's Unicity (*tawhid*), is understandable considering that taking oneself as an authority effaces the authority of Allah. Abu'l Hassan is advocating for Allah's Unicity (*tawhid*) in two ways. Firstly, by abrogating self-choice the individual is effaced through a denial of self-reliance and, in turn, the alternative is trust and reliance on Allah. On this point Ibn Ata'illah writes that "if you wish to enter into the presence of God ... then that will not be possible for you so long as other than God lords it over your heart, for verily, you belong to whosoever has authority over you."[35] Secondly, the possibility of choice presupposes multiplicity which is reaffirmed through self-choice. The Qur'an states "thy Sustainer creates whatever He wills; and He chooses [for mankind] whatever is best for them" (28:68). Regarding this, Ibn Ata'illah writes that since "it is He who creates what He wills, so He manages them how He wills,"[36] indicating that knowledge of creation's ontological inefficiency, as he takes this Qur'anic passage to specify, should be sufficient to abrogate self-direction and self-reliance. For Ibn Ata'illah[37] the verse "is, then, He who creates comparable to any [being] that cannot create" (16: 17) closes the possibility of further disputing this point.

However, it is not always clear, especially for the novice, what course of action affirms Allah's Unicity (*tawhid*). For this Ibn Ata'illah prescribes keeping company with those who have reached the goal of the Sufi path, as well as those who are striving towards it. One reason for this is that to

---

34 *Kitab at-Tanwir*.
35 *Miftah al-Falah*, p. 103 – 04.
36 *Kitab at-Tanwir*.
37 *Kitab at-Tanwir*.

act in accordance with Allah's Will requires good etiquette (*adab*), which can only be gained progressively, starting with those who show good etiquette (*adab*) towards Allah and those who are striving to. Regarding the company one keeps, Ibn Ata'illah writes that "from the characteristics of the animal-self (*nafs*), is that it desires to become like, imitate and take on the characteristics of who it accompanies" such that "your companionship of the heedless help it to become heedless."[38] Thus, through good company an individual is able to develop their etiquette (*adab*) through imitation and correction of spiritually detrimental actions. However, he is quick to point out that merely attaining the company of others is not enough for "company is a form, and *adab* [etiquette] is its *ruh* [spirit]," indicating that etiquette (*adab*) is the internal compliment of company, such that "if you join the form and the *ruh* [spirit], you will benefit of their company" yet without its internal compliment "your company is a corpse."[39] This indicates that company is only spiritually beneficial if their example is used to help establish and maintain etiquette (*adab*) within oneself.

Ibn Ata'illah is insistent on being scrupulous in choosing the right company. He states "do not keep company with anyone whose state does not inspire you and whose speech does not lead you to God."[40] He further demarcates the minimum criteria for those whose company is to be kept, stating,

Shaykh Abu'l Hassan said: "There are four etiquettes, that if they are abandoned by the seeker of Allah engaged with worldly means, then attach no importance to him, be

---

38 *Kitab al-Tanwir*.
39 *Unwan al-Tawfiq*, p. 8.
40 *Kitab al-Hikam*, 31.

he even the most knowledgeable of men. They are: avoiding closeness with oppressors, giving preference to the people of the hereafter, giving consoling charity to the poverty-stricken, and sticking to performing the five prayers in congregation."[41]

While each of these, to varying degrees, are obvious signs of piety, their combination marks the minimum etiquette (*adab*) for inspiring others and leading them to realise their inherent contingency and ontological poverty. While Ibn Ata'illah draws on the Qur'an and the Hadith in justifying each of the four properties as virtues, consistent across each justification is the idea that these properties maintain and strengthen, for the individual who observes them, the means of realising and embodying creations inherent ontological poverty. By avoiding oppressors the practice of religion is secure, the people of the other world, here meaning "the friends of Allah (*awliya*),"[42] aid in the implementation of etiquette (*adab*), the poor are a symbolic reminder of each creation's own ontological poverty and their aid helps in detaching from contingent things, while maintaining the congregational prayers both strengthens the resolve of the attendees and removes each individual from their worldly pursuits to refocus and reorient themselves towards Allah.[43] These four properties ensure for those who observe them the minimum for constancy in etiquette (*adab*) such that, without even one of these, their spiritual development would stagnate and could not be considered as fitting company for those who desire further spiritual development.

---

41 *Kitab al-Tanwir.*
42 *Kitab al-Tanwir.*
43 *Kitab al-Tanwir.*

In implementing etiquette (*adab*) the company of others is informative. For spiritual development Ibn Ata'illah recommends that an individual keep company with an individual "who casts off secondary causes and turns away from hindrances" and has "realised the reality of *la ilaha ill'Allah Muhammadan Rasulu'llah* [there is no god but Allah and Muhammad is the Messenger of Allah]."[44] Their "casting off secondary causes" is a direct indication of their company with, and good etiquette (*adab*) towards, Allah and their realisation of the *kalimah* is indicative of their embodiment of Allah's Unicity (*tawhid*). The reasoning behind keeping such company is that an individual with this degree of spiritual development is able to "make you recognise the Path and he will surmount the steep roads for you and remove impediments from your heart."[45] Those individuals who have undergone this sort of spiritual development know the road and are able to steer the aspirant around various stumbling blocks which can cause impediment, such that "when the seeker finds a guide, then let him obey what he orders him to do, and let him abstain from what he prohibits or restrains him from doing."[46] In doing so, the aspirant is able shorten the 'journey' due to their avoiding impediments. For these reasons, amongst others, Ibn Ata'illah advises "get his company and have *adab* [etiquette] in his assembly."[47]

Yet Ibn Ata'illah is clear that such company is not the goal. Keeping good company is meant to be a means to having company with Allah. Ibn Ata'illah writes "prepare for this behaviour with your brothers ... so that it will become

---

44   *Unwan al-Tawfiq*, p. 7
45   *Unwan al-Tawfiq*, p. 7.
46   *Miftah al-Falah*, p. 94.
47   *Unwan al-Tawfiq*, p. 7.

a stairway for you by which you obtain access to behaving with the Lord of heaven."[48] The reason why good company is a preliminary measure is because such individuals "take on the character of their Master, as it is related, 'take on the good character of Allah'."[49] The importance of this passage is threefold in that a) it shows that the ultimate example for etiquette (adab) is Allah, b) by taking on "the character of their Master" those travelling the Sufi path strive for harmony between the contingent and the absolute, and c) following on from the previous point, it is through etiquette (adab) that Allah's Unicity (tawhid) is affirmed and, in a sense, experienced within multiplicity. Ibn Ata'illah can be read as commenting on this last point when he states that "when you see Allah as the Doer in all you see all beings as agreeable,"[50] for in knowing that creation acts in accordance with (tawhid), as Allah is the Doer, nothing can be considered disagreeable for this would be contending with Allah.

Etiquette (adab) culminates in developing a good etiquette towards Allah. Ibn Ata'illah quotes a Hadith that states "God Most High says, 'I am of the same thinking as my slave is towards Me,'"[51] which can be seen as a key to Ibn Ata'illah's ethics. This Hadith gives impetus to develop and implement etiquette (adab), for the way the slave thinks of Allah will be returned to them. To think good of Allah involves knowledge of Allah and, as "whoever knows himself knows his Lord," this involves both knowledge of Allah's Unicity (tawhid) and knowledge of creation's inherent ontological poverty. To ensure that such knowledge improves each individual's thinking of Allah, Ibn Ata'illah writes "if you

---
48 *Unwan al-Tawfiq*, p. 10.
49 *Unwan al-Tawfiq*, p .11.
50 *Unwan al-Tawfiq*, p. 11.
51 *Miftah al-Falah*, p. 59 – 60.

have not improved your thinking of Him because of His nature, improve it because of His treatment of you."[52] As "the reward of deeds dependsupon the intentions,"[53] by improving one's thinking of Allah, as a result of knowledge, the intentions are correspondingly raised and, in turn, better etiquette is developed.

Whilst etiquette (*adab*) with Allah can be seen as a particular tier of etiquette, above other such tiers, it is also to be understood as the zenith in the hierarchy of tiers for it encompasses all subsequent tiers. There is a Hadith Qudsi within which Allah states

O son of Adam, I asked you for food and you fed Me not. He will say: O Lord, and how should I feed You when You are the Lord of the worlds? He will say: Did you not know that My slave So-and-so asked you for food and you fed him not? Did you not know that had you fed him you would surely have found that with Me?[54]

This can be read as a clear indication that maintaining good manners with creation is, in accordance with Allah's Oneness (*tawhid*), maintaining them with Allah. However, Ibn Ata'illah shows an awareness of the difficulty of a) maintaining an awareness of this implication and b) maintaining a corresponding degree of etiquette. He writes that "outwardly, creatures (*al-akwan*) are an illusion (*ghirra*), but, inwardly, they are an admonition (*'ibra*)"[55] indicating that a) abiding with creatures, rather than Allah, is an admonition from Allah for it indicates a weakness of the awareness of His Unicity (*tawhid*) and b) when abiding with

---

52 *Kitab al-Hikam*, p. 31.
53 *Sahih al-Bukhari* (Hadith # 1).
54 *Hadith Qudsi* (Hadith # 18).
55 *Kitab al-Hikam*, p. 36.

Allah, it is through creatures that Allah's admonition comes, hence the necessity of a soteriological semiotics. Furthermore, Ibn Ata'illah states that "if you want to know your standing with Him, look at where He has made you abide now,"[56] indicating that one's position within creation is indicative of one's relation with Allah. The development of etiquette (*adab*) with Allah does not result in an ontological effacement of creatures. Rather, the realisation that "creatures (*al-akwan*) are an illusion (*ghirra*)" is an epistemological reorientation which leaves creation's contingent 'reality' intact while realising that they are a pedagogical trope that enacts a soteriological semiotics. Thus, the primacy and unity of Allah is affirmed through engagement with the multiplicity of ontologically contingent creatures.

While much more could be written on the teaching of Ibn Ata'illah, two things become apparent from this brief overview. These are the relevance and the beauty of the teaching of Shaykh Ibn Ata'illah. By capturing the heart of the Sufi path within his works, and by providing a practical approach, Ibn Ata'illah's lucid prose transcends historical and geographical locality. By outlining a method of soteriological semiotics, while emphasising the importance of keeping company with those who can read the signs, Shaykh Ibn Ata'illah's teaching will remain relevant for every seeker who desires to read the book of nature and see their Lord's communication therein. That his relevance is escalating in the modern world can be seen through the ever-increasing diversity of languages that his works are being translated into and studied. The succinctness with which Ibn Ata'illah captures his teaching and conveys that of his predecessors ensures for works that encapsulate the Sufi path in a beautiful and readable manner. While, at the

[56] *Kitab al Hikam*, p. 35.

same time, the teaching espoused therein encourages and aids his readers to pierce the forms that surround them to perceive the beauty of the Divine unfolding through creation. These alone ensure the perennial flourishing of the teaching of Shaykh Ibn Ata'illah.

Bibliography

Botros, S. M 1976, *Abu al-'Abbas al-Mursi: A Study of Some Aspects of His Mystical Thought*, unpublished M.A. thesis, McGill University.

Al-Bukhari, *Sahih al-Bukhari* 9 vols., trans. M. M. Khan 1997, Darussalam, Riyadh.

Cook, A. B. S. 2017, *Ibn Ata'illah, Muslim Sufi Saint and Gift of Heaven*, Cambridge Scholars Publishing, Newcastle upon Tyne.

Cornell, V. J. 1996, *The Way of Abu Madyan*, The Islamic Texts Society, Cambridge.

1998, *Realm of the Saint: Power and Authority in Moroccan Sufism*, University of Texas Press, Austin.

Danner, M. A. K. 1996, *The Key to Salvation*, The Islamic Texts Society, Cambridge.

Danner, V. 1973, *Sufi Aphorisms*, E. J. Brill, Leiden.

1978, *The Book of Wisdom*, Paulist Press, New York.

Dunlop, D. M. 1945, 'A Spanish Muslim Saint: Abu'l-'Abbas Al-Mursi', *The Muslim World*, vol 35, pp. 181 – 196.

Durkee, A. N. 2005, *The School of the Shadhdhuliyyah: Vol 1 Orisons*, The Other Press, Malaysia.

Geoffroy, E. (ed.) 2005, *Une voie soufie dans le monde: la Shâdhiliyya*, Maisonneuve & Larose, Paris.

Hadith Qudsi, tans. E. Ibrahim and D. Johnson-Davies n.d., Millat Book Centre, India.

Honerkamp, K., 'A Biography of Abû l-Hasan al-Shâdhilî dating from the Fourteenth Century', in E. Geoffroy (ed.) 2005, pp. 73 – 87.

Ibn Ata'illah, *Kitab al-Hikam*, trans. in V. Danner 1973.

Lata'if al-Minan, trans. in N. Roberts 2005.

Miftah al-Falah wa Misbah al-Arwah, trans. in M. A. K. Danner 1996.

Unwan al-Tawfiq fi adab al-Tariq, in A. A. R. al-Tarjumana (trans.) 2005, pp. 6 – 15.

Jackson, S. A. 2005, *Islam and the Blackamerican*, Oxford University Press, New York.

2012, *Sufism for Non-Sufis?*, Oxford University Press, New York.

Renard, J. 1986, *Ibn 'Abbād of Ronda Letters of the Sūfī Path*, Paulist Press, New Jersey.

Roberts, N. 2005, *The Subtle Blessings in the Saintly Lives of Abu al-Abbas al-Mursi & His Master Abu al-Hasan*, Fons Vitae, Louisville.

Al-Sabbagh, I., *The Mystical Teachings of al-Shadhili*, trans. Douglas, E. H. 1993, State University of New York Press, Albany.

Shoshan, B. 1993, *Popular Culture in Medieval Cairo*, Cambridge University Press, Cambridge.

Al-Tarjumana, A. A. R. (trans.) 2005, *Self-Knowledge Commentaries on Sufic Songs*, Madinah Press, Capetown.

Trimingham, J. S. 1998, *The Sufi Orders in Islam*, Oxford University Press, New York.

Williams, K. 2018, *The Pure Intention: On Knowledge of the Unique Name*, The Islamic Texts Society, Cambridge.

2. Shaykh Ibn Ata'illah's Introduction

The praise belongs to Allah, who alone is responsible for creating and managing all affairs. He is Alone in commandment and decree. The King, in whose kingdom neither assistant nor minister is known. Who possess all – nothing escapes His ownership, be it big or small. The Sacred One, so perfect in His Attributes, there remains no similarity nor peer with His creation. The Knowing of All, from whose glance the deepest of thoughts are not hidden. "**Does He who created not know? He is the Subtle, the Aware.**"[1] He who encompasses the beginning of all things as well as their final outcomes. The All-Hearing, it makes no difference to Him if voices are pronounced or less than whispered. The perpetual Provider, who favours His creation by bringing to them their nourishment. The Self-Sufficient, who alone suffices for them in all their states and conditions. The Bestower, the One who gifted the living their life. The All-Powerful, and He returns life to them after their deaths. The Reckoner, and He will repay them in full for their good and their evil on the Day they arrive before Him.

Glorified be He as God, who so generously enriches His slaves even before they come into existence. He undertook the distribution of their sustenance whether they accepted Him or not. To every existent thing He outstretched His gifts and bestowals. He preserves the existence of the

---

1   Quran 67:14

universe by way of His eternality.² He is clearly visible through His wisdom on His earth and by His power in His heaven.

I testify that there is no god, except Allah ﷻ alone, without partner – in the manner of a slave who has entrusted his affairs to His judgement and surrendered to His decree and plan. And I testify that Muhammad ﷺ is His slave and messenger, chosen above all His prophets. He was distinguished by acquiring an overflowing of Allah's gifts and bounties, he is both precursor and seal, and none other than he can claim this honour. He is the intercessor of all slaves, on the Day when *Al-Haqq*³ ﷻ gathers them to allot His judgement. May Allah continually bless him, his family, and his loyal companions and grant them abundant peace.

Pay heed, my brother, may Allah make you from those He loves, and gift you with His closeness, and allow you to experience the sweetness of the drink of His beloved slaves, and safeguard you by preserving the connection between Him and you. May He not turn away from you, and may He unite you with the slaves He favoured with His glad tidings, those who became broken-hearted on their understanding the reality of **"Sight comprehends Him not…"**⁴ Then He consoled them with His lights, He opened for them the garden of His friendship and bestowed on their hearts the wafting of its breezes. He made them recognise His managing of their affairs since pre-eternity and so they surrendered the reins over to Him. He revealed to them the subtle kindnesses in His decrees, so they transcended

---

2 If His assistance was cut-off from His creation for even an instant, all creation would cease to exist.

3 From the beautiful names of Allah. Literally – The Reality.

4 Quran 6:103

disputation and stubbornness against Him. Thus, they surrendered to Him and entrusted all their affairs to Him, fully knowing that no slave attains the pleasure of Allah ﷻ except by being pleased with Him. None reaches sincere slave-hood except by submitting to His decree. So, the thought of (seeking the aid of) other than Him does not come to their minds, nor are they touched by unease and distress. As the poet said:

> *The calamites of the age do not strike them*
> *Upon their mouths are bridles halting complaint*

Allah's decrees flow over them and all the while they praise His majesty and surrender to His command. As the poet said:

> *He sends misfortunes to strike down upon you*
> *Yet your heart is to Him in complete prostration*

Now, whoever seeks closeness with Allah ﷻ must do so by its proper door and gain access via the proper means. The most pressing matter, which is necessary for you to rid yourself of and be purified from, is your desire to control your affairs and to disagree with Allah's decrees. To expound on this point, I have put together this book and have named it '*Al-Tanweer fi Isqat Al-Tadbeer*'[5] – so that its name be in accordance with its contents and its words match its meanings. I ask Allah ﷻ that He make it only for the purpose of pleasing His Noble Self, that He accept it by His

---

5   The title is difficult to render into English but carries the meaning of being a light-giving manual on how to abolish the desire to manage or control our affairs according to our own wishes and instead hand them over to Allah, especially when His decree contradicts what we wish for and to entirely trust His decisions regarding them. The desired outcome is to increase the state of slave-hood (*'ubudiyya*) within the aspirant.

all-embracing and ever-flowing kindness, that He benefits through it both the elite (in faith) and the common man – May He accept by His love for Muhammad, upon him be peace.

Indeed, to bring about His Will, He is All-Powerful, and He is most worthy and capable of responding.

3. Setting Out

Allah, the Most High, states, "**But no, by your Nurturing Lord**[6] **(O Muhammad), they will not believe until they make you the judge between them in their disputes, and find no resistance in their selves to what you have decreed, and they surrender will full submission**"[7] And He, be He Glorified states, "**And your Nurturing Lord creates what He wills, and chooses, no choice have they. Glory be to Allah and exalted is He above the partners they ascribe!**"[8] And the Glorious states, "**Or shall man have whatsoever he longs for? Yet unto Allah belong the Hereafter and this world.**"[9]

The Messenger ﷺ said, "*He who tastes the sweetness of faith is the one pleased with Allah as Lord, Islam as religion, and Muhammad as Prophet.*"[10] And said the Messenger ﷺ, "*Worship Allah with contentment, and if you cannot, then with patience over what you dislike.*" There are other such verses and *hadiths*[11] that, whether explicitly or by alluding to, point to the abandoning of a desire to control, and worry over, the running of one's affairs in opposition to Allah's decrees.

---

6   The word *Rabb* has been translated throughout this work as 'Nurturing Lord' as it is a more precise translation than simply 'Lord'. See al-Baydawi's exegesis (*tafseer*) on Surah Fatihah, translated by Shaykh Gibril Fouad Haddad.
7   Quran 4:65
8   Quran 28:68
9   Quran 53:24-25
10   Sahih Muslim.
11   Sayings and narrations from the Prophet ﷺ.

While those of deeper knowledge (*ma'rifa*) have said – *Whoever abandons the managing of their affairs, their affairs are managed for them (i.e. by Allah)*. While Shaykh Abu'l Hassan Al-Shadhili, may Allah be pleased with him, said *"If you cannot abandon (your desire to have control over the outcome of your affairs), then manage yourself so that you do not manage (Allah's affairs)."* He also said, *"Abandon your own choosing regarding your affairs, rather choose not to choose – no, even flee from having no choice – no, flee from even your fleeing, and from each and every thing except Allah ﷻ. For it is in reality your Nurturing Lord who creates what He wills, and He is the one who chooses."*

Let us return to the words of the Most High in the verse initially mentioned – **"But no, by your Nurturing Lord (O Muhammad), they will not believe until they make you the judge between them in their disputes, and find no resistance in their selves to what you have decreed, and they surrender will full submission."** In it is an indication that true faith is only acquired by someone when Allah ﷻ and His Messenger ﷺ rule over them in their matters of speech, actions, in their taking, in their leaving, in their loving and in their aversion. This includes the religious obligations as well as submitting to His Divine decrees. Submission and obedience are necessary upon every believer unequivocally. The religious obligations are the commands and prohibitions (of the *Shariah*) which are binding responsibilities upon every slave. The Divine decrees are those matters that He decreed to fall upon you and are outside of your control. Hence, you cannot acquire true faith except by these two matters; obedience to His commands and surrender to His overpowering decrees.

Notice first that He did not negate the belief of those

who do not judge (by Allah's command) nor of those who do judge but still find unacceptance in their selves – until He took an oath by alluding to His special nurturing of His Messenger ﷺ, out of His tenderness, care, honouring and consideration for him. For Allah ﷻ did not say – No, by *the* Nurturing Lord – He only said, "**But no, by *your* Nurturing Lord (O Muhammad), they will not believe until they make you the judge between them in their disputes…**"

This verse is also emphasised by this oath, and this emphasis from Allah, be He Glorified, is due to His knowing full well that the inner selves are in the habit of loving when they overpower others in disputes and win over them, despite whether the truth is for them or against them.

The verse expresses the importance of the Messenger ﷺ with Allah ﷻ. For Allah ﷻ made His judgement the same as the Messenger's judgement and His decree the same as his decree. It is required from the slave to submit to the Prophet's judgement and comply with his command. Their faith in Allah's divinity is not accepted until they submit to the rulings of His Messenger ﷺ – since he is as his Nurturing Lord described him, "**Nor does he speak out of his own desire. It is nothing but a revelation revealed.**"[12] The Messenger's ruling is the ruling of Allah ﷻ and his decision is the decision of Allah ﷻ. The Glorified states, "**Truly those who pledge allegiance to you pledge allegiance only to Allah.**"[13] He stressed it moreover with His words, "**The hand of Allah is over their hands.**"[14]

The other indication in the verse to the Prophet's great stature and the high honour of his rank is when

---
12 Quran 53:3-4
13 Quran 48:10
14 Quran 48:10

Allah ﷻ states, **"By *your* Nurturing Lord..."** This shows how Allah ﷻ attaches the Messenger ﷺ to Himself. He mentions similarly in another verse, **"Kaf. Ha. Ya. Ayn. Saad. A reminder of the Mercy of *your* Nurturing Lord to *His* slave, Zachariah."**[15] So Al-Haqq ﷻ affiliates Himself to Muhammad ﷺ directly and to Zachariah ﷺ in the third person so that all slaves would know the difference between their two stations (with Allah) and the distance between the two, high ranks.

Now, He, be He Glorified, did not suffice to say that people are believers just by submitting to His judgements outwardly. Rather, He stipulated that there should be no inner frustration or uneasiness (i.e. Allah says in the verse, **"and (they) find no resistance in their selves"**). That is, they should feel no anguish or constriction in themselves towards the judgements of His Messenger ﷺ, no matter if the judgement was against them or for them.

This inner disunity is due only to the absence of inner-light (*nur*) and the presence of other attachments (in their hearts) – hence this frustration and constriction. The real believers are not like this. Their hearts are brimming with the light of faith, are expanded, and are opened by inner-light from *Al-Wasi'* (The Truly Vast One) and *Al-Aleem* (The All-Knowing One). He has stretched out His lights to them from His overflowing, immeasurable bounty. Their hearts have been well-prepared for the arrival of His decrees, and they entrust all matters to Him, not letting their own disapproval or even approval have any say in the matter.

---

15 Quran 19:1-2

4. A Detour

Know that *Al-Haqq* ﷻ, when He wishes to strengthen a slave to be able to bear what He has decreed upon them out of His wisdom, He dresses them with lights from His names and clothes them with His manners.[16] So, His decrees will descend, but His lights (to strengthen them) have already preceded. The slave's strength to bear those decrees is only from his Nurturing Lord and not from his self. Thus, one is capable to carry fate's burdens and have patience over its hardships.

Indeed, what helps them to bear the burden of His decrees is the arrival of His lights.

But if you like you could also say – *what helps them carry the load of Divine rulings is the opening of the door of understanding.*

Or you could say – *what strengthens them to bear calamities is the arrival of His gifts.*

Or you could say – *what strengthens them to bear Divine decrees is realising the wisdom behind His choice.*

Or you could say – *what gives them patience over His rulings is their knowing that He knows all.*

---

16   i.e. the slaves are moulded with the manners of Allah ﷻ. Hence the slave becomes patient, forbearing, generous, noble, kind, and merciful etc.

Or you could say – *what gives them patience over His actions is the splendour of His beauty.*

Or you could say – *their patience over their fate is due to their knowing that patience brings about contentment and pleasure.*

Or you could say – *what gives them patience over Allah's decrees is the removal of His veils and coverings.*

Or you could say – *what strengthens them to carry the burdens of Divine commandments is the arrival of the secrets of intimate knowledge (of Allah).*

Or you could say – *what gives them patience over His decrees is their knowledge of what those decrees contain of kindness and charity towards them.*

These are then ten reasons that bring about patience in the slave and strengthen him upon the decrees of his Master when they appear. Allah ﷻ alone is the One who bestows these gifts from His overflowing kindness. He is the benefactor of this all upon the chosen of His slaves. Let us now speak on each of these ten reasons briefly so that their benefits might be realised accordingly, and the advantages of repetition might be acquired consequently.

The First

What helps them to bear the burden of His decrees is the arrival of His lights. These blessings, when they arrive, reveal to the slave the closeness of *Al-Haqq* ﷻ to him. They realise these decrees do not come except from Him. The slave's knowledge that these decrees come directly from their Master is a cause of solace for them and bolsters their patience.

Have you not heard what Allah ﷻ said to His Messenger ﷺ, "**Be patient with the judgement of your Nurturing Lord, for you are before our eyes**"?[17] That is, it is not the decree of anyone's but His and, because of this, it should not torment you. Rather, it is the decree of your Master, faithful in His kindness and care upon you.

Lightened for me is what I meet of difficulty
Because it is You, dear Lord who decrees and examines

And it is not for man to regulate Allah's affair
Nor can he take from Allah what he desires.

A relevant parable is of a man in a dark room. Suddenly, something hits him, yet he does not know what it is or from where it came. A lamp is lit and he sees it was his Shaykh or leader. Hence his knowledge of this brings about his patience in the matter.

The Second

What helps them carry the load of Divine rulings is the opening of the door of understanding. For when Allah ﷻ wills a certain decree to fall upon His slave, and He has given the slave understanding of the wisdom behind that decree, then know that He, be He Glorified, wants to carry the burden off the slave's shoulders. Understanding brings your focus back to Allah ﷻ, makes Him your only goal, and induces your trust upon Him.

---

17   Quran 52:48

The Glorious states, "**And whosoever trusts in Allah, He suffices him.**"[18] That is, Allah suffices their needs, He protects them, He stands by them against others, and He watches over them.

In fact, being given understanding from Allah ﷻ unveils the reality of what it means to be a slave to Allah. The Most Glorified states, "**Does not Allah suffice His slave?**"[19] In fact all these ten statements revolve around the gift of understanding and are only variations of it.

The Third

What strengthens them to bear calamities is the arrival of His gifts. Indeed, your recollection of Allah's previous gifts upon you helps you bear the arrival of calamities. So just as He decrees for you the things you love, have patience over what He would love to see from you. Have you not heard the words of the Most High "**And when an affliction befell you (O believers), though you wrought an affliction twice its like, did you say – From where is this?**"[20] So, Al-Haqq ﷻ consoled them of their defeat[21] by (reminding them of) their victory. This is like previous blessings which, when remembered at the moment of tribulation, lighten the burden upon the slave brought close to Him.

Also, He makes them realise the great reward He has kept in store for them within that calamity and that gives them fortitude. As does the strength and tranquility which He sends down upon their hearts. As does what He sends

---

18   Quran 65:3
19   Quran 39:36
20   Quran 3:165
21   i.e. their defeat at the battle of Uhud after gaining victory at Badr.

upon them from subtle kindnesses and favours. So much so, that some of the Companions would say to their sicknesses, *"Intensify in your grip!"* While one of those with intimate knowledge would say, *"I have become so sick, but I love that the (spiritual) gifts and secrets of Allah continue to descend."* But this is not the place for delving into that.

The Fourth

What strengthens them to bear Divine decrees is realising the wisdom behind His choice. The slave, upon witnessing His excellent choosing, understands that it is not the purpose of *Al-Haqq* ﷻ to pain His slave because He is especially merciful to them, **"And He is Especially-Merciful to the believers."**[22]

The Messenger ﷺ once saw a woman with her child and asked his companions, *"Do you think this woman would throw her child into fire?"*

They replied, *"No, O Messenger of Allah."*

He said, *"And Allah is more compassionate to His believing slave than she is to her child."*

Rather, He decrees upon you these difficulties because of what they necessitate of blessings and bounties. Have you not heard the words of the Glorious **"Surely, the steadfast will certainly be given their reward without measure"**?[23]

If *Al-Haqq* ﷻ was to leave His decrees to the whims of His slaves, His favours would be prevented, and they

---

22   Quran 33:43
23   Quran 39:10

would be prevented from entering His paradise. So, all praise and gratitude are to Him for His excellence in choosing.

Have you not heard the words of the Most Glorified **"But it may be that you hate a thing though it be good for you, and it may be that you love a thing though it be evil for you"**?[24] A compassionate father would surely drive his son to the blade of the surgeon – and not for the desire to cause pain. The well-meaning doctor treats you with stinging medicine, even when it troubles you. If he consented to your wishes, you would forfeit your healing.

As for the one who is prevented from something and recognises that as a blessing, then this is not withholding at all but bestowal. It is like a merciful mother who prevents her child from overeating out of fear of indigestion and gluttony. Because of this Shaykh Abu'l Hassan Al-Shadhili, may Allah be pleased with him, said, *"Know that Al-Haqq does not withhold from you out of a refusal to give, but as a mercy and kindness for you."*

So, the withholding of Allah is in fact His gifting, yet none realises this hidden gift except a truthful person (*siddeeq*). From the words we have recorded in another book are – *"Certainly, what will lighten from your shoulders the pain of calamity, is your knowledge that it is He, be He glorified, who is the one who trials you."*[25] So, the One who directed fate upon you is the same who has excellence of choice regarding your affair.

---

24 Quran 2:216
25 *Kitab Al-Hikam*

The Fifth

What gives them patience over His rulings is their knowing that He knows all. That is, the slave knows that Al-Haqq ﷻ is well acquainted with what He has tested the slave with. This knowledge lightens the burden of the calamity for him. Have you not heard the words of the Glorious **"Be patient with the judgement of your Nurturing Lord, for you are before Our eyes"**?[26] That is, *what you – O Muhammad – have experienced from the disbelievers from the Quraysh, of stubbornness and denial, is not concealed from Us.*

Related to this, is the well-known story of a man whipped ninety-nine times, yet he did not let out a single sigh. But, on the hundredth strike, he cried out. He was asked about this and replied, *"The one for whose sake I was bearing the whippings for was in the gathering looking on – until the ninety-ninth whip. When he turned away (and no longer witnessed my ordeal), I then sensed the pain."*

The Sixth

What gives them patience over His actions is the splendour of His beauty. Al-Haqq ﷻ removes the sourness of difficulties from them when He manifests signs of His beauty to His slaves during those troubles. He lets them taste and experience from the sweetness of the manifestation.[27] Perhaps that delight will completely overpower them, leaving no trace of pain. Sufficient for you to understand this are the words of Allah **"Then when they saw him, they so admired him, they proceeded cutting their hands all the**

---

26   Quran 52:48
27   i.e. their contemplating and recollection of Allah, that the Beautiful One is rememebering them in His decrees, wisdom and actions. And Allah knows best.

while exclaiming – 'Allah be praised! This is no human being; this is but an angel of nobility'."[28]

The Seventh

Their patience over their fate is due to their knowing that patience brings about contentment and pleasure. Whoever remains patient upon the decrees of Allah ﷻ, it will lead to acquiring contentment from Allah ﷻ. So, they bear its sourness to seek the resulting contentment. Much like bitter medicine is sipped in the hope it will lead to healing.

The Eighth

What gives them patience over Allah's decrees is the removal of His veils and coverings. Al-Haqq ﷻ, when He wishes to remove the burden which He has placed upon His slaves, uncovers the veils from the insight of their hearts. The slave recognises the closeness of Allah, and that delight makes one oblivious to pain.

If Al-Haqq ﷻ was to manifest His beauty and perfection to the people of hellfire, it would make them oblivious to their punishment. Just as if He were to veil Himself from the people of Paradise, all happiness would cease to exist for them.

Punishment is then the presence of veils between Allah ﷻ and His creation. The degree of punishment is according to the degree of His veiling. Bliss is only in His revealing and manifestations. Its joy is dependent on the intensity of His manifestation.

---

[28] Quran 12:31. Referring to the Prophet Joseph ﷺ. When the wealthy women of Egypt cast their eyes upon him, instead of the fruit before them they were meant to cut, they began cutting their hands and did not even realise it out of their fascination of the Prophet's beauty.

The Ninth

What strengthens them to carry the burdens of Divine commandments is the arrival of the secrets of intimate knowledge (of Allah). All imposed obligations are taxing upon the slave. These include abiding by His commands, restraining from His prohibitions, patience with His decrees, and gratitude for His blessings. These obligations then revolve around four matters: obedience, sin, blessings, and trials. They are indeed four, having not fifth.

All four circumstances demand an obligation from you that is due to Allah ﷻ. Due to Him because of His being Lord and Master. His due upon you concerning obedience is that you recognise His favour on you in regard to it (i.e. His empowering you to abide by obedience in the first place). His right upon you regarding sins is your seeking of forgiveness over what you have committed. His right upon you regarding trials is showing patience to Him throughout them. And His right upon you regarding blessings is your gratitude throughout.

Further, what will lighten all these burdens upon you is proper understanding. If you recognise that obedience returns and yields benefits to you, it will grant you steadfastness in performing acts of obedience. If you know that persistence in sin and wandering into them necessitates punishment from Allah – either later (in the Hereafter or later in your life) or immediately by the removal of the lights of faith – it would be a motive for you to abandon them. Likewise, if you understood that patience returns to you its fruits, and lowers into your reach its blessings, you would hasten to it and rely upon it. If you knew that gratitude comprises of an increase in blessings from Allah

– for He says, "**If you give thanks, I shall surely grant you increase...**"[29] – it would be a reason for your diligence and your rising towards Him. We shall, Allah willing, expound on these four matters near the end of this book and dedicate a chapter to it.

The Tenth

What gives them patience over His decrees is their knowledge of what He has placed in those decrees of kindness and charity towards themselves. Indeed, *Al-Haqq* ﷻ has embedded His kindness and mercy within the disliked things that befall you. Have you not heard the words of the Most High "**But it may be that you hate a thing though it be good for you, and it may be that you love a thing though it be evil for you**"?[30] Or the words of His Messenger ﷺ, "*Paradise is surrounded by what is disliked and Hellfire is surrounded by what is desirous*"?

Within trials, sicknesses, and poverty are secrets of His mercy that none understand except those of spiritual insight. Do you not see that trials and strife calm and subdue one's animal-self (*nafs*), humiliate it, and jolt it out of its heedless seeking of desires?

Indeed, with afflictions occurs humility, and with humility occurs victory – "**Allah certainly gave you (O believers) victory at Badr, when you were lowly.**"[31] But to delve into that would take us out of the purpose of this book.

---

29 Quran 14:7
30 Quran 2:216
31 Quran: 3:123

5. Back on the Path

Let us return to the verse in which the Glorious states, "**But no, by your Nurturing Lord (O Muhammad), they will not believe until they make you the judge between them in their disputes, and find no resistance in their selves to what you have decreed, and they surrender will full submission.**"

Know the relevant times are three: before Allah's judgement, during it, and after it. As for before it, slave-hood to Allah ﷻ requires resorting to His judgement. As for during and after, slave-hood consists of having no feelings of frustration, since some rulings may induce feelings of bitterness within you. If you were to be discontent with His judgement, it would only be submission to the judgement outwardly and aversion to it inwardly. There is no place for that regarding Allah's judgement.

One might ask – If no resistance is shown against Allah's judgement, one would have fully surrendered. Then what is the purpose of His repeating "**...and they surrender with full submission**" at the end of the verse? It is already mentioned that they are free from internal resistance and conflict, so it is already deduced they are in a state of submission. Why is it repeated?

The reply to that is that "**they surrender will full submission**" applies to all your affairs. If you argued that that is already obvious by the Most High's words – "**until they make you (O Muhammad) the judge,**" then the rebuttal is that the judging initially referred to in the verse is limited to the arbitration of disputes since He links it with "**...between them in their disputes.**"

The verse then revolves around three matters:

The first relates to arbitration or judging between disputes.

The second relates to the absence of feelings of frustration or opposition to those judgements.

The third relates to complete and absolute surrender in their inner-selves for both that decision and *all other Divine decrees that befall them*. It is the mentioning of what is specific before what is general.[32] So understand!

The second, relevant verse we mentioned was "**And your Lord creates what He wills, and chooses, no choice have they. Glory be to Allah and exalted is He above the partners they ascribe!**" It contains multiple benefits.

His words "**And your Lord creates what He wills**" are an obligation upon the slave to not interfere with Allah's managing of your affairs. Since it is He who creates what He wills, so He manages them how He wills. Likewise, one who does not create has no claim to manage what is created. "**Is He Who creates like one who creates not? Will you not, then, reflect?**"[33]

As for His words "**...and (He) chooses...**" expresses His exclusivity in choosing (for the management of His creation). He is not forced or impelled towards His actions,

---

32   Such ordering is often used as a rhetorical device.
33   Quran 16:17

rather they come out of His will and choice. In that is found the requirement upon the slave to delegate management and choosing over to Him since what is for Him cannot be for you.

His words "**...no choice have they**" has two aspects. The first is that it is not fitting that slaves have any choice in the matter of His decree. They can never claim to be better at choosing than the Glorious ﷻ. The second is that they have no choice in the matter period. It is as if He says – *We have not given them the choice in the first place nor given them precedence in it over Us.*

His words "**...the partners they ascribe**" exalts Allah ﷻ over the idea that His slaves have any choice or authority alongside His choice. The verse makes evident that whoever claims to have a choice in Allah's managing of affairs, alongside Him, is a polytheist *(mushrik)*. A claimant of divinity for himself made evident through his very state – even if he denies it with his tongue.

The third, relevant verse consists of the Most High's words "**Or shall man have whatsoever he longs for? Yet unto Allah belong the Hereafter and this world.**" It also indicates the abandoning of your own self-direction.

"**Or shall man have whatsoever he longs for?**" That is – *it is not appropriate that slaves have anything, except what We have prepared for them*. A point which is accentuated by the Most High then stating, "**Yet unto Allah belong the Hereafter and this world.**" It enjoins upon the slave to abandon management alongside His management. If the Hereafter is for Him as well as this world, then humankind has no part in them. Neither is it fitting that people administer and manage what are not their possessions. It is only fitting that the One who owns the two worlds be the one to manage them, and that is Allah, the Glorious.

Consider also the words of the Prophet ﷺ, *"He who tastes the sweetness of faith is the one pleased with Allah as Lord, Islam as religion, and Muhammad as Prophet."* It too contains multiple benefits.

His words, upon him be peace, *"He who tastes the sweetness of faith is the one pleased with Allah as Lord..."* contain proof that whoever does not have this quality does not taste the sweetness of faith and cannot appreciate its delight. Such a one's faith is only a body with no soul. An empty shell. A conception of the mind with no truth behind it.

On the other hand, this phrase indicates that if hearts are free of the sicknesses of heedlessness and preoccupation with desires, they enjoy the sweetness of understanding just as others enjoy the delights of foods. Such sweetness is only tasted by one pleased with Allah ﷻ as his Lord. They are those who surrender to Him, obey His commands, and throw the reins of control over to the excellent determination and choice of Allah ﷻ – far from the delusions of their own managing and choice. Such find the sweetness of life and true relief, by surrendering their burdens over to Allah ﷻ.

When one is pleased with Allah ﷻ, one receives Allah's pleasure, as He states, **"Allah is content with them and they content with Him."**[34] If one is blessed with Allah's pleasure, Allah ﷻ brings about its sweetness in the heart to show the slave the value of what He honoured him with. Hence, the slave can recognise the kindness of Allah upon

---

34 Quran 98:8

him.

Yet, there is no being pleased with Allah, except with understanding, and there is no understanding except with light *(nur)*, and there is no light except with being brought close to Allah, and there is no closeness except with heedfulness. So, when heedfulness was bestowed upon the slave, gifts and favours from His treasures followed. When Allah's support and light reaches the slave, his heart is cleansed from (spiritual) sicknesses and disorder. He becomes capable of perception and tastes the sweetness of faith due to his, now, unimpaired awareness and soundness of understanding.

But if one's heart is diseased with heedlessness of Allah ﷻ, he would not be aware of such sweetness. Fever, at times, causes the taste of sugar to be bitter – a distortion of reality. Only when the heart is cured of its sicknesses, does it understand things as they truly are. It then can sense the sweetness of faith, the delight of obedience, and the bitterness of being removed from Allah ﷻ and disobedience to Him.

The heart which tastes the sweetness of faith is in delight and grateful for recognising the favour of its Nurturing Lord. The sweetness compels it to seek the means that will preserve this faith and boost its delight. As for the heart that tastes the sweetness of obedience, it ensures consistency in obedience, as well as witnessing the kindness of Allah ﷻ. While tasting the bitterness of disbelief and disobedience necessitates that the heart flees from them and loses its passion for them. One then achieves purity from sin and from yearning for it.

Realise that not every person who abandons sin also

abandons the desire for that sin, yet alone becomes averse to it. It is the light of the heart that guides one to recognise that disobedience towards Allah ﷻ and heedlessness of Him is a deadly poison. The hearts of the believers flee from any discord with Allah, just as you flee from poison.

Returning to the *hadith*, his words, "...*Islam as religion*..." denote that if one is pleased with Islam as religion, then one is pleased with what Allah is pleased with and with His excellent choosing. The Most Glorified states, **"Truly the religion in the sight of Allah is Islam."**[35] He also states, **"Whosoever seeks a religion other than Islam, it shall never be accepted of him."**[36] He also states, **"Allah has chosen for you the religion, so die not except as Muslims."**[37]

These verses necessitate obedience to His commands, refraining from His prohibitions, enjoining good, prohibiting evil, and having passion enough for the religion that if one sees a denier trying to insinuate falsehood into it, one refutes him with Islam's proofs and extinguishes the effect of that lie on himself with his faith.

Finally, his words, "...*and Muhammad as Prophet*," necessitate that whoever is pleased with Muhammad ﷺ as his prophet, should be his supporter, take on his character and customs, mould himself to his values, be abstinent to this world while seeking the world beyond this one, forgive the offender, overlook harm done to oneself, as well as imitate his other virtues. One might then fulfil the pledge of allegiance to the Prophet ﷺ through word and by action, through taking and leaving, loving and disliking, both

---
35   Quran 3:19
36   Quran 3:85
37   Quran 2: 132

outwardly and inwardly.

Whoever is pleased with Allah ﷻ, surrenders to Him. Whoever is pleased with Islam acts upon it. Whoever is pleased with Muhammad ﷺ follows him. None of these can exist without the others. It is inconceivable that one is pleased with Allah ﷻ as Lord and not with Islam as religion. Or with Islam as religion but not Muhammad ﷺ as prophet. It is obvious enough to need no explanation.

6. The Stations of Certainty

If you have so far understood, then know – the stations of certainty are nine. They are repentance *(taubah)*, abstinence *(zuhd)*, patience *(sabr)*, gratitude *(shukr)*, fear *(khawf)*, hope *(raja')*, trust *(tawakkul)*, love *(mahabbah)*, and contentment *(rida')*. None of these stations can be attained except by abandoning the managing of, and having choice in, Allah's affairs.

The one in a state of repentance *(taubah)* necessarily repents from his sins. But he must also repent from trying to manage his Lord's affairs, for that is amongst the greatest of sins of the heart. *Taubah*, is in fact, repenting to Allah ﷻ from everything He does not like to see in you. He would not be pleased to see you trying to interfere with His affairs as it is joining partners *(shirk)* to His sole Lordship, to His exclusivity as the Nurturer. Further, it is ingratitude and denial to the blessing of the intelligence. Likewise, He is not pleased by ingratitude. How can the repentance of a slave be sound when he is worried about how his worldly affairs are to be managed and is oblivious to the excellent care and nurturing of his Guardian ﷻ?

Neither is the station of abstinence *(zuhd)* attained except by doing away with the worry over Allah's managing. Since, from what *zuhd* requires abandonment of and abstinence in, is abstinence of any opposition to Allah's decrees or His managing of your affairs.

There are two types of *zuhd*. One is outer and

apparent and the other is inner and hidden. As for the outer and apparent, it is the known abstinence from different kinds of permissible things like food, clothing, and the like. But the hidden abstinence is freeing oneself from the yearning for power, fame, and the like. This latter type also includes abstaining from the yearning to control Allah's decrees.

Likewise, neither patience *(sabr)* nor gratitude *(shukr)* are valid except with the dropping of one's managing with Allah ﷻ. The patient one shows restraint and fortitude over what Allah ﷻ would not like to see from him. From amongst that which He does not like, is administering alongside Him and having a choice over how His dominion should be run.

Patience too is of different types: self-control over the forbidden, perseverance in fulfilling His commandments, and restraint from management over, and having choice in, His dominion. If you wanted, you could describe it as patience in turning away from what is worldly and patience in worshipping – and from the demands of worship, is not managing alongside Allah ﷻ.

Likewise, gratitude *(shukr)* is not attained except when a slave abandons managing Allah's affairs. Imam Al-Junaid ؓ said, *"Gratitude is that Allah is not disobeyed through His blessings."* If it was not for the intellect, through which He distinguished you and made as a means for you to reach your full potential, you could never (assume to) self-direct your affairs. Just as inanimate objects and animals have no concern over managing Allah's affairs due to their absence of intellect. It is the intellect that concerns itself with consequences that occur in the future.

Self-direction also contradicts the stations of fear

(*khawf*) and hope (*raja'*). A healthy fear of Allah ﷻ, when it strikes the heart, prevents it from taking lightly any opposition to His decrees. As for hope, the hopeful have their hearts full of joy with Allah ﷻ and their time is spent by being busy with Him. What time do they have to manage Allah's affairs?!

Self-direction also contradicts the station of trust (*tawakkul*). The one who entrusts himself to Allah ﷻ, throws the reins over to Him and relies on Him in all affairs. This necessitates there be no administering alongside Him and surrendering to the flow of His decree. The connection is the most obvious here in this station as well as the station of contentment (*rida'*).

Then there is the station of love (*mahabbah*). The lovers are engrossed in the love of their Beloved ﷻ. Abandoning their own will for the Beloved's will is the essence of their goal. Nor do the lovers have the convenience to plan Allah's affairs because of their preoccupation with being in love with Him. That is why it has been said, *"Whoever tastes a little of the pure love of Allah becomes unconcerned with everything else."*

So too does the station of contentment (*rida'*) contradict having a choice in Allah's managing of affairs. That is clear and needs no extrapolation. The one pleased with Allah ﷻ is content and satisfied with His planning and management, so why would he manage and administer what he is in complete contentment with? Do you not know the light of *rida'* washes away the filth of self-direction from the heart? The one pleased with Allah ﷻ has his path made easy to accept His decrees and abandons administering alongside Him. The excellent choice of their Master suffices for the slave. So understand.

7. On the Methods to Abstain from Self-Direction

Know that certain means will help you rid yourself of managing and having choice alongside Allah ﷻ.

The First

The first is your realisation of Allah's previous managing and planning for you. That is, that you know Allah ﷻ was administering your affairs before you were even doing so yourself. Just as He was managing for you before you existed, and nothing of your managing was aiding Him, likewise He is managing for you after your coming into existence. So be to Him like you were and He shall be for you like He was (in His excellent management and choice for you).

Abu'l Hussayn Al-Hallaj ؓ said, "*Be for me like You were for me when I was not.*" He asked that Allah manage his affairs after his coming into this world just as He was managing them before that. For Allah ﷻ was taking care of the affairs of all His slaves in His knowledge before they came into existence. So, if the slave was non-existent at that time (in which the administering of his entire existence was being organised), the claim the slave has any real management over his life collapses.

If you question how one's life can be managed at a

time they are non-existent, then know that all things exist in the knowledge of Allah ﷻ, even if they do not have material existence. So, *Al-Haqq*, be He glorified, oversees its management in respect to its existence in His knowledge. This matter has incredible depth, but this is not the place to roam its valleys.

A Signpost

Know that *Al-Haqq*, be He glorified, has watched over you, managing and attending to you through all stages of your existence with benevolence and kindness. First, He established His excellent choice for you on the Day of Decrees, the day when He said, "**'Am I not your Nurturing Lord?' they said 'You are certainly, we bear witness'.**"[38] From His excellent arranging for you that day was His acquainting Himself with you and you recognised Him. He manifested Himself to you and you witnessed Him. It was He who made you speak and inspired you with the response that affirmed that He is indeed your Nurturer and Lord and that He is one and alone.

Then He made you a drop of sperm deposited in the loins of your fathers. He took the responsibility for you there, managing and preserving you as well as the one you were inside of. He continued His support to you through the medium of your father and his fathers all the way back to your father Adam ﷺ. He then cast you into the womb of your mother and He took care of you with His excellent oversight. He made the womb an earth in which your nourishment and growth could take place and a storehouse

---

38   Quran 7:172

from where you could receive your life.

He combined and then united the two (sperm and ovum), upon which Divine wisdom demonstrated the secret of existence being built upon pairs. He then made you into a blood clot ready for whatever Allah, be He glorified, wanted to bestow upon you. Then into a lump of flesh in which He cleft your form and established your shape. Then He blew into you your spirit (*ruh*). He nourished you in the womb through blood, His sustenance entering into you before you even exited out into the world. He kept you safe in the womb of your mother until your body members strengthened and your shape solidified so that you could make your emergence to what He decreed, both for and against you, so that you could come into this home and come to know His abounding favours and justice upon you.

When He brought you into this world, and He – be He glorified – knew that you could not chew food with the absence of molars, yet alone any teeth at all, He made flow two breasts of gentle nourishment and entrusted them to the mercy in your mother's heart. Every time the milk stopped flowing, the mercy He placed for you in her heart would urge the milk to flow on, unceasingly and without fail. Then He busied your father and mother in ensuring your welfare, in showering kindnesses upon you, and looking upon you with the eye of love.

Is this anything other than His compassion that He confers upon His slaves in the guise of fathers and mothers, through which He makes known His kindness and love? In reality, nothing supported you but His Nurturing Lordship. Nothing favoured you, but His Divinity.

He enjoined upon your father to undertake your care until you came of age, which compelled him to treat you with kindness. Allah ﷻ lifted the pen of recording your responsibilities until the time of your maturity and understanding. Till you became middle-aged or elderly, His bestowals and bounties did not cease. Then, He calls back your soul, gathers you to Him and He makes you stand right before Him. Then, He delivers you from His punishment and He enters you into His reward. Then He removes the veils between Himself and you! Then, He prepares for you a throne amongst a gathering of His friends (*awliya*) and loved ones!

The Glorious states, **"Truly the pious are amidst Gardens and a stream, upon a seat of truth before an Omnipotent King."**[39] Then which of His kindnesses will you thank Him for? Which of His favours or generosities can you keep in mind? Listen to His words, be He Glorified, **"Whatever blessing you have, it is from Allah."**[40] Know that you have never left, nor can you ever leave His kindness and blessings.

If you desire a declaration of the successive stages of your development and life, hear the Glorified's words, **"And indeed We created man from a draught of clay. Then We made him a drop in a secure dwelling place. Then of the drop We created a blood clot, then of the blood clot We created a lump of flesh, then of the lump of flesh We created bones and We clothed the bones with flesh; then We brought him into being as another creation. Blessed is Allah, the best of creators! Then indeed you shall die thereafter. Then surely you shall be raised up on the Day**

---

39 Quran 54:54-55
40 Quran 16:53

of Resurrection."[41] Flashes of light will appear to you to illuminate its meanings.

In all this is what compels you, O slave, to surrender to Him and trust upon Him. What will aid you to do this is abandoning the management of His affairs and abstaining from contesting His decrees and Allah alone provides success.

* * * * *

The Second

Know that giving regard to your own management instead of Allah's management is your ignorance regarding what is best for you. The believer has recognised that if he leaves the managing to Allah ﷻ, he will secure for himself the best managing of his affairs. For He states, **"And whosoever trusts in Allah, He suffices him."**[42] So your management lies in abandoning management and your concern for yourself lies in abandoning your concern for yourself. Understand the words of the Most Glorious **"come into houses by their (proper) doors."**[43] So the door to Allah's excellent running of your affairs is abandoning the management of His decrees concerning yourself.

The Third

The third is that you realise that Divine decrees do not

---

41   Quran 23:12-16
42   Quran 65:3
43   Quran 2:189

always flow according to your planning and management. In fact, the majority of what occurs you did not plan for and how little of what you plan for actually occurs! The intelligent do not build their houses upon unstable ground. When will your house ever be completed while Divine decrees tear it down?

> *On what day will the building be completed*
> *If you build it up and someone else pulls it down?*

If you plan but Divine decrees run contrary to your plan, then what is the benefit of planning not supported by Divine decree? Rather, the real management of affairs can only be by the One who holds the reins of all decrees in His hands. Hence the poet said:

> *When I saw His decrees in such smooth-running flow*
> *Then without worry or distrust, I can honestly say –*
>
> *I trust totally upon Him who created me*
> *And throw myself in with that smooth-running flow*

The Fourth

The fourth is your realisation that He is responsible for managing His kingdom, its high and low, hidden and visible. Just as you have charged Him to be responsible for His throne, His podium (*kursi*), His heavens and His earth, likewise delegate to Him the oversight of your existence.

Your existence compared to those worlds is as nothing. For the seven heavens and seven earths compared to His podium (*kursi*) are like a ring lost in a desert. His podium, His seven heavens and seven earths together compared to His throne are like a ring lost in a desert. What are you then amid His kingdom?

Your concern over yourself and your attempt of controlling all your affairs is your ignorance of Allah ﷻ. The matter is how the Glorified explained, "**They did not measure Allah with His true measure.**"[44] If the slave knew his Nurturing Lord, he would be too embarrassed to manage alongside Him. If you have fallen into the quagmire of self-direction, it is because you are veiled from Him.

For those of certain faith, when the perception of their hearts is unveiled, they witness themselves as managed not managers, dispatched not dispatchers, incited not inciters.

Such are the inhabitants of the Highest Assembly,[45] who witness the emergence of Allah's absolute power, the permeating domination of His will, the concord between His power and what it overwhelms, and between His will and what it seeks out. Since secondary causes are removed from their perspectives, they are purified of making false claims (of attributing deeds, feats, power etc. to themselves or creation). That is due to their unimpaired observation of reality and confrontation with it.

That is why the Most Glorified states, "**Surely We shall inherit the earth and whatsoever is upon it.**"[46] This verse is praise of the angels and indicates they are purified from claiming ownership over what Allah ﷻ entrusted to them. They do not claim that they are the source of what was attributed to them. For if they did, He would have said – *We shall inherit the earth and the heavens...* Rather, they attribute

---

44   Quran 6:91
45   *al-Mala' ul-A'la*, the heavenly assembly of angels according to Ibn Kathir and others.
46   Quran 19:40

everything to Him. Their bewilderment of, and infatuation with, His power prevents them from relying on anything besides Him.

So, just as you have entrusted the running of His heavens and His earth to Him, hand over to Him His running of your existence. **"Surely the creation of the heavens and the earth is greater than the creation of mankind."**[47]

The Fifth

It is that you realise you are a possession of Allah and you do not manage what is not yours. What you do not own, you do not manage its affairs. If you, O slave, do not dispute among yourselves over rights of ownership – and in reality, you own nothing except what He assigned to you and have no true ownership other than a legal right that His law ascribes to you without any merit on your part that warrants it – then it is more fitting and proper that you do not dispute with Allah over His possessions.

To add to that, the Most Glorious states, **"Truly Allah has purchased from the believers their souls and their wealth in exchange for the Garden being theirs."**[48] How can there be a dispute over the administering of something after its sale? What you have sold requires you to hand it over and to raise no dispute over its management. For to manage and administer it would be a nullification of the sale contract.

Once I entered the presence of Shaykh Abu'l Abbas Al-Mursi, may Allah be pleased with him, and complained to him about some of my affairs. He said *"If your self truly*

---

47   Quran 40:57
48   Quran 9:111

belongs to you, then put it in order as you please. But you will never be able to do so. If it belongs to its Originator, hand it over to Him and He will put it in order, as He wills." Then he said, *"Relief is in resignation to Allah and in abandoning the management alongside Him – and that is true slave-hood (to Allah)."*

Ibrahim ibn Adham, may Allah be pleased with him, said, *"One night I slept missing my daily supplications (wird) and regretted that when I awoke. Over the next three days, I was overcome with sleep and missed some of my obligatory prayers. When I awoke I heard a voice saying:*

> *Anything you commit can be forgiven*
> *Except the turning away from Us*
>
> *We have forgiven you what has passed*
> *But what has passed you was greater still*

Then it was said to me, 'O Ibrahim, be a slave!' So, I committed myself to being a slave to Allah and found relief."

The Sixth

The sixth is your knowledge that you are a guest of Allah ﷻ. The world is a home that belongs to Allah ﷻ and you only tarry here a short while. From the proper manners of the guest is not to worry about the host's running of his guesthouse.

It was said to Shaykh Abu Madyan, may Allah be pleased with him, *"O my master. Why is it we see other shaykhs occupying themselves with causes and means of the world (asbab), yet we do not see you doing so?"*

The Shaykh replied, *"My brother, judge me fairly. The world belongs to Allah. We tarry here only as His guests."*

The Messenger, upon him be peace said, *"Being a guest is for three days."* Likewise, we are guests with Allah ﷻ for three days. But the Glorified states, **"And truly a day with your Lord is as a thousand years of that which you reckon."**[49] So out of those 3000 years of our being His guests is what we spend on His earth, and He will complete what remains from that in the next world out of His favour, and then increase upon that, with everlasting life.

The Seventh

The seventh is your realising that Allah is Self-Sufficient from all things and does not need you. Have you not heard His words **"Allah, there is no god but He, the Living, the Self-Subsisting"**?[50]

He is Allah, Most Glorified, the Self-Sufficient One of this world and the next. He alone sustains this world with His nourishing and bestowal. He alone sustains the next world with His reward and recompense.

When the slave recognises his Nurturing Lord's self-sufficiency and His power in executing His affairs, he throws the reins over to Him, falls prostrate before Him, hands himself over in surrender to his Master, and looks forward to whatever comes upon him from his Master's will and decree.

The Eighth

The eighth is the slave's busying himself with worship and the duties of slave-hood, which is what is demanded from one's life as He states, **"And worship your**

49	Quran 22:47
50	Quran 2:255

Nurturing Lord, till the certainty (death) comes upon you."[51]

Hence, if the slave directs his energy to the demands of being Allah's slave, it will preoccupy him from concerning himself with Allah's management of his life and worry over it. Shaykh Abu'l Hassan Al-Shadhili ﷺ said, *"Know that there is upon you, at every moment, something of slave-hood due to Al-Haqq as required by His Lordship."* The slave is obliged to perform and be responsible for this worship. Even over the breaths he takes, which are a trust from *Al-Haqq* ﷻ. What time does one then have to overlook the priority of fulfilling Allah's rights so that one can begin managing the affairs of one's worldly interests, fortunes and goals?

No one attains the special favour of Allah, except by abandoning one's selfish interests and abstaining from them, by expending one's energy to reach closeness to Allah ﷻ, by taking all means to remain in harmony with His will and being diligent in His service and dealings with Him. According to the level of disregard for your selfish desires, will Allah ﷻ bring you closer to Him.

That is why Shaykh Abu'l Hassan ﷺ said, *"O you, racing on the path to your success, yearning to be in His presence and by His side! Reduce your concern for your outer*[52] *if you desire your inner illuminated with the secrets of the kingdoms of your Nurturing Lord."*

The Ninth

The ninth is that you are a slave, owned by a Master. It is binding on the slave that he not be worried about

---

51 Quran 15:99
52 Your material and selfish desires.

being in the slave-hood of his Master when the Master is characterised by great generosity, having no fault or flaw. The essence of being in the station of slave-hood is trust in Allah and surrender to Him. This entirely contradicts trying to manage His affairs.

Rather, it is incumbent on the slave that he serves the Master, and the Master bestows His favours upon the slave. The slave must serve, and the Master looks after him out of His grace. Understand His words "**And bid your family to prayer and be steadfast therein. We ask no provision of you; We provide for you.**"[53] That is, serve Us, and We are responsible for allocating to you your sustenance.

The Tenth

The tenth is realising your ignorance over the outcome of affairs. Perhaps you planned a matter thinking it to be in your interests, but it was to your detriment. Or perhaps you received benefits from your difficulties. Or hardships from what you thought was for your benefit. Or injuries and harm in the guise of happiness. Or happiness in the guise of harm. Perhaps a gift was hidden within a tragedy or a tragedy within a gift. Or perhaps you profited from the hands of your enemies. Or were harmed by the hands of your friends.

If such is reality, then how can any intelligent person try and manage affairs alongside Allah , when he does not know where happiness lies so he might grasp it or where the harm lies so he might avoid it? That is why Shaykh Abu'l Hassan said, *"O Allah, we have been powerless in repelling harm from ourselves when we know it is harmful. How can we have any success over what we do not know to be harmful?!"*

But suffices for you the words of Allah be He glorified **"...it may be that you hate a thing though it be good for you, and it may be that you love a thing though it be evil for you. Allah knows, and you know not.**"[54]

How often did you, O slave, desire a thing but He diverted it away? You found grief in your heart and frustration within until the reality of the matter was uncovered, and you recognised Allah, the Glorious, taking care of you through His most excellent concern for you. He did so in a manner you could not imagine, choosing for you from whence you could not know. How reprehensible then it is that a seeker of Allah (*mureed*) does not understand that, or a slave does not surrender to Him. Become as the poet said:

How often I desired what You turned away from me
How often You remained to me, more than me, devoted

So, I resolve upon myself to ignore every thought
And hand it over to You, let it be Your preference

And that You never see me together with Your prohibition
For Your Greatness and Immensity is deep in my heart hidden

It has been related that from amongst the righteous was he who, whenever he was told about some trial or misfortune afflicting him would simply reply, "*It is good.*" It just so happened one night, a wolf came along and took off with his rooster. When he was notified he replied, "*It is good.*" The same day his dog was wounded and died. He simply replied, "*It is good.*" Then his old and exhausted

---

54   Quran 2:216

donkey perished but he only said, "*It is good,*" annoying his household considerably.

That night, a band of marauding bedouins raided his neighbourhood, slaughtering everyone. Everyone, that is, except this man and his family. The raiders could only make out the inhabitants in the darkness of night by the crow of a rooster, or the barking of a dog, or the braying of a donkey. Since for him, they had all died, their death was his life. So, glory belongs to the All-Wise Planner and Manager!

But how shameful of a slave is he who does not recognise the excellence of Allah's managing, planning, and choosing, except after the fact. As for the elect of Allah's slaves, they are in a class of their own. They understand the purposes of Allah ﷻ and bear witness to His excellent management of affairs before even the consequences become apparent. But even they are of different stations.

The First Station

Those who corrected and made good their opinion about Allah ﷻ and surrendered to Him after He made them accustomed to His excellent managing and kindness.

The Second Station

Those who corrected and made good their opinion about Allah ﷻ after He made them realise that worry, managing alongside Him, and disputing with His decrees does not repel what He has decreed. Nor does it win for them what He has not decreed for them.

The Third Station

Those who corrected and made good their opinion

about Allah ﷻ after hearing the words His Messenger ﷺ spoke on behalf of Him – "*I am with My slave as he thinks of Me.*" So, their good opinion of Allah ﷻ is a prayer and means in itself through which they beseech Allah ﷻ. They hope He deals with them according to the good opinion they hold of Him. Certainly, Allah ﷻ has even eased the path to His favour for the believers if they think of Him according to the verse "**Allah desires ease for you, and He does not desire hardship for you.**"[55]

The Fourth Station

Yet, more elevated than all these stations, is the surrender to Him and entrusting of affairs to Him, for the sole reason that that is *Al-Haqq's* right and what He is worthy of. Not because of any personal desire or motive from the slave.

The first group are still tied to a personal motive. One who submits to Allah ﷻ because of His continual kindnesses and bestowals, has submitted for the reason of those habitual blessings of days gone by. If they were not, neither would be his submission.

The second group is similar. For abandoning the management of one's affairs just because there is no benefit in self-direction is not leaving it purely and solely for Allah's sake. Such a slave, if he had found some benefit in his planning and management, might very well have never abandoned it.

As for the third group, the slave who surrenders to Allah ﷻ, holding a good opinion of Him so He would treat him according to those good thoughts, then he too strives

---

[55] Quran 2:185

for his personal benefit. He is afraid those favours may be lost if he was to deviate from his surrender to Allah ﷻ.

Rather, he truly has a good opinion of Allah ﷻ, who surrenders to Him and makes his opinion good about Him (and His decrees) just because of the greatness of Divinity and attributes of God-ship. This, then, is the slave who demonstrates the reality of the affair! He is worthiest to be imitated. The Messenger ﷺ alluded to them, *"Certainly, Allah has slaves for whom a single glorification they utter is equal to the mountain of Uhud (in reward)."*

Allah, be He Glorified, made a covenant with all His slaves to forsake managing alongside Him when He stated, **"And when your Nurturing Lord took from the Children of Adam, from their loins, their progeny and made them bear witness concerning themselves, 'Am I not your Nurturing Lord?' they said, 'You are certainly, we bear witness...'"**[56] For when they affirmed that He is indeed their Nurturing Lord and Master, it necessitated abandoning vying with Him in the running of His affairs. This contract existed even before the animal-self (*nafs*) existed. The animal-self is the source of uneasiness and management against Allah's management. If the slave remained upon that initial state in which the veils were removed and Allah's presence witnessed, never would the slave dare manage Allah's affairs. But when the veils were drawn, contending with Allah ﷻ manifested itself and agitation followed. Hence, those with intimate knowledge from Allah ﷻ, who witness the secrets of His kingdom, never try to manage alongside Him. Their contemplation of Allah ﷻ blesses them with this insight. It renders apart any eagerness to contend with Him. How can a slave vie with Allah ﷻ when he is continually

---

56   Quran 7:172

contemplating Him and understands the intensity of His Magnificence!?

A Point of Benefit

Know that self-direction and preferring your choice therein, is no little matter. Rather, it is of grave consequence. If we consider Adam, upon him be peace, we find that what drove him to eat from the (forbidden) tree was his attempt to manage for himself. Look to what Satan said to him and Eve, as related by Allah, "**'Your Lord has only forbidden you this tree, lest you should become angels, or among those who abide forever'.**"[57]

So, Adam pondered. He knew that eternity by the side of Allah is the greatest objective and ascension from the limits of man to the superior qualities of angels, or as he thought them to be superior. When Adam managed and planned for himself in this manner, he ate from the tree. It was only because of his planning and speculating over the command of Allah.

The design of *Al-Haqq*, however, was that He would send Adam down to earth and appoint him as His representative (*khalifah*) there. Although it appeared as descension, it was in fact ascension.

Shaykh Abu'l Hassan said, "*I swear by Allah, Allah did not send Adam down to earth to take away from him. He only sent him to earth to perfect him.*" Adam, be he blessed, always continued to advance closer to Allah. He was elevated through the ascension of being brought close to Allah and being chosen by Him (as a Prophet) just as he was elevated through the ascension of being humbled and

---

57   Quran 7:20

made submissive (to Allah) – and that is the more complete distinction. Every believer must recognise that the Prophets and Messengers are not carried from one state to another, except the second is closer to perfection than the first. Understand the words of the Most High "**And indeed the last is better for you than the first.**"[58] Regarding this verse, Ibn Attiya mentions "...*and the second state is better for you (O Muhammad) than the first state.*"

If you have understood so far, then know the management of affairs belongs to *Al-Haqq* and His will overrules. His plan came into effect that the children of Adam populate the earth and that there appear the righteous as well as the clear oppressors to themselves. Out of the planning of His wisdom was the fruition of His plan and its being made manifest in this observed and worldly realm (*alem al-shahadah*). *Al-Haqq* desired that Adam's eating from the tree be the reason for his descent onto Earth and his descent onto earth be the reason to display his status as Allah's representative – a status He gifted upon him through that descent. Hence Shaykh Abu'l Hassan said, "*By Allah, Allah had sent down Adam to the Earth before He created him when He, be He Glorified, said –* '**I am placing a representative upon the earth**'."[59]

From the excellent planning and management of Allah for Adam was his eating from the tree, his descent to earth, and finally his being honoured by Allah with the mantle of *khilafah* and leadership among men.

Since we have finished our discussion here (on the means to abandon self-direction), let us investigate the

---
58 Quran 93:4
59 Quran 2:30

benefits and gifts bestowed upon Adam ﷺ amid this event to understand that Allah's special people have a unique relationship with Him for He plans and manages for them in a way He does not do for others.

8. A Detour

There are many pearls in Adam's eating from the tree and his descent to earth.

The First

Adam and Eve ﷺ were well acquainted with Allah's sustenance, gifts, kindnesses, and blessings in Paradise. So, *Al-Haqq* ﷻ willed, from the kindness hidden in His running of affairs, that they eat from the tree, so that they also become acquainted with His forbearance, His covering, His forgiveness, repentance and their being chosen by Him.

The Second

As for forbearance, He did not hasten to punish them at the time of their action. The Forbearing One does not hasten to punish you over your deeds, rather bears patiently with you so that He may forgive and bless you or that He finally may punish and take vengeance.

The Third

He acquainted them with His covering (*sitr*). When they ate from the tree and their shame became apparent to them – as they were suddenly deprived of the garments of Paradise – He allowed them to cover themselves with its leaves. As He said, be He glorified, "**...and when they tasted of the tree, their nakedness was exposed to them, and they began to sew together the leaves of the Garden to**

cover themselves."⁶⁰ That was out of His covering.

The Fourth

Al-Haqq wanted Adam to recognise his being chosen by Allah. From this realisation sprang the stations of repentance to Him and receiving guidance from Him. *Al-Haqq* willed that Adam recognise that he was chosen as well as Allah's care for him. He allowed the eating of the tree but He did not turn away from Adam because of it. Neither did He withdraw His assistance and protection. His love and care became apparent for Adam. As one of the righteous said, *"For whom love and care have preceded, no sin will harm him (i.e. their sin will lead to humility and repentance)."* Many a love has survived one's disagreement, but what of the absolute and true love that persists for you from the Source of Love, regardless of your opposition or conformity?

As for His words, be He glorified, **"Then his Nurturing Lord chose him (Adam)"**⁶¹ – they do not signify that *Al-Haqq* chose Adam later, after eating from the tree, but *Al-Haqq* chose Adam before Adam's existence. What occurred after the oversight (of eating from the tree) was the sign of Adam's being chosen came to light. That is the meaning of His words **"Then his Nurturing Lord chose him,"** that is, the effect of his being chosen and the special care he received became apparent. His repentance to Allah and his receiving guidance from Allah was facilitated.

So, the verse **"Then his Nurturing Lord chose him, and turned to him (in forgiveness) and guided (him)"**⁶²

60	Quran 7:22
61	Quran 20:122
62	Ibid

refers to three things that were made known by this event: Adam's being chosen, repentance to Allah – which is the result of being chosen and finally, guidance – which is the result of repentance. So understand.

Upon his being sent down to earth, he became acquainted with Allah's wisdom just as he had known Allah's power in Paradise.[63] For this world is the place of taking means and taking advantage of instruments. When Adam ﷺ descended to earth he learnt harvesting, farming, and whatever else he required for his living. Through this Allah ﷻ brought about what He had warned Adam ﷺ about before his descent to earth, **"So let him (Satan) not expel the two of you from the Garden, such that you would be put to toil."**[64]

What is meant by the word "*tashqaa*" (toil) in this verse is being fatigued (in the toiling for livelihood), not (another possibility that it refers to) being miserable. Proof of this is that "*tashqaa*" is in the single form[65] (and so refers only to Adam). It is not in the dual form (in which case it would also be referring to Eve). That is so since responsibility and toiling for livelihood primarily rests upon men, not women.

---

63 This world is where Allah's wisdom has a predominant manifestation. That is why we see such a strong (albeit only apparent) relationship between cause and effect. To attain, we need to make the effort, struggle, and understand it as a means of attainment. However, in the Hereafter, the people of Paradise will just wish for something and it will appear before them – hence, Allah's power is manifested more greatly in that realm.
64 Quran 20:117
65 In Arabic, verbs can refer to one do-er (single form), two do-ers (dual form) or three and more (plural form). The verb for *tashqaa* is in the single form and not the dual, in which case it would have referred to both Adam and Eve, upon them be peace.

The Most High states, **"Men are guardians of women."**[66]

If the intended meaning of "*tashqaa*" was misery due to being distanced and veiled from Allah ﷻ, He would have said – *that the two of you become miserable (tashqayaa)*. Since Adam ﷺ is singled out here, it points to another meaning, not misery from being distanced from Allah ﷻ. Even if the word appeared in the dual form (addressing them both), we would only understand it beautifully and respectfully, returning to our initial interpretation that it refers only to physical fatigue and toil (and not Adam and Eve's being distanced from Allah).

A Noteworthy Point

Know that Adam's eating from the tree was not because of his stubbornness or his being in disharmony with Allah ﷻ. It was either because he forgot and so unwittingly reached out for the fruit, which is the opinion of some scholars derived from the Glorified's words, **"And We indeed made a pact with Adam afore time, but he forgot"**[67] – or he ate knowingly but only because Satan said to him, **"Your Lord has only forbidden you this tree, lest you should become angels, or among those who abide [forever]."**[68] It was because of his love and infatuation with Allah ﷻ that he desired what would lead to eternity by His side. He desired the qualities of angels as Adam – upon him be peace – witnessed the closeness of the angels to Allah ﷻ. He desired to eat from the tree to reach angelhood, which is a better state – or as he thought. Even the people of knowledge and intimacy are at odds as to who are of a higher rank with Allah – the angels or prophets.

66	Quran 4:34
67	Quran 20:115
68	Quran 7:20

Satan further added to his deceit, as Allah ﷻ states, **"And he swore unto them, 'Truly I am a sincere adviser unto you'."**[69] Adam, peace be upon him said, *"I did not imagine anyone would make a false oath by the name of Allah."* It was as Allah ﷻ said, **"Thus he lured them on through deception."**[70]

A Noteworthy Point

Know that Adam, blessings of Allah be upon him, would not need to relieve himself from what he ate. Rather, it would exit his body as perspiration with the smell of musk – just as the people of Paradise will do when they enter it. But when he ate from the forbidden tree, he felt the need to relieve himself.

It was said to him, *"O Adam, where will you do it? On these (lavish) cushions or those (adorned) curtains? Or by the coast of these (delightful) rivers? Descend to the earth where such an act is befitting!"*

If that was the effect of a misstep by Adam ﷺ, how can sins not affect the sinner? So understand.

A Parable

Know that everything forbidden by Allah ﷻ is a forbidden tree and the presence of Allah ﷻ is Paradise. Then it is said to the 'Adam of your heart' and the 'Eve of your animal-self (*nafs*)' – **"...approach not this tree, lest you be among the wrongdoers."**[71]

However, Adam ﷺ was blessed with Allah's

---
69 Quran 7:21
70 Quran 7:22
71 Quran 2:35

guardianship when he ate from the tree, he descended to earth to assume the responsibility of *khilafah*. But you, if you eat from the tree of forbidden fruit, will descend to the earth of being distanced from Allah, so understand! If you eat from a forbidden tree, you will be exiled from the paradise of being in harmony (with Allah), fall upon the dirt of separation (from Him) and your heart will be made miserable. When distanced from Allah, it is the heart that is made miserable not the animal-self (*nafs*). The animal-self relishes in being distanced (from Allah) because it finds its path open to what is agreeable to it, of passions, desires, idle pastimes, and heedlessness.

A Clarification

Know that Allah revealed Himself to Adam by creating him out of nothing. So, Adam called on Him – O *All-Powerful (Ya Qadeer)*! Then He made Himself known by the choosing and selecting of His will, Adam called on Him saying – O *He Who Wills (Ya Mureed)*! Then He introduced Himself to him by His wisdom when He forbade him from eating from the tree, so he called out to Him – O *Most Wise (Ya Hakeem)*! Then He decreed that he eat from the tree, so Adam called out to Him – O *He who Compells (Ya Qahir)*! Then He did not hasten to punish him, so he called out to Him – O *Forbearing One (Ya Haleem)*! Then He did not disgrace him for it (but made him His representative and prophet) so he called out to Him – O *Veiler (Ya Sattar)*! Then He forgave him and accepted his repentance, so he called out to Him – O *He Who Excessively Forgives (Ya Tawwab)*! Then Allah made Adam realise that his eating from the tree never reduced His love for him, so he called out to Him – O *Most Loving (Ya Wadud)*! Then He sent him down to the earth and He facilitated for him the means of livelihood, so he called out to Him – O *Tenderly Kind One (Ya Lateef)*! Then He strengthened Adam ﷺ to perform what He demanded from him (of worship), so he called out to Him – O *Most Mighty (Ya Qawiy)*! Then He made Adam ﷺ see deeper into the secrets of why the tree was forbidden, the eating from it, and the descent unto earth, so he called out to Him with more conviction – O *Most Wise One (Ya Hakeem)*! Then He gave him victory over the ever-plotting enemy (Satan), so he called out to Him – O *Bestower of Victory (Ya Naseer)*! Then He aided him over the burden and responsibility of worship, so he called out to Him – O *He who Supports (Ya Dhaheer)*!

Never did Allah ﷻ send him down to earth, except to perfect his knowledge of Allah ﷻ and to establish him with the duties of worship. Therefore, two forms of slave-hood were perfected in Adam, upon him be peace. The slave-hood of recognising and knowing Allah ﷻ and the slave-hood of performing duties and responsibilities. How great was the favour of Allah ﷻ upon him! How abundant His kindness! So understand!

9. Back on the Path

Know that the most majestic station a slave can attain is (complete) slave-hood to Allah. All other stations are but support and aid to this station. The words of Allah are evidence that the station of slave-hood is the most honourable station, the Most Glorious states, "**Glory be to Him Who carried *His slave* by night...**"[72], "**...if you believe in Allah and what We sent down upon *Our slave*...**"[73], "**A reminder of the mercy of your Nurturing Lord upon *His slave*...**"[74], "**...when the *slave of Allah* rose to call upon Him...**"[75]

Also, when the Messenger of Allah was given the choice of either being a prophet and king or a slave and messenger, he chose slave-hood to Allah.[76] In all this is the surest evidence that it is the most virtuous of stations and greatest in closeness with Allah.

The Messenger said, "*I am but a slave. I do not eat reclining. I am but a slave. I eat as slaves eat.*" He also said, "I

---

72 Quran 17:1
73 Quran 8:41
74 Quran 19:2
75 Quran: 72:19
76 Abu Huraira reported: The Angel Gabriel was with the Prophet, peace and blessings be upon him, and he looked towards the sky as an angel descended. Gabriel said, "Verily, this angel has not come down since the day he was created." The angel said, "O Muhammad, your Lord has sent me to you with the offer that I make you a prophet-king or a slave-messenger." Gabriel said, "Be humble before your Lord, O Muhammad." The Prophet said, "**Rather, I will be a slave-messenger**." Musnad Imam Ahmad 7120

am the master of the children of Adam, with no pride." I heard our Shaykh, Abu'l Abbas ﷺ, saying, *"'With no pride' means I do not pride myself with being their master, my pride is only in my slave-hood to Allah."* It is for slave-hood that man was first created. The Most Glorified states, **"I did not create jinn and mankind, save for My servitude."**[77]

Actions of worship are the outer expression of slave-hood, but slave-hood remains its soul. If you have understood this, then know that the spirit of slave-hood and its secret is only abandoning one's choice and opposition against Allah's decrees.

Slave-hood to Allah ﷻ is then abandoning one's claim to manage the affairs that fall under Allah's Lordship. If the station of slave-hood to Allah ﷻ, the noblest of stations, is not attained except with the abandonment of managing Allah's affairs, it becomes incumbent upon the slave to abandon it. One must take the road of surrender to Allah and commit matters to Him in order to reach that most perfect of stations and walk that most excellent path.

The Messenger of Allah ﷺ once heard Abu Bakr ﷺ reciting the Quran softly while Umar ﷺ was raising his voice in recitation. He asked Abu Bakr ﷺ, *"Why have you lowered your voice?"*

He replied, *"For sure my voice reaches the One I whisper to."*

He then asked Umar ﷺ, *"Why have you raised your voice?"*

"To awaken the heedless and ward off Satan," he replied.

The Prophet ﷺ said to Abu Bakr, *"Raise your voice a little."*

---

77   Quran 51:56

Then he turned to Umar and said, "*Lower your voice a little.*" Our Shaykh, Abu'l Abbas, would say, "*Here the Messenger wanted to pull them out of their own aims and into the Messenger's aim for them.*"

Note

Understand from this *hadith* – may Allah have mercy on you – that leaving one's will (for the will of Allah) is the most excellent of worship. Both Abu Bakr ؓ and Umar ؓ explained to the Messenger ﷺ their sound intentions when he asked them. Yet, even so, the Messenger ﷺ directed them, despite their pure intentions, to the choice of the Messenger of Allah ﷺ.

A Beneficial Point

Know that when the Children of Israel entered the desert they were nourished with (the foods of) *manna* and *salwa*. It was Allah ﷻ who chose that sustenance for them. They acquired it from the fountain of His generosity without toil or fatigue. But their animal-selves, heavy with old habits, together with their ignorance of Allah's managing for them, preferred what they were accustomed to eating. They said, **"'O Moses, we shall not endure one food, so call upon your Lord for us, that He may bring forth for us some of what the earth grows: its herbs, its cucumbers, its garlic, its lentils, its onions.' He said 'Would you substitute what is lesser for what is better? Go down to any town, and you will have what you ask for.' So they were struck with abasement and poverty, and earned a burden of wrath from Allah."**[78]

They turned their backs on what Allah ﷻ chose for

---

78 Quran 2:61

them, preferring instead what they chose for themselves. It was said to them rebukingly, "**Would you substitute what is lesser for what is better?**" The literal explanation to which is – *Do you desire garlic, lentils, and onions over manna and salwa? When the taste of manna and salwa is better and is attained without any difficulty on your part?* While from the secrets of the verse is – *Would you prefer your own desires and choosing over Allah's choosing for you? Would you substitute what is inferior and what you desire for what is better, that which Allah desires for you?* "*Go down to any town*" for what you desire is only worthy to be found down there. A secret of this wording is – *descend from the heaven of trusting in Us and Our excellent choice in running your affairs to the dirt of your own choice and self-direction*. A state of humiliation and wretchedness fitting with your choosing and managing of affairs alongside Allah ﷻ.

If this nation (of Muhammad) were gathered in that desert, due to the presence of their light (*nur*) and deep understanding, never would they utter the words the Children of Israel did. Do you not see that the Children of Israel said to Moses ﷺ at the beginning of the affair, it being the reason for their exile to the desert, "**We shall never enter it (the Holy Land), so long as they remain therein. So go forth, you and your Lord, and fight! We shall stay right here, sitting.**"[79] While at the end of their affair they said, "**O Moses, we shall not endure one food, so call upon your Lord for us...**"

Initially they refused to obey the order of Allah ﷻ and in the end they preferred to choose for themselves something other than what Allah ﷻ had chosen. How often was there evidence in their actions that they were in contradiction to

---

79 Quran 5:24

reality and indifferent to the straight path? An example of which is their saying, "**Show us Allah openly.**"[80] Or their saying to Moses ﷺ, before even the moisture on their feet had dried from crossing through the sea that had been split open for them, "**Make for us a god as they have gods,**" when passing by a people worshipping idols. They were certainly as Moses, upon him be peace, remarked, "**Truly you are an ignorant people.**"[81] Likewise the words of the Most High, "**And when We lifted the mountain above them, as if it were a canopy, and they thought it would fall upon them, 'Take hold of that which We have given you with strength, and remember what is therein, that perhaps you attain piety'.**"[82]

As for this nation (of Muhammad ﷺ), the mountain of awe for Allah and His greatness has been raised over their hearts, so they grasped the Quran and were supported by what it contains. Likewise, they were preserved from worshipping the cow (which the early Children of Israel fell into), and were saved from other than that, because Allah ﷻ chose this nation just as He chose *for this* nation, and praised it, "**You are the best community brought forth unto mankind...**"[83] Also He states, "**Thus did We make you a middle community, that you may be witnesses for mankind...**"[84] That is you follow the best and most balanced way.

Thus, it becomes clear that managing and having choice alongside Allah ﷻ are from the most severe sins and offences. If you want to win Allah's choosing for you

---

80	Quran 4:153
81	Ibid
82	Quran: 7:171
83	Quran 3:110
84	Quran 2:143

then abandon having choice over His decrees. If you desire Allah's excellent managing of affairs to be in your favour, then do not let managing of His affairs be seen from you. If you desire to reach the goal, then it entails you having no goal other than His!

That is why when it was said to Abu Yazeed Al-Bistami ﷺ, "*What do you wish for?*" He replied, "*I wish that I do not wish!*" That is, he had no wish or request from Allah, other than having no wish in opposition to Allah's wish. He knew that the abandonment of one's desire is the most excellent of miracles (*karamah*) and the most honoured distinction. It may so happen that someone attains outward miracles yet hidden within him is his own self-direction. The true miracle is only in the abandoning of managing Allah's affairs and trusting and committing to the judgement of Allah ﷻ.

In this regard, Shaykh Abu'l Hassan ﷺ said, "*There are only two comprehensive and encompassing miracles.*[85] *The first is the miracle of faith, increased by certainty and witnessing the truth. The other is the miracle of performing deeds in obedience and imitation (of the Prophet) while avoiding claims about one's righteousness and deceiving one's self. Whoever is given them, then wishes for something other than them, is a liar and a dishonest slave or has misunderstandings of knowledge and proper action. He is like someone who is given an audience with a king who is pleased with him. Yet, the man desires instead the assembly of animals and casts away the cloak of the king's approval. Every miracle not accompanied by being pleased with Allah, and Allah's pleasure with the slave, is but a deception designed to gradually lead astray, or its claimant has a shortcoming, or he*

---

85   The reference is to a *karamah*, a miracle given to a righteous slave of Allah, as opposed to a *mu'jizah*, a miracle give to a prophet.

is one destined to be destroyed." A miracle is no miracle until it is accompanied by being pleased with Allah ﷻ and that necessitates the abandonment of managing His affairs as well as one's choice, preferring instead His choice.

Some have commented that when Abu Yazeed ﷺ wished to have no wish, this itself was a wish. Such are the words of one with no intimate knowledge of Allah ﷻ. Abu Yazeed, may Allah be pleased with him, wished to have no wish because Allah ﷻ desires that neither he, nor any other slave, have a desire other than His desire. Abu Yazeed's wish was to be in harmony with what Allah ﷻ desired to see from him.

Shaykh Abu'l Hassan said, "*Choosing and selecting from the Divine law is not from your choosing, you are but hearing and obeying. Understanding this is the domain of His slaves that have special knowledge from Him and that have intimate understanding of Him. It is a world-in-itself in which knowledge of reality descends from Allah ﷻ for the one ripe enough to receive it.*"

The Shaykh directs our attention to the fact that choosing to perform actions from the Divine law (*shariah*) does not contradict the state of slave-hood to Allah ﷻ, when one's faith is founded on abandoning one's choice alongside Allah's. He mentions this so that an intelligence, deficient in grasping realities, might not be deceived in thinking that choosing to perform religious duties, litanies, and voluntary worship would take the slave out of pure slave-hood to Allah, because of their thinking that the slave played a part in choosing.

The Shaykh also stated, "*Having a choice of, and*

organising yourself with, the demands of the shariah is not from your choosing. You are only addressed to abandon your managing and choosing for yourself. Not to leave off Allah's and His Messenger's managing for you." So understand!

Thus, Abu Yazid ﷺ was justified in his wishing to have no wish because that was what Allah ﷻ desired from him. This wish of his did not take him out of proper slavehood to Allah. If you have understood this, then you have realised that the path to Allah ﷻ is through the wiping away of one's wishes and denying one's own will (in opposition to Allah's). To the extent that Shaykh Abu'l Hassan said, *"No friend of Allah reaches that state while there remains any trace of his own managing and choosing."*

I heard our Shaykh, Abu'l Abbas ﷺ saying, *"No friend of Allah reaches Allah until he even gives up his desire to reach Allah."* What he meant by this, and Allah ﷻ knows best, is the abandonment of one's desire to reach Allah ﷻ because of the proper conduct due to Him (*adab* with Allah), not because of apathy or disinterest. Nor because of one's believing they are not worthy of reaching Him, nor because of one's belittling of himself as he gets closer to Him. Not through disinterest, nor out of complacency, nor by preoccupation to anything other than Him, should one give up on the desire to reach closeness to Allah ﷻ.

Then, if you desire brilliance and illumination, upon you is the abandonment of managing alongside Allah ﷻ. Journey to Allah as the righteous did, you will attain what they attained. Travel down their road and follow their way. **"Throw down your staff"**[86] for this is the sacred valley. In a

---

86   Quran 28:31. The verse mentions the incident when Allah ﷻ ordered Moses ﷺ to throw down his staff in the sacred valley of Tuwa. Here, Imam Ibn Ata'illah ﷺ appears to use it as a metaphor for

similar vein, I composed the following lines to some of my brothers:

> *O my Companion, the caravan has set out swiftly*
> *Yet here we stand, where are you heading?*
>
> *Are you happy to sit behind after them –*
> *Held down by desires contending?*
>
> *Listen to the heavens and earth, their tongue is plain*
> *That all within them will come to their ending*
>
> *None see the right course of action save one –*
> *Purged from greed, not fooled by its coveting*
>
> *For whoever catches sight of things truly sees*
> *Creations are naught next to He who envisioned their creating*
>
> *Yes, in His valley there are lights for those wishing to enter*
> *And the realisation of secrets for those who are returning*
>
> *Arise and see all things and the light embracing them*
> *Allow its shine towards you today, be dawning*
>
> *Be His slave, cast the reins to His command*
> *And beware of your scheming, how is it befitting –*
>
> *That you plan each detail, but Someone Else is governing?*
> *Will the slave then be to the might of God, contending?*
>
> *So cast it off! Those desires and each of your own volitions*
> *That is the highest goal! I hope your heart is listening*
>
> *Such was the road of earlier caravans that followed –*
> *The footprints laid before them, so follow who is following*

---

casting away your own management and choice alongside Allah's.

Let him cry who seeks a smile from his beloved
Yet none comes his way, not even a beam fleeting

Yes, let him weep, he who is still weeping
And his time in trifling amusement, he, who is still losing.

Know – may Allah grant you success – that Allah ﷻ has slaves who have successfully abandoned management alongside Him, through His disciplining, cultivating and teaching. These lights abolished their desire to control their affairs. Their knowledge and grasp of secrets wreaked havoc on having a choice alongside His choice. They tarried in the station of contentment (with Allah) and attained its bliss. So much so, they cried out to seek Allah's help out of fear that its sweetness might distract them – lest they become attached to the station of contentment (and not to Allah), or wish to remain there forever or end up depending on it.

Shaykh Abu'l Hassan ﷺ narrates the following, "*At the beginning of my journeying to Allah, I would manage and plan which good deeds to perform. Sometimes I would say to myself – stick to the wilderness and deserts.[87] Other times I would say – return to the cities and townships to accompany the scholars and elect. Then I was told about a certain friend of Allah residing on a mountain top. I climbed it and arrived by nightfall. I disliked to call upon him at such a late hour (so waited outside) and heard him saying, 'O Allah, some people requested of You that they be given authority over Your creation and You granted them that and they were pleased with You because of it. O Allah, I ask You that You turn people away from me so that they find no other refuge except You.'*

I said to myself – from what ocean has this Shaykh scooped up

---

87   To separate from the sins involved with mixing with the common people and for contemplation of Allah.

these pearls!? I waited until the sky brightened before entering upon him. I greeted him and said, 'How are you, my master?'

He replied, 'I complain to Allah about the frost of (the station of) contentment and submission to him, just as you complain about the burn of your planning and choosing!'

I said, 'My master, as for my complaint about the burn of my planning and choosing, I have indeed tasted it and am experiencing it. But I do not understand what you mean by the frost of contentment and submission?'

He said, 'I fear that its sweetness will distract and entice me from Allah.'

I said, 'My master, I heard you saying yesterday – O Allah, some people requested of You that they be leaders over Your creation and You granted them that and they were pleased with You because of it. O Allah, I ask You that You turn people away from me so that they find no other refuge except You…?'

He smiled and said, 'My son, do not say – give me authority over Your creation. But say – O Allah, You, Yourself, be for me. Do not you see that if Allah is with you, everything is with you? What cowardly fear is it otherwise (to seek refuge in other than Him)!?'"

A Beneficial Point

Know, that the demise of Noah's son was only due to his reliance on his own managing and displeasure with the managing of Allah ﷻ when Allah ﷻ chose for Noah ﷺ and his companions of his ship. "**And Noah called out to his son, who remained aloof, 'O my son! Embark with us, and be not with the disbelievers.' He said, 'I shall take refuge on a mountain; it will protect me from the water.' He** said, 'There is no protector on this day from the Command of Allah, save for the one upon whom He has Mercy'."⁸⁸

In essence, Noah's son sought refuge in the mountain of his own intellect. The physical mountain he sought refuge in was a symbol of this inner reality. It was as Allah, Most High stated, **"and the waves came between them, and he was among the drowned."**⁸⁹ Such it was outwardly by the flood and such it was inwardly by being cut-off from Allah.

So take heed, O slave. When the waves of fate crash upon you, do not seek refuge in the mountain of your intellect lest you drown in the ocean of seperation from Allah. Rather, return to the ship of Allah's refuge and trust upon Him – **"And whosoever holds fast to Allah is indeed guided unto a straight path."**⁹⁰ **"And whosoever trusts in Allah, He suffices him."**⁹¹ If you do so, then that victorious ship will ascend to the mountain of safety and security. Then you would descend in Allah's care and enjoy the blessedness of being connected with Him, for you and **"the nations that are with you"**⁹² – that is the worlds of your existence.⁹³ Understand this and do not be heedless. Worship your Nurturing Lord and do not be from the ignorant.

By now you would have realised that abandoning one's management and choice alongside Allah's is from the most important matters that those of certain faith observe.

88	Quran 11:42-43
89	Ibid
90	Quran 3:101
91	Quran 65:3
92	Quran 11:48
93	i.e. you would enjoy Allah's blessing in all your inner faculties, such as your mind, heart, soul, *nafs* etc – and Allah knows best.

It is the goal of those constant in worship and the most honourable adornment of those with intimate knowledge (*arifeen*).

Once I asked one of those with intimate knowledge, while we were by the Ka'aba, *"In which direction is your return?"*

He replied, *"I have a habit (in dealing) with Allah, that I let not my will preceed my feet."*[94]

One of the Shaykhs said, *"If the people of Paradise have entered Paradise, and the people of the Fire entered the Fire, and I remained behind, I would have no preference as to which of the two abodes my judgement would determine for me."*[95] This is the state of a slave whose own choice and wishes have been completely removed so that there remains no will except Allah's will.

One of the righteous said, *"I have awoken with my desires found squarely within the decrees of Allah."* While Abu Hafs al Haddad ؑ said, *"For forty years, Allah has not placed me in a state which I disliked. Nor have I been annoyed when he moved me to another."* While another said, *"For forty years I wished to abandon my own wish, but could not attain what I wished for!"*

Such are the hearts that Allah ؑ has taken guardianship over. Have you not heard the words of the Most Glorified, **"'As for My slaves, truly you (Satan) have no authority over them.' And your Nurturing Lord suffices as a Guardian"**?[96] Their realisation of the

---

94   i.e. wherever Allah opens the way for me, I go.
95   i.e. I am content with whatever my Master chooses.
96   Quran 17:65

station of slave-hood, prevented them from having their own choice alongside His Lordship. It saved them from approaching sin and deficiency.

The Most Glorified states, **"Truly he (Satan) has no authority over those who believe and trust in their Nurturing Lord."**[97] Satan has no authority over hearts, one might ask, then how does he persist with his whisperings of self-direction? How does he induce confusion into their hearts? The Quranic verse clarifies that whoever corrects his faith and trust in Allah ﷻ, then Satan has no power over him. For Satan only approaches you from one of two directions. Either by inducing doubts in your faith or by seducing you to trust upon creation. As for his whispering of doubts in one's belief, true faith annihilates it. As for trust in the creation, the reliance upon Allah ﷻ purifies it.

A Point to Consider

Thoughts of opposing Allah's decrees may occur in a believer. But Allah ﷻ does not abandon him to the clutches of those thoughts. Have you not heard His words, be He glorified, **"Allah is the Protector of those who believe. He brings them out of the darknesses into the light"**?[98]

Al-Haqq ﷻ rescues believers from the darknesses of self-drection and into the brilliant lights of trust in Allah ﷻ. He casts out the delusion of their anxieties by the truth of their trust. He shakes their self-direction at its foundations and brings down its walls. As He has said, and He is Most Elevated, **"Nay, but We cast truth against falsehood, and it crushes it, and, behold, it vanishes."**[99]

97	Quran 16:99
98	Quran 2:257
99	Quran 21:18

If anxiousness and thoughts of self-direction come to a believer, then they are borrowed (from Satan) and not rooted in one's heart. They are fleeting with no real existence. For the light of faith is what has settled in the hearts of believers and its rays have enveloped them. Its gleams have eased their hearts. This residing faith refuses that anything else should settle by its side.

The occurrence of such thoughts is only natural so that the phantom of self-direction may appear. It awakens their hearts thereby and the phantom disperses, nothing more than a dream.

Allah, the Glorified states, **"Truly those who are pious, when they are touched by a visitation from Satan, they (actively) remember; so behold, they see."**[100] In this verse, there are multiple lessons.

The First

The Glorified's words **"Truly those who are pious, when they are touched by a visitation from Satan, they (actively) remember"** indicate that their original state is one of being free from the whisper of Satan. If a fleeting thought does reveal itself, then sometimes it is only to make known the arsenal of faith placed within you.

The Second

He said, **"when they are touched"** and did not say – *when they are taken hold of* or *when they are seized*. Touching is contact without grabbing hold of and without force. The phrase indicates that thoughts of desire and whim are not deep-rooted in their hearts, they touch them in passing and

---

[100] Quran 7:201

do not seize or grab hold of them like they do disbelievers. Satan dominates the disbelievers and stealthily steals from the hearts of the believers the moment their minds slumber over the guarding of their hearts. Yet when they awaken, their hearts dispatch the armies of seeking forgiveness, humility to Allah and poverty before Him. They thus retrieve from Satan what he stole and seize back what he pillaged.

The Third

In His words **"when they are touched by a visitation"** there is an indication that it is something temporary. That Satan cannot come to hearts that are continually awake and alert. He only induces a dream-like vision of heedlessness and desire upon hearts in the moment of their slumber due to oversight. Whoever does not sleep, no dream will appear to him.

The Fourth

He said, **"when they are touched by a visitation from Satan"** and did not say – *when they are touched by the arrival or lodging of Satan*. Because a visitor has no right to call it home. The evil thought is but a symbolic likeness, not real existence. The Glorified informs thereby, that they are not harmful to the righteous (*muttaqeen*). What Satan casts upon their hearts is like the dream you see in your sleep, when you awake, it disappears.

The Fifth

He said "**they (actively) remember (*tadhakur*)**"[101] and did not say – *they mention (dhikr)*. It is an indication that mentioning is not enough in expelling heedlessness when the heart itself is in a state of heedlessness. It is only remembrance deep in the heart with contemplation and meditation that repels heedlessness, even if one does not say anything with their tongue. For the arena of mentioning (*dhikr*) is the tongue, while that of remembrance (*tadhakur*) is the heart. When the whisper of desire occurs, it occurs upon hearts not tongues. What expels it is only the contemplation of the heart which purifies the place the thought occurs and extinguishes its effect.

The Sixth

He said, "**they (actively) remember**" without mentioning what it is they remember. For instance, He did not say they remember Paradise, or the Fire, or punishment, or something else. This is indeed sublime. Effective remembrance to remove the whispers of desires from the hearts of the righteous is different for each person and according to their ranks. For all have consciousness (*taqwa*) of Allah, whether they be prophets, messengers, the truthful (*siddiqeen*), friends of Allah (*awliya*) or the righteous (*saliheen*). But the *taqwa* of each varies according to their station. Even the strength of their remembrance varies accordingly. If only the recollection of one thing was mentioned it would only apply to those whose recollection of that thing was effective. If, for example, He mentioned – *they remember the reward* or *they remember previous blessings*, others would then miss out

---

101 i.e. they remember with contemplation and presence with both mind and heart.

on the fruits of the verse. The Glorified willed that nothing be explicitly mentioned regarding what they remember so that all stations be included together. So understand!

The Seventh

The Glorified states, "**they remember; so behold (*fa-ithaa*), they see**" and did not say – *they remember then (fa) they see*. Or He did not say – *they remember and after (thumma) they see*. Or He did not say – *they remember while (wa) they see*.

As for the expression – *they remember while (wa) they see* – it does not hold the meaning that their seeing the right path was because of their remembrance. The purpose of the verse is to indicate that seeing correctly is due to proper remembrance so that the slaves may be motivated to resort to it.

As for His not choosing the words – *they remember and after (thumma) they see* – it is since this expression also does not carry a strong indication of a relationship between remembering and seeing correctly. It imparts a meaning of there being a delay in their seeing clearly, which is against the gist of the verse. While the purpose of *Al-Haqq* ﷻ in the verse is to convey that the seeing aright immediately follows their remembrance.

Likewise, He did not use the expression – *they remember and then (fa) they see* – since it holds a meaning of one thing following another (without a relationship of cause and effect). Rather He chose the expression, be He glorified, "**they remember; so behold (*fa-ithaa*), they see.**" Thus, He indicated that their foresight never left them, in praise of them and illustrating His favour upon them. Just as you might say – *Zaid remembered the matter correctly*. That is, the matter was stored away soundly in his mind and he realised it only now. Likewise, the righteous always remained seeing aright. All that occurred was in the moment of the visitation of the thoughts of desire, the light of their entrenched foresight was cloaked. Yet when their hearts awaken, the Glorified expels the heedlessness and the sun of insight shines brightly.

The Eighth

In this verse and other similar ones, there is mercy for the righteous and kindness for the believers. For if He said – *those who are righteous, no visitation from Satan touches them* – no one would be included in the righteous except the Divinely protected. *Al-Haqq* ﷻ wished to expand the circle of His mercy when He said, "**Truly those who are pious, when they are touched by a visitation...**" He informs you that the occurrence of negative thoughts upon the righteous does not take them out of the band of the righteous as long as they are as He described them – quick to remember, returning to Him with contemplation.

Another verse that expands the hopes of His slaves and is full of mercy is "**Truly Allah loves those who repent, and He loves those who purify themselves.**"[102] He did not say – *He loves those who do not sin*. If He had, how few would be included in His love? But *Al-Haqq* ﷻ knew the nature of His slaves and their tendency to heedlessness and what their creation necessitated of opposing desires and predispositions.

The Most Glorious also states, "**Allah desires to lighten (your burden) for you, for man was created weak.**"[103]

| 102 | Quran 2:222 |
| 103 | Quran 4:28 |

Some scholars have said it means mankind is incapable of controlling their desires when they are enticed by them. He also states, "**He knows you best, from when He brought you forth from the earth...**"[104] Due to His knowledge of human beings being overpowered by error, He opened the door of repentance, pointed towards it and invited them to enter through it. He promised to receive them there if they repent and accept them if they return to Him.

The Messenger ﷺ said, "*All the children of Adam fall into error, and the best of those who fall in error are those who turn to Allah in repentance.*" The Messenger ﷺ has thus informed you that falling into error is a necessity of your existence, rather it is the essence of your existence.

The Most High also states, "**and who, when they commit an indecency or wrong themselves, remember Allah and then seek forgiveness for their sins—and who forgives sins but Allah?—and who do not knowingly persist in what they have done.**"[105] He did not say something like – *those who do not do indecency*.

The Most Glorious also states, "**who shun grave sins and indecencies and who, when they are angry, they forgive.**"[106] He did not say – *those who have no anger*. So understand, may Allah have mercy upon you. These are evident secrets and observable matters.

The Ninth

The ninth concerns the clarification of the ranks of those who contemplate amongst the righteous. When

---

104	Quran 53:32
105	Quran 3:135
106	Quran 42:37

an evil thought from Satan touches the righteous, their piety does not let them insist on the disobedience of their Master. Rather it brings them back to Him through their remembrance. Their deep remembrance is of the following types:

One who contemplates the reward (Allah has promised).

One who contemplates the punishment.

One who contemplates the standing (before his Lord) to be judged.

One who contemplates Allah's previous kindnesses and is ashamed to disobey Him.

One who contemplates Allah's future blessings upon one and is ashamed to repay it with ingratitude.

One who contemplates the closeness of Allah ﷻ to one.

One who contemplates that *Al-Haqq* ﷻ completely encompasses and surrounds one.

One who contemplates that *Al-Haqq* ﷻ is glancing at one now.

One who contemplates the covenant one took with Him (before being sent to this world).

One who contemplates the goal of annihilating one's desires and seeing only Allah ﷻ.

One who contemplates the harm of disobedience

and so shuns it.

One who contemplates the benefits of obedience and its associated honour and so takes its path.

One who contemplates that *Al-Haqq* is sustaining and empowering one at every moment.

One who contemplates the grandeur of *Al-Haqq* and His majestic authority.

As well as other types of remembrance and they have no limit. We only mentioned what we have to familiarise you with the states of the righteous and motivate you towards some of the stations of those of deep knowledge. So understand.

The Tenth

It is possible that what is meant by "**a visitation**" in the Most Glorious's words "**Truly those who are pious, when they are touched by a visitation from Satan…**" – is a fleeting doubt or thought occurring via the animal-self (*nafs*) by the inciting of Satan. It is called a visitation (*tayf*) because it wanders about (*yateefu*) the heart. In another reading (*qira'a*) of the verse, it is "**… when they are touched by a wanderer[107] from Satan…**" Each reading becomes an explanation for the other. The disturbing thought wanders about the heart and if it finds a way to sneak in, it is through a weak point in the fortress of faith, otherwise, it leaves.

The parable of the stations of faith and the light which surrounds them is that of high walls and a fortress

---

107   *taif* instead of *tayf*.

surrounding a city. The walls are akin to this light. The fortress is the station of faith whose territory is the heart. Whoever has a fortress of certain belief to surround his heart, who rectifies the stations[108] of his faith, which are like barriers of light, then Satan has no means to reach him nor a place to call home.

Have you not heard the words of the Most High, **"As for My slaves, truly you (O Satan) have no authority over them"**?[109] That is to say – *Satan has no authority over them since they corrected their slave-hood to Me by not contesting My decrees nor by challenging My managing of affairs. Rather they trusted Me and to Me, they surrendered.* Because of that *Al-Haqq* took responsibility for their care, their success, and their protection. They directed their worries to Him and He sufficed them from needing any other.

Now, it was said to one of those with intimate knowledge (*arifeen*), *"How is your struggle with Satan?"*

He replied, *"And who is Satan? We are a people directing our concern only with Allah. He suffices us against those other than Him."*

I heard our Shaykh, Abu'l Abbas, may Allah be pleased with him saying *"When Al-Haqq, be He Glorified, said, '****Truly Satan is an enemy unto you; so take him as an enemy****'[110] – one group understood from it that Allah is requesting enmity with Satan from them, so they directed their concern and their enmity towards him. But that distracted them from attaining the love of the Beloved . Another group understood that the*

---

108   Such as repentance, abstinence, patience, love etc. They were previously discussed by the Imam.
109   Quran 17:65
110   Quran 35:6

verse was indicating that Satan is indeed to you an enemy, but I (i.e. I, Allah, in contrast) am your beloved. So, they occupied themselves with attaining Allah's love and He sufficed them against all others."

If they seek refuge in Allah ﷻ from Satan, it is because Allah ﷻ commanded them to do so. They do not believe that anyone other than Allah has true power. How could they believe otherwise when they hear Him saying, **"It is only Allah who decides. He has commanded that you worship none but Him."**[111] The Most Glorious also states, **"Surely the scheme of Satan is ever feeble."** And He, the Most Glorious, states, **"As for My slaves, truly you (O Satan) have no authority over them."** And the Most High states, **"Truly he (Satan) has no authority over those who believe and trust in their Nurturing Lord."**[112] And the Most High states, **"And whosoever trusts in Allah, He suffices him."**[113] And the Most Glorious states, **"Allah is the Protector of those who believe. He brings them out of the darknesses and into the light."**[114] And He states, be He Glorified, **"...and it is incumbent upon Us to help the believers."**[115] These verses and others similar to them are nourishment to the hearts of the believers and it is their clear support. If they seek refuge in Allah ﷻ from Satan it is by Allah's command. If they vanquish Satan with the light of faith it is only by Allah's support. If they are safe from Satan's schemes, then it is only by Allah's blessings and benevolence.

Shaykh Abu'l Hassan ﷺ said, *"I was together with a*

111	Quran 12:40
112	Quran 16:99
113	Quran 65:3
114	Quran 2:257
115	Quran 30: 47

man in my travels. He advised me saying, 'There are no words more helpful in performing good deeds than (saying) – *There is no power or might except Allah. And there is no deed more helpful, other than fleeing towards Allah and seeking refuge with Him –* **And whosoever holds fast to Allah is indeed guided unto a straight path.'**[116]

Then the man said, 'In the name of Allah, I flee to Allah, I seek refuge in Him and there is no power or might except through Allah. And who forgives sins except for Allah!?'

Then he extrapolated, '"In the Name of Allah" is a saying with the tongue originating from the heart. "Then flee to Allah" describes the state of the spirit (ruh) and the inner-heart (sirr). "I have sought refuge in Allah" describes the state of the intellect and animal-self (nafs). "There is no power or might except through Allah" describes the King and His command. "Who forgives sins except for Allah" is saying – My Nurturing Lord, I seek refuge in you from the works of Satan, he is a clear, misguiding enemy.'

Then he spoke addressing Satan, 'This is Allah's informing us of you, and I believe in Allah and with Him, I have my trust. I seek refuge in Allah from you and if He had not commanded me to, I would not do so, for who are you that I seek Allah's protection from you?'"

If you have understood, may Allah have mercy upon you, then you have realised that Satan is too wretched and contemptible in their hearts that they ascribe to him the power to bring about his will. The wisdom in the creation of Satan is that he be the focus to which disobedience, disbelief, heedlessness, and forgetfulness are attributed. Have you not heard His words "**...and nothing made me**

---

116   Quran 3:101

neglect to mention it, save Satan..."[117] or **"This is the work of Satan"**?[118] The secret of bringing about Satan is so that he can be used to clean up the dirtiness of attributing (unpleasantries to Allah). That is why one of those with intimate knowledge said, *"Satan is the (dirty) rag of this world."*

Shaykh Abu'l Hassan said, *"Satan is like the male and the animal-self (nafs) is like the female and the occurrence of sin between them is like a baby born to a mother and father. They do not create the baby, but from them, it does appear."*

What the Shaykh intends by these words is that an intelligent person does not doubt that a child is not a creation of the father and mother. Rather, it is attributed to them only because it appeared from them. Likewise, the believer does not doubt that sin is not the creation of Satan nor the animal-self. It only appears from them and is not created by them. The appearance of the sin from them ascribes it to them only by extension. The One to whom the creation and bringing forth can be ascribed is only Allah. Just as He creates deeds of obedience out of His overflowing bounty, likewise He is the Creator of disobedience out of His justice. For He states, **"Say, 'All is from Allah.' What is with these people that they hardly understand any word?"**[119] And He states, **"Allah is the Creator of all things..."**[120] And He states, be He glorified, **"Is there a creator other than Allah..."** And the Glorified states, **"Is He Who creates like one who creates**

---

117   Quran 18:63. What Joshua said to Moses after losing the fish in their journey to meet Khidr.

118   Quran 28:15. What Moses said after striking and unintentionally killing a man from the Egyptians.

119   Quran 4:78

120   Quran 13:16

not? Will you not, then, reflect?"[121]

These verses rebuke the arguments of heretics who claim Allah ﷻ creates acts of obedience but not those of disobedience. He also states, be He glorified, "**...it is Allah Who created you and whatever you do...**"[122] If they argue and say that the Glorious also says, "**Truly Allah commands not indecency**"[123] – then there is no contradiction here because His command is different from His decree.

If they retort that the Glorified states, "**Whatever good befalls you, it is from Allah, and whatever evil befalls you, it is from yourself**"[124] – then the response is that in this verse Allah ﷻ is teaching His slaves the proper courtesy (*adab*) with Him. He commanded us to attribute goodness to Him for that is what befits Him. He commanded us to attribute evil to ourselves for that is befitting of us. This is based on the proper etiquette as demonstrated by Khidr ﷺ.

Khidr ﷺ said, "**As for the ship ... *I desired* to damage it.**"[125] But then he says in regards to the wall he mended – "**it belonged to two orphan boys ... and *your Nurturing Lord desired* that they should reach their maturity and extract their treasure.**"[126] So if there appeared anything unsavoury he attributed it to himself. While all merit and goodness he attributed to his Master.

Similar was Abraham ﷺ, for he never said – *when Allah makes me sick, He is the One who cures me* – rather, he

---

121	Quran 16:17
122	Quran 37:96
123	Quran 7:27
124	Quran 4:79
125	Quran 18:79
126	Quran 18:82

said, **"and when *I become sick*, He is the One who cures me."**[127] He thus attributed sickness to himself and healing to his Nurturing Lord, even though it is indeed Allah ﷻ who is the true Creator of, and Agent in all that.

So, the Most High's words **"Whatever good befalls you, it is from Allah,"** refer to His creating and bringing forth. As for **"and whatever evil befalls you, it is from yourself"** it is in terms of association and linking (the evil to yourself).

Just as the Messenger, upon him be peace said, *"Goodness is in Your hands and no evil is from You!"* Of course, the Messenger ﷺ knew well that Allah ﷻ is the Creator of all good and evil, the beneficial and the harmful. But he abided by the proper etiquette of expression and said, *"Goodness is in Your hands and no evil is from You!"* Just as we have explained. So understand!

If they then say that *Al-Haqq* is far above creating sin because it is shameless, and *Al-Haqq* is far too Holy to create shameless things, we reply that – performing sins is shameful when it is concerning the slaves since it is in opposition to His command. Shamelessness does not extend to the one who prohibits it, but only to the one commanded to avoid it. Just as goodness cannot be attributed to the slaves because they are commanded to do good and it is a binding order upon them. So understand!

It is necessary that *Al-Haqq*, be He glorified, be far exalted over this misguided attempt to exalt Him. When they say that Allah ﷻ is far above creating sin, we reply – rather, He is far elevated from something occurring in

---

127   Quran 26:80

His Kingdom which He does not will. So understand, may Allah guide us and you to the correct and guided path and establish us firmly upon proper religion.

10. Elaboration on the Manner of Abandoning Self-Direction & Disputation of Divine Decrees

Allah, be He Glorified, states, "**And who shuns the religion of Abraham but a foolish soul? We chose him in the world and in the Hereafter he shall be among the righteous. And when his Nurturing Lord said unto him, 'Submit!' he said, 'I submit to the Nurturing Lord of the worlds'.**"[128] And He states, "**Truly the religion in the sight of Allah is Islam (the religion of submission).**"[129] And He states, "**the religion of your father Abraham. He named you Muslims (those who submit), aforetime.**"[130] And He states, "**...so submit unto Him.**"[131] And He states, "**So if they dispute with you, say, 'I submit my face to Allah, and so too those who follow me'.**"[132] And He states, "**And whosoever submits his face to Allah and is virtuous has indeed grasped the most unfailing handhold.**"[133] And He states, "**'Take me as a submitter (Muslim) unto Yourself, and admit me to the company of the righteous'.**"[134] And

---

128	Quran 2: 130-131
129	Quran 3:19
130	Quran 22:78
131	Quran 22: 34
132	Quran 3:20
133	Quran 31:22
134	Quran 12:101

He states, "**(Say) I am the first of those who submit (i.e. the Muslims).**"[135] There are also other similar verses.

Know that this repetition of Islam (submission) indicates its great honour and weight. Submission has both an outer and inner reality. The external submission is to act following Allah's commands. Its inner submission is the absence of opposition to His decrees.

Islam has an aspect related to outer forms and an aspect related to the heart. The latter is the absence of opposition and is complete submission (to Allah). The actions of Islam are like a body and submission to Him is as its soul. Islam is the outward appearance and submission is its inner reality. The Muslim is then one who submits absolutely to Allah ﷻ. They can be seen to be obedient to His commands outwardly, while inwardly are completely resigned to His power and control.

The realisation of this station of submission occurs with the abandonment of managing Allah's affairs and committing them to Him, having no qualm whether He overrules one's wishes or consents to them. Whoever claims Islam requires this submission and resignation to Allah ﷻ – "**Bring your proof, if you are truthful.**"[136]

Have you not heard Abraham's reply, "**And when his Nurturing Lord said unto him, 'Submit!' he said, 'I submit to the Nurturing Lord of the worlds'.**"?[137]

When he was flung by a catapult (into a great fire

---

135 Quran 6:163
136 Quran 2:111. The Imam includes this verse to indicate that your submission to Allah's will is a proof of your Islam.
137 Quran 2:131

ignited by his people), the angels cried out, *"Our Nurturing Lord! Here is your friend in such a situation that You know better about!"*

Al-Haqq replied, *"Descend to him, dear Gabriel and if he seeks your help, help him. Otherwise, leave Me and My friend."*

When Gabriel, upon him be peace, arrived at the horizon, he called out to Abraham, *"Do you have any need?"*

Abraham replied, *"From you, I have no need. But from Allah, then indeed."*

Gabriel said, *"Ask Him!"*

But Abraham only replied, *"His knowledge of my situation suffices me from having to ask Him."*

He did not seek support from anyone besides Allah nor did his attention even incline to other than Him. Rather, he surrendered to His decree, relying on Allah's management for him rather than his own management for himself. He relied on *Al-Haqq's* care for him, rather than his own care for himself. He relied on *Al-Haqq's* knowledge, be He glorified, rather than his asking of Him, fully recognising that *Al-Haqq* is most kind in managing all his affairs. And so, Allah praised him **"...and Abraham, who fulfilled"**[138] and saved him from the fire – **"We said, 'O Fire! Be coolness and peace for Abraham'."**[139]

The scholars have mentioned that if *Al-Haqq* did not say to the fire to be **"peace for Abraham,"** the coldness of the fire would have harmed him and so the fire became

---

138 Quran 53:37
139 Quran 21:69

cool and soothing. Those with knowledge of the stories of the Prophets have also mentioned that every fire at that moment, whether in the east or west, suppressed itself thinking it was the fire being addressed. It has also been said that the fire only burnt off the chains of Abraham ﷺ.

A Lofty Point

Look at the words of Abraham ﷺ when Gabriel ﷺ asked, *"Do you have any need?"* He replied, *"From you, I have no need."* Notice he did not say – *I have no need*. That is because the station of prophethood and friendship with Allah ﷻ requires complete and frank servitude. The station of slave-hood requires expressing one's needs to Allah ﷻ and standing before Him in a state of poverty. Being in this state required Abraham ﷺ to say, *"From you, I have no need."* That is, I am needy of Allah but not from yourself (O Gabriel). His words combined this poverty to Allah ﷻ as well as the removal of any hope in other than Him.

The matter is not as some have claimed – *"A Sufi is not a Sufi until he does not ask Allah of his need."* These words are not in accordance with the great Sufi scholars who are in imitation of the Prophet ﷺ. Rather, these words mean that the Sufi has understood that Allah ﷻ has already taken care of all his needs before his being created. So, their asking Allah does not bring about what has already been concluded in pre-eternity. Also, the absence of need does not necessarily mean the absence of one's poverty (before Allah).

Another interpretation of *"A Sufi is not a Sufi until he does not ask Allah of his need"* is that, by his asking of Allah ﷻ, his concern is not over the thing he asks for. For there is a wide difference between the one who seeks Allah ﷻ from the one who seeks *from* Allah ﷻ. Or perhaps even, what is meant by the statement, is that one has entrusted all affairs to Allah ﷻ through submission to Him. In which case, one has no desire except what Allah ﷻ desires.

Another Lofty Point

When Gabriel ﷺ said to Abraham ﷺ, *"Do you have any need?"* and he replied, *"From you, I have no need. But from Allah, then indeed,"* Gabriel ﷺ knew that Abraham ﷺ would not seek his help while his heart was absorbed only with Allah ﷻ. So, Gabriel urged him, *"Ask Him!"* As if to say – *If you will not seek my help because you have no attachment to intermediaries (to Allah's power), then ask your Nurturing Lord for He is indeed closer to you than even I am.*

It was then that Abraham ﷺ replied, *"His knowledge of my situation suffices me from having to ask Him."* As if to say – *I pondered deeper and found my Nurturing Lord closer to me than even my needing to ask Him. Rather, I see my asking Him as just another intermediary. I do not want to grasp on to anything other than Him. I realised that* Al-Haqq, *be He glorified, is All-Knowing and need not be reminded by my asking. It is impossible to think He does not know. I have found sufficiency in His knowledge before and above my asking of Him. I know that He, out of His kindness, will not abandon me in any affair!* This is what it means to have sufficiency with Allah ﷻ and to imbibe meaning to the saying *"Sufficient is Allah for me* (hasbiAllah)."

Our Shaykh ﷺ used to say about the words of Allah **"...and Abraham, who fulfilled"** – that Abraham ﷺ loyally fulfilled the meaning of *'Sufficient is Allah for me'*. While others have mentioned that because he handed over his food to his guests, his son to sacrifice, and his body to fire, *Al-Haqq* praised him with "**...and Abraham, who fulfilled**."

A Lofty Point

When *Al-Haqq* declared about Adam ﷺ and his descendants, "**I am placing a vicegerent upon the earth**," the Angels replied, "**Will You place therein one who will work corruption therein, and shed blood, while we hymn Your praises and sanctify You?**" To which He replied, "**Truly I know what you know not**."[140] Abraham's refusal to seek Gabriel's help when he was thrown into fire was a rebuttal from Allah (to their earlier objection when Adam was created). It was as if He was saying – *O you who said,* "**Will You place therein one who will work corruption therein, and shed blood...**," *do you see my slave now?* Hence the secret in "**Truly I know what you know not**" became apparent.

In the same manner, the Prophet ﷺ mentioned, *"The Angels of night and day observe you (in turns). Then when those that remained with you ascend, Allah asks them, while He is more knowing, 'How have you left my slave?'*

They reply, 'We came to them and they were praying and we left them while they were praying'." Shaykh Abu'l Hassan said, "*It was as if* Al-Haqq *says to them –* O *you who said,* "**Will You place therein one who will work corruption therein...**," *how have you left my slave?*"

It is as if the intention of *Al-Haqq* ﷻ in sending Gabriel ﷺ to Abraham ﷺ was to show the status of His friend to His angels and solidify the nobility of Abraham's rank and grandeur.

---

140   Quran 2:30

How is it possible for Abraham ﷺ to seek aid from anything other than Him when he was not looking towards anything but Him, nor was he in contemplation of anything other than Him? Abraham ﷺ was only given the title "the Friend" because the love of Allah ﷻ had permeated his innermost heart (*sirr*) as well as Allah's grandeur and oneness. No space remained in it for anything else. As the poet said:

> *Everything to do with You has permeated my soul*
> *And that is how the Friend became a friend*
>
> *Whenever I speak, You are my words*
> *When I am silent You are my heart's burning thirst.*

A Signpost

Know that *Al-Haqq* ﷻ expanded the innermost heart (*sirr*) of Abraham ﷺ with the light of contentment with Him, outstretched to Abraham ﷺ the spirit of submission, and protected his heart from the inclination to sin. The fire did not become cool and peaceful for him except when his heart was handed over to Allah ﷻ in surrender. Since when there is surrender, peace ensues. It was from the reform of the inner state that such honour and greatness appeared. Understand from this, O believer, that whoever surrenders to Allah ﷻ amidst trials, Allah ﷻ will repay its thorns with fruits and its terror with tranquillity.

So when Satan hurls you in the catapult of tribulation, and the creation discloses itself to you saying, *"Do you have any need?"* Then reply, *"From you, I have no need. But from*

Allah, then indeed!"

If creation was to then suggest to you, *"Ask Him!"* Reply, *"His knowledge of my situation suffices me from having to ask Him."*

Allah will make the fires of this world cool and tranquil for you and bestow upon you favours and honours. This is the way of guidance Allah has opened through His Prophets and Messengers. The believers walked in their footsteps and the certain in faith stuck diligently to their path. As He said, be He glorified, **"Say, this is my way. I call unto Allah with clear sight — I, and those who follow me.**"[141]

He also states in the matter of Prophet Jonah, **"So We answered him and saved him from grief. Thus, do We save the believers."**[142] That is to say – *likewise, We save the believers who follow his elevated way.* Those who seek out Allah's light (*nur*) with humility and poverty. Those who are clothed with submissiveness and recognise they have no power or might of their own.

※ ※ ※ ※ ※

---

141   Quran 12:108
142   Quran: 21:88

In the story of Abraham ﷺ is a message to the heedful and guidance for the thoughtful. Whoever abandons their concern for the management of their affairs, then Allah ﷻ Himself takes charge over it for them with His most excellent managing.

Do you not see that Abraham ﷺ did not choose for his own self? He did not worry for himself but cast the reins over to Allah ﷻ, delivering them completely over to Him. When he did so, relying upon Him in all his affairs, the result of his surrender was his safety, honour, and the perpetual praise ascribed to his name through the annals of time.

Further, Allah ﷻ commanded us to not leave Abraham's religion and that we observe the meaning of the name he gave us, "**...the religion of your father Abraham. He named you Muslims (those who submit) aforetime...**"[143] So anyone who considers themselves Abrahamic must be free of giving precedence to their own managing and be empty of disputation with Allah. "**And who shuns the religion of Abraham, but a foolish soul?**"[144]

Abraham's creed necessitates the enstrusting of affairs to Allah ﷻ and surrendering in the face of His decrees. Know that the goal is that besides Allah, you have no other goal. In this vein, I composed the following poem:

> *My desire from you is your abandoning desire*
> *If about the road that leads to Me, you enquire*
>
> *Cast away your hopes in creation in earnest*
> *Will you not have faith in what I promised?*

---

143 Quran 22:78
144 Quran: 2:130

Until when will you My majesty ignore?
The bond of care I keep alive, love I outpour

Until when will you at My wonders gaze
And still, wander down every road in a haze?

Until when will you abandon seeking My paradise?
By your life, how far off you've been enticed!

My love for you is ancient, don't you see?
On the Day of Alast[145] you said – Only Me

Is now there another lord that you vow
Will save you from sorrow tomorrow or now?

Weak is all creation, keep in mind, O seeker
The weak calls out for help from the weaker

All creation exists only by My power
I display a spectacle wherever I desire!

What in My house, in My kingdom, in My dominion
To other than Me, do you place your trust in?

See for yourself with eyes free of lies –
Does not every creation announce that it dies?

From death to death does it travel
And you too, no doubt, tread the same gravel

My cloak is on you, from disgrace yourself save
Wear it always do not depend upon slaves

Forward all your hopes to My door

---

145 The Day of *Alast* when Allah ﷻ asked all the Children of Adam **"Am I not your Nurturing Lord (Rabb)?"** (*Alastu bi Rabbikum*). They replied, **"Indeed You are, we bear witness."**

And come to Me being of arrogance poor

Understand and live by your humble nature
The loyal to Me sees impossible treasure

Be to Us a slave – and a slave is pleased
With whatever it is the Master decrees

Shall I veil your lowliness with My beauty
And you repay it with ignorance unduly?

Are you then equal to Me in My Kingdom
That you dispute My decrees, how loathsome!

If you then desire to be with Me dearly
Forsake your nafs, it is indeed the enemy

Drown in the ocean of fana'[146], maybe you will see Us
Prepare Us that We are yours on the Day of Justice

Be a seeker of only Us, if you would bargain
A rich reward from a Most Generous Guardian

And so be not on anyone besides Us depending
For on this day it is We that are directing.

Know that self-direction is of two types: the praiseworthy and the blameworthy. As for the blameworthy, it is every managing where you rely on yourself to acquire some worldly benefit – not for Allah ﷻ and not relying upon His reality. It includes deliberating to perform a sin or acquiring a worldly benefit out of heedlessness, or even acts

---

146 *fana'*: In Sufi terminology, it refers to the annihilation of the desires of the animal-self (*nafs*) but also has other dimensions of meaning. It can also refer to the spiritual state of seeing only Allah's existence and being blind to all worldy causes.

of obedience but to show off, or to acquire fame and the such. All of which is blameworthy as it brings about punishment or veiling (between you and Allah). Whoever recognises the blessing of the mind is ashamed before Allah ﷻ to exhaust his intelligence in any scheme that does not bring about His closeness and is not a means to capture His love.

The mind is the greatest of bounties Allah ﷻ bestowed upon His slaves. For He, be He glorified, created all things and blessed them first with being created and then with the continuation of existence. These two blessings are present in everything and necessary for every existent thing: the blessings of being created and continual existence. Perhaps this is what is intended from the Glorified's words, **"My mercy encompasses all things."**[147]

Yet since all things have their share of being created and continuation in existence, *Al-Haqq* ﷻ willed to distinguish some of His creations over others to show the efficacy of His will and the profoundness of His volition. So, He distinguished some of His creations with growth like that of plants and living beings – both animal and human. His power was thus manifested more intensely than in those creations that do not grow.

When these three groups of creation were all classified with the characteristic of growth, He distinguished human beings with life and included the animals in that also. So, His power shined more intensely than it did so in plants.

Then He willed to distinguish humans further and bestowed upon them the intellect, giving preference

---

147   Quran 7:156

to them over other animals and completing His favours upon mankind. Through the mind, by its insightfulness, illumination and light, the profits of this world and the hereafter are acquired.

Expending the blessing of the mind on planning and managing only for this world, which has no value in and of itself with Allah ﷻ, is ingratitude for the blessing of the mind. While to direct your intellect to rectify your state in your final abode is to be grateful to the One who showed kindness to you and illuminated you with His light. It is more worthy of you, more becoming, excellent and honourable. So do not expend your intelligence, which Allah favoured you with, in managing and planning this world. It is as the Messenger of Allah ﷺ informed us, *"The world is a decaying corpse."*

This world is as he ﷺ described it during his conversation with Dahhak ﷺ, when the Prophet ﷺ asked him, *"What do you eat?"*

Dahhak replied, *"Meat and milk, O Messenger of Allah."*

The Messenger ﷺ asked, *"And what does it become?"*

"It becomes as you know O Messenger of Allah."

He commented, *"Indeed, Allah has made what exits from the children of Adam a parable for this world."* He ﷺ also said, *"If this world was equal to a fly's wing in the sight of Allah, He would not have given a disbeliever a draught of water."*

The similitude of one who expends his intellect in managing only for this world, which is as just described, is like one who was given a majestic and mighty sword by a king. One which the king did not allow most of his subjects to carry. It is to be used to fight the king's enemies and was bestowed so that the wielder of the sword may be beautified by carrying it. Instead, the wielder of the sword begins to strike it against a carcass until it becomes blunt and it loses its splendour and brilliance. It would only be befitting that the king takes back the sword from the wielder, punish him further for his awful behaviour, and bars him from the king's reception in the future.

Hence, self-direction is of two types; the praiseworthy and the blameworthy. The praiseworthy is when your planning and deliberating brings you closer to Allah ﷻ. Such as contemplating how to fulfil the rights of fellow human beings and creations, like being honourable and forgiving. Or how one might perfect one's repentance to the Nurturing Lord of the worlds. Or pondering on what will lead to the suppression of wayward desires and passions and the seductions of Satan. All of this is praiseworthy, no doubt. In this regard, the Messenger ﷺ said, "*An hour's contemplation is better than the worship of 70 years.*"

Self-direction for this world is of two types: managing this world for the sake of this world and the other is managing this world for the sake of the Hereafter. Managing this world for the sake of this world is that you concern yourself with all worldly means to boast and be arrogant. The sign of which is that every time you experience an increase in worldly benefits, it only increases you in heedlessness and being deceived by it. One's concerns then distract him from obedience and lead to disobedience.

As for the management of the world for the sake of the hereafter, it is the administering of a merchant so that his earnings are permissible (*halal*). He spends what remains upon the poor and the downtrodden and protects his honour by not needing to ask from anyone else. A sign of one who seeks the world only for Allah ﷻ is that he does not assign importance to himself nor does he hoard his wealth. Rather, he supports and prefers others.

The one who is abstinent from this lowly world also has two signs: one sign when he loses and another sign when he gains wealth. As for when he gains wealth, the sign is preferring others and charity. The sign of the abstinent one when he loses wealth is feeling the relief of being free of it. Charity is gratitude for the blessing of gain. Relief is gratitude for the blessing of loss. That is the fruit of understanding Allah's purposes and intimate knowledge. For just as *Al-Haqq* ﷻ had blessed you in gaining it, likewise He has blessed you in averting it from you, rather His blessing in averting it is more complete and bounteous.

Sufyan Al-Thawri ﷺ once said, "*Certainly the blessings of Allah in what He has prevented me of this world is more excellent than His blessings of what He has given me of this world.*"

While Shaykh Abu'l Hassan ﷺ related, "*I saw (Abu Bakr) As-Siddiq, may Allah be pleased with him, in my dream and he said, 'Do you know what is the sign of the love for this world leaving the heart?'*

I replied, 'I do not know?'

He answered, 'The sign of the love for this world leaving one's heart is being charitable with it when you have it and to feel relieved when you do not'."

It becomes clear that not every seeker of this world is blameworthy, but the blameworthy is he who seeks the world for his self and not for his Nurturing Lord. That is, those who seek the world for their standing in this world, not in the hereafter. People then are of two types: a slave who seeks this world for this world and a slave who seeks this world for the hereafter. I heard Shaykh Abu'l Abbas, may Allah be pleased with him, saying, *"The true knower (of Allah) has no portion of this world. For him, this world is for his hereafter and his hereafter is for his Nurturing Lord."*

The Companions ﷺ and the pious predecessors were established on this principle. For every time they involved themselves with the means and measures of this world, they sought to gain ever closer to Allah ﷻ and attain His pleasure by it. They did not aim thereby to attain this world, its adornments or its pleasures. That is how *Al-Haqq* describes them, "**Muhammad is the Messenger of Allah. Those who are with him are harsh against the disbelievers, merciful to one another. You see them bowing, prostrating, seeking bounty from Allah and (His) contentment; their mark upon their faces is from the effect of prostration.**"[148]

In another verse, He states, "**(It is) in houses that Allah has permitted to be raised and wherein His Name is remembered. He is therein glorified, morning and evening, by men whom neither trade nor buying and selling distract from the remembrance of Allah, the performance of prayer, and the giving of alms, fearing a day when eyes and hearts will be turned about.**"[149]

He also states, be He glorified, "**Among the believers**

---

148   Quran 48:29
149   Quran 24:36-37

are men who have been true to that which they pledged unto Allah. Among them are those who have fulfilled their vow, and among them are those who wait, and they have not changed in the least."[150] There are also other similar verses.

What do you think (is the lofty status) of a people whom Allah had chosen for the companionship of His Messenger and selected to be the addressees of His speech as it was being revealed? There is no believer, until the Day of Resurrection, except he is infinitely indebted to the Companions. Every believer has been supported through their efforts. For they are the ones who carried the Messenger's wisdom and rulings to us, clarified the permissible and the forbidden, taught the elect and the common man, opened many a territory and land and overpowered the people of polytheism and tyranny. Certainly, with truth, the Messenger said, *"My companions are like stars, whichever you follow, you will be guided."*

Allah described them in the first verse above with favourable qualities and He states they were "**seeking bounty from Allah and (His) contentment**." Allah, who is well acquainted with the secrets of the world as well as its evident matters, indicates by these words that what they attained of this world and what they aimed for was nothing other than the noble face of Allah and His abundant bounties.

The Glorified said concerning them, "**Make yourself (O Muhammed) patient with those who call upon their Nurturing Lord morning and evening, desiring His face.**" He informs us that the Companions did not desire anything

---

150 Quran 33:23

except His face nor have any other goal except a path that led to Him.

He states in another verse, "**He is therein glorified, morning and evening, by men whom neither trade nor buying and selling distract from the remembrance of Allah.**" This verse is an indication that He purified their innermost hearts and perfected the lights upon them. Hence, this world had no place in their hearts nor did it scratch the surface of their faith. How could this world enter into hearts full of His love and in which the lights of His closeness shine so intensely?

He, be He glorified, also states, "**As for My slaves, truly you (O Satan) have no authority over them.**"[151] If the world had any power over their hearts then Satan would certainly have had power over them also. For Satan can not possibly have power over a heart illuminated by abstinence and swept clean of the filth of worldly desire. The Glorified's words "**As for My slaves, truly you (O Satan) have no authority over them,**" allude to the meaning of – *neither Satan nor anything else from creation has any power over their hearts for the power of My greatness in their hearts forbids that anything holds sway over them except Me.*

Al-Haqq states, "**neither trade nor buying and selling distract (them) from the remembrance of Allah.**" Notice He did not forbid them to trade. Rather, the verse points to the permissibility of trading and business from the connotation of the verse, which is clear if you ponder prudently. Have you not heard His words, "**establish prayer, and pay the *zakat* (alms-tax)**"?[152] If He had forbidden

---

151 Quran: 17: 65
152 Quran: 21:73

them wealth He would have forbidden them the means to it, which are business and trade. But He states, "**and pay the *zakat*.**" So His enjoining *zakat* upon the Companions is evidence that they were still praised with the aforementioned characteristics even though they had wealth. Allah praised them even when they were wealthy since they observed the rights of their Master regarding their wealth.

Abdullah ibn Utbah relates, "*Uthman ibn Affan had in his possession on the day he was martyred, 150,000 gold dinars and 1,000,000 silver dirhams, and lands to the value of 200,000 gold dinars. While the wealth of Zubayr reached 50,000 golden dinars and 1000 horses and 1000 servants. Amr ibn al-As left behind 300,000 gold dinars. The wealth of Abdul Rahman ibn Auf is well known and need not be mentioned. The world was in the palm of their hands but not in their hearts. They were patient when they did not have it and grateful to Allah when they gained it.*"

Al-Haqq only tested them with poverty in their early days of Islam so that their light could be perfected and the innermost reaches of their hearts be purified, after which He changed their circumstances. For if they were given such wealth beforehand, love for it might have settled in their hearts. But once their certainty of faith became deep-rooted and established and they were granted wealth, they gave out that wealth like trustworthy treasurers. And they abided by the words of Allah, "**…and spend from that over which He has appointed you as trustees.**"[153]

In the same vein, we can understand why the Companions were forbidden from going to holy war (*jihad*) in the early days of Islam. Allah commanded them,

---

153   Quran 57:7

"**So pardon and forbear, until Allah comes with His Command.**"[154] If war was permitted to them in the earlier days, then perhaps the one new to Islam would ascribe victory to himself subtly, not realising that he was doing so. But (they were left to mature) to the extent that whenever Ali was struck in battle, he would pause to cool off from any possible anger before striking back. He feared that if he struck back immediately after he might be doing so with some joy of seeking revenge. This he did out of his intimate knowledge and his understanding of the schemes and tricks of the animal-self (*nafs*) and its traps, may Allah be pleased with him. The Companions gave huge importance and concern to the states of their hearts, the sincerity of their deeds, and had great caution so that nothing be found in their actions that was not for seeking the pleasure of Allah, Most High.

The world was in the hands of the Companions, not in their hearts. Such was evident by their disinterest in this world and their charity in it. They were the ones about whom *Al-Haqq* states, "**They prefer others over themselves, even if they be impoverished.**"[155] Once a Companion gifted the head of a sheep to another, who thought, "*So and so is more deserving of it*," so he offered it to someone else. The next companion it was gifted to also said the same thing and gifted it to another. So it continued to change hands until it returned to the original owner, after going through seven or so others.

What is enough for you to understand their generosity is the incident when Umar donated half his wealth and Abu Bakr donated all of his. Or when

---

154   Quran 2:109
155   Quran 59:9

Abdul Rahman ibn Auf ﷺ donated 700 camels loaded with goods. Or when Uthman ﷺ equipped the entire "army of distress."[156] There are many other instances of their lofty deeds and the brilliance of their inner states.

As for the verse "**Among the believers are men who have been true to that which they pledged unto Allah. Among them are those who have fulfilled their vow, and among them are those who wait, and they have not changed in the least**," it informs us of the deep and hidden sincerity that none could be aware of except *Al-Haqq* ﷻ. This verse is a great praise and a weighty honour. For men only see the outer form of deeds, but the verse vindicates both the deeds of the Companions and their inner sincerity and confirms their praiseworthy qualities and feats.

It becomes clear from all this that one's managing of affairs is of two types: managing worldly affairs for the sake of this world like the heedless, estranged from Allah, or the managing of worldly affairs for the sake of the Hereafter like the state of the honoured Companions and pious predecessors.

---

156   Abdur-Rahman bin Khabbab narrated: "I witnessed the Prophet ﷺ while he was encouraging support for the 'army of distress' (the battle of *Tabuk*). Uthman bin Affan stood and said: 'O Messenger of Allah! I will take the responsibility of one-hundred camels, including their saddles and water-skins, in the path of Allah.' Then the Prophet urged support for the army again. So Uthman stood the second time and said: 'O Messenger of Allah! I will take the responsibility of two-hundred camels, including their saddles and water-skins, in the path of Allah.' Then the Prophet urged support for the army agains. So Uthman bin 'Affan stood and said: 'O Messenger of Allah I will take the responsibility of three-hundred camels, including their saddles and water-skins, in the path of Allah.' I saw the Messenger of Allah ﷺ descend from the pulpit while he was saying: 'It does not matter what Uthman does after this, it does not matter what Uthman does after this'(i.e. his place in Paradise is secured)." Jami' at-Tirmidhi 3700

The words of Umar, may Allah be pleased with him, give credence to this when he said, "*I arranged the army while I was performing my prayer.*" Since the managing and planning of Umar ﷺ was based on witnessing reality and complete preoccupation (with Allah), his managing of affairs was only for Allah's sake. It did not break or take anything away from his prayer.

You might ask – You have claimed that none of the Companions was desirous of this world but *Al-Haqq*, be He Glorified, did reveal about them on the Day of *Uhud*, stating, "**Among you are those who desire this world, and among you are those who desire the Hereafter.**"[157] To the extent that even the Companions ﷺ said, "*We did not think that any of us desired the world until His Word (this verse) was revealed.*"

Know – may Allah grant you success in understanding this and make you of those who pay heed to it – that it is incumbent upon every believer to have positive and good thoughts about the Companions ﷺ. The believer should believe in their virtue and adorn them with the best possible interpretations of their sayings, actions and all their states, both during the life of the Messenger ﷺ and after his passing. For *Al-Haqq* declared their excellence and purity absolutely and He did not limit it to a specific time to the exclusion of others. Likewise, is the Messenger's praise of them, "*My Companions are like the stars, whichever one you follow, you will be guided.*"

As for the verse "**Among you are those who desire this world, and among you are those who desire the Hereafter,**" there are two responses.

---

157   Quran 3:152

The First Response

The verse is referring to the fact that from amongst you is one who desires the world for the sake of the Hereafter. Like those who desired the booty of war so they could use it for Allah's sake, spending it on goodness and charity. The verse then continues to say that there is also amongst you one whose intention is different – one who desires to acquire the virtue of *jihad*, nothing else. Such a one does not incline towards the war booty. So, the matter is one of there being the virtuous among you and then the more virtuous. There is amongst you he who is complete of faith and then there is the more perfect.

The Second Response

The Master can say whatever He wishes to His slave. We must observe proper decency to His slave because the slave has a relationship with Allah ﷻ. Not everything that the Master says to His slave should be insisted upon and spoken of by other slaves. The Master can say whatever He wills to encourage His slave and motivate him towards His design and purpose. We should abide by the limits of proper behaviour with His slaves. If you examine the Noble Book, you would find many such examples. For instance, in *Surah Abasa*, about which Sayidah A'isha, may Allah be pleased with her said, "*If the Messenger of Allah were to conceal anything from revelation it would be this chapter.*"

Nevertheless, it is settled from the states of the Companions that what is meant by the praiseworthy abandoning of self-direction is not to abandon the means of this world but rather to seek thereby, obedience to one's Master and to work towards the Hereafter. The self-direction that has been prohibited, is the managing and concern of this world only for this world. A sign of this is that Allah is disobeyed in relation to one's self-direction and no differentiation is made between the forbidden and the permissible.

A Benefit

Know that things are blameworthy or praised according to what they lead to. So blameworthy self-direction is what keeps you busy from Allah ﷻ, makes you neglect His service and prevents you from being occupied with Him. While praiseworthy self-direction leads you closer to Allah ﷻ and attains His pleasure. It is hence completely different.

Likewise, this world is not to be criticised in totality. Nor is it to be praised in totality. The blameworthy aspect of it is what keeps you away from your Master and prevents your preparation for the Hereafter. As some of the true knowers of Allah ﷻ have said, *"Everything that occupies you from Allah whether it be family or wealth or children, brings you loss. While the praiseworthy is what supports you to act in His obedience and moves you in His service."* In short, what results in the praiseworthy, is praiseworthy in itself and what results in the blameworthy is blameworthy in itself.

It has also been narrated from the Messenger of Allah ﷺ, *"The world is a decaying corpse."* He also said, *"The world is cursed. Cursed is whatever is in it, except the remembrance of Allah and what is related to that, and the scholar and the student."* These *hadiths* require disapproval of, and repulsion from this world.

But he ﷺ also mentioned, *"Do not revile the world.*

What an excellent riding animal it is for the believer. By it he reaches goodness and is saved from evil." The world which the Messenger ﷺ cursed is the world that preoccupies one from Allah ﷻ. Hence he mentioned the exception in the *hadith "...except the remembrance of Allah and what is related to that, and the scholar and the student."* By these words he explained the remembrance of Allah ﷻ is not considered to be from this world. While his words *"Do not revile the world"* refers to such things that connect you with Allah ﷻ. That is why he said, *"What an excellent riding animal it is for the believer."* He praised it in its aspect of being a riding animal, not a for its being a deceiving, burdensome home.

If you have understood so far, then you have realised that abandoning self-direction is not abandoning the means of the world so that one becomes unfruitful or a burden among men. In such a case, one would only be acting in ignorance to Allah's wisdom, Who created worldly means and made available the use of worldy opportunities and measures.

It has been narrated that the Prophet Jesus, upon him be peace, passed by a monk worshipping in isolation and asked, *"From where do you eat?"*

He said, *"My brother feeds me."*

Jesus ﷺ replied, *"Your brother is more worshipful than you."*

That is to say – *Your brother, even though he is in the markets, is more worshipful than you. For he is the one who allows you to worship and frees you time for it.*

How is it possible for us to not involve ourselves with worldly means after the revelation of His words, be

He glorified, "**Allah has permitted buying and selling and forbidden usury.**"[158] Also His words, "**And take witnesses when you buy and sell between yourselves.**"[159] Also the Prophet's saying, *"The most excellent of what a believer eats is what his right hand has earned. For David was a prophet of Allah and would eat from the toils of his labour."* He also said, *"The most excellent of earnings are those of a labourer with his own hands so long he is trustworthy."* He also said, *"The trustworthy, truthful Muslim will be amongst the martyrs on the Day of Resurrection."*

So how can anyone after this look down upon the worldly means? The blameworthy is only what occupies you away from Allah and prevents you from His remembrance. Even if you were to abandon the worldly means and yet, were still heedless of Allah, then you would still be in a blameworthy state. Also, misfortunes do not only affect those who involve themselves with worldly means, they may also touch those who renounce worldly means, "**There is no protector on this day from the Command of Allah, save for the one upon whom He has Mercy.**"[160]

In fact, misfortunes may be even more intense among those who have renounced the world. For calamities may strike those who busy themselves with worldly means, all the while they do not make any claims of righteousness. They appear outwardly as they are inwardly and have humility with their recognition of their shortcomings and cognisance of the superior virtue of those who have renounced the world. But the calamities that strike those that renounce the world may be self-admiration, arrogance, showing off,

---

158	Quran 2:275
159	Quran 2:282
160	Quran 11:43

faking or putting on a show for mankind by appearing to obey Allah ﷻ when actually seeking some benefit from them. Or perhaps their calamity may be reliance and trust upon the creation. A sign of this is that he criticises people when they do not honour him and blames them when they do not serve him. The one immersed in the worldly means, despite his heedlessness, is then in a better state than him.

May Allah ﷻ correct and rectify our intentions and purify our animal selves from such calamities. We can rely only on His bounty and His kindness.

A Signpost

You might understand from the previous discussion that the one who abandons the worldly means and the one who occupies himself with them are of the same rank. But the matter is not as such. Allah ﷻ makes the one who frees himself for His worship and spends his time for Allah ﷻ like the one who is pious and occupies himself with the world. If we were to consider one man busy with worldly means and another who abandons them, and if they are on equal footing in regards to their knowledge of Allah, then the one who abandons worldly means is more excellent and his state is more elevated and complete.

That is why some of the righteous with intimate knowledge said, *"The example of the one invested in worldly means and the one divested of them are like two slaves of a king. He says to one, 'Work and eat from the fruit of your labour.' He says to the other, 'Remain in my presence and service and I will look after your wants and needs.' The latter's position is more prestigious and sublime. It is more indicative of the king's care and regard for him."*

Further, it is difficult to be safe from disobedience and remain pure in worship when occupied with worldly means because it requires associating with what is conflicting (to the Divine laws) and mixing with the people of heedlessness and sin.

The most effective factor that will help you in your obedience to Allah is witnessing the obedient ones. The most powerful thing that draws you toward sin is witnessing the sinners. As the Prophet said, *"A man is upon the religion of his close friend. So let each of you look to whom he befriends."* The poet also says:

> *Ask not about a man but ask about his companion*
> *Every companion has for his guide, his companion*

From the characteristics of the animal-self (*nafs*), is that it desires to become like, imitate and take on the characteristics of who it accompanies. So your companionship of the heedless helps your animal-self to become heedless. But the animal-self is inclined to heedlessness by its nature, so what would be its state when it is goaded on by mixing with the heedless?

You may find that your animal-self, dear brother – may Allah give you success – is in different states from when you leave home and when you return. When you go out for the day, spiritual lights shine brighter in you, your chest is at ease and you are motivated towards acts of worship and abstinence from this world. But you find that when you return home, you are no longer in the same state. What was with you is there no longer. This is due to nothing but the filth of disobedience and the heart's absorption of the darkness of worldly means.

The negative effects on the heart from engaging in worldly means and the sins arising from them, continue to affect the heart for some time afterwards. If their negative effects did not persist, hearts would not be hindered in their journeying to Allah ﷻ. Their negative effects are like fire. Perhaps the flame has abated but black ashes still remain. So the one absorbed in material causes needs to work towards knowledge and piety (*taqwa*). Knowledge will teach him the difference between the permitted and the forbidden while *taqwa* will stop him from committing sins. One certainly requires legal knowledge of what is permitted related to trading, contracts, and expenditure, along with the rulings of other religious obligations.

11. A Detour

A discussion on the matters that those who involve themselves with worldly means must abide by.

The First

One should have a strong resolve with Allah ﷻ before setting out of one's house to forgive others one may deal with. Places of business are prone to quarrelling and bargaining. The Messenger of Allah ﷺ said, *"Are any of you capable of being like Abu Dhamdham? He would say when leaving his house, 'O Allah, I have given away my prestige as a charity to the Muslims'."*

The Second

One should perform ablution (*wudu*) and prayer before leaving one's house, asking Allah ﷻ for protection when setting out. A person can have no idea about what has been decreed for him on that day. The one who sets out for the places of business is like one who sets out to the battlefield. It is incumbent upon the believer to don the armour of Allah's protection and take up the shield of trusting in Him, to save himself from the arrows of his enemies (satans from men and *jinn*). He states, **"And whosoever holds fast to Allah is indeed guided unto a straight path."**[161] He also states, **"And whosoever trusts in Allah, He suffices him."**[162]

---

161 Quran 3:101
162 Quran 65:3

The Third

When one leaves one's house, one should place it, his family and its contents in the care of Allah ﷻ for He is most fitting and worthy of preserving them for him. He would do well to remember the words of Allah, "**But Allah is the best of keepers, and He is the most Merciful of the merciful.**"[163] As well as the words of the Prophet ﷺ, "*O Allah, you are the Companion in travel and the Caretaker of the family left behind.*" If one entrusts them to Allah ﷻ, one has seen to it that he will return and find them as he loves to see them, and as they love to see him.

One of the righteous travelled, while his wife was pregnant, saying, "*O Allah, I have entrusted to you what is in her womb.*" His wife passed away while he was absent and when he returned he asked about her and was told she died, still pregnant. When night arrived he saw a light from the cemetery. On approaching it, he saw it coming from her grave, and behold he found his baby by it. He heard a voice saying, "*O man! You entrusted the baby to Us and here it is. If you had entrusted its mother to Us too, you would have found them both, safe together.*"

The Fourth

It is recommended for one to say when leaving one's house, "*In the Name of Allah. I place my trust in Allah. There is no power or might save through Allah.*" For that will make Satan lose all hope in him.

The Fifth

One should enjoin good and forbid against evil. Let

---

163   Quran 12:64

one do so as a gratitude for the blessings of strength and piety which one is bestowed with. Let him remember the words of Allah ﷻ, **"Those who, were We to establish them upon the earth, would perform the prayer, give the alms, and enjoin right and forbid wrong. And unto Allah is the end of all affairs."**[164]

For whoever can enjoin good and forbid evil without the fear of harm reaching him, his honour or wealth, then he is among those established on the earth. It becomes necessary for him enjoin good and forbid evil. If however one cannot enjoin good and forbid evil without harm reaching him before he does so, or he believes that harm will reach him, then one is no longer obligated and he may avoid it.

The Sixth

One should walk with composure and humility due to His words, **"The slaves of the Compassionate are those who walk humbly upon the earth."**[165] Neither is this limited to walking, rather all your actions should be accompanied with composure and governed by consciousness.

The Seventh

One should remember Allah in his workplace. It has been narrated from the Messenger ﷺ, *"He who remembers Allah in the markets is like the living amongst the dead."* One of the pious predecessors would ride his mule to the market to only remember Allah and then return, having no purpose other than that.

The Eighth

---

164   Quran 22:41
165   Quran 25:63

Trade and earning a living should not prevent one from rising to perform the prayers in their proper times in congregation. If he misses out on this because he is preoccupied with work, it warrants the anger of his Master and removes blessings from his earnings. One should be ashamed that *Al-Haqq* sees him prioritising his interests above the rights of his Nurturing Lord.

From the pious predecessors, there was he who would be in the middle of his craft and as he raised his hammer he would suddenly hear the call to prayer. He would throw the hammer behind his back so it not be considered a preoccupation when he had been called to the service of his Nurturing Lord.

On hearing the caller to prayer, one would do well to recall "**O our people! Answer Allah's caller.**"[166] Also the words of the Most High, "**O you who believe! Respond to Allah and the Messenger when he calls you unto that which will give you life.**"[167] And His words, "**Respond to your Nurturing Lord.**"[168]

Sayidah A'isha, may Allah be pleased with her, said, *"The Messenger of Allah would be in his house mending the sandal or helping the servant until the call was made for prayer. At which point he arose as if he did not know us."*

The Ninth

One should avoid taking oaths and exaggerating in selling one's goods or services. For that has been severely warned against. The Messenger of Allah has said, *"The*

166	Quran 46:31
167	Quran 8:24
168	Quran 42:47

merchants are wicked, except one who is upright and honest."

The Tenth

One should withhold one's tongue from backbiting. Remember the words of Allah **"nor backbite one another. Would any of you desire to eat the dead flesh of his brother?"**[169] One should recognise that the listener of backbiting is just one of two backbiters. So if someone is talked about in your presence you should forbid it. If they do not listen, you should get up and leave. Being ashamed in front of others should not prevent one from fulfilling what is due to the Real King . It is more worthy that one is ashamed before Allah and tries to please Him. **"But Allah and His Messenger are worthier of being pleased by them."**[170] It has been narrated from the Messenger , *"Indeed backbiting is worse than a Muslim committing fornication thirty six times."*

Shaykh Abu'l Hassan said, *"There are four etiquettes, that if they are abandoned by the seeker of Allah engaged with worldly means, then attach no importance to him, be he even the most knowledgeable of men. They are: avoiding closeness with oppressors, giving preference to the people of the hereafter, giving consoling charity to the poverty-stricken, and sticking to performing the five prayers in congregation."*

He spoke the truth, may Allah be pleased with him. Indeed, avoidance of oppressors reveals the light of faith, and one is saved from the punishment of Allah, **"And incline not toward the wrongdoers, lest the Fire should touch you."**[171]

---

169   Quran 49:12
170   Quran 9:62
171   Quran 11:113

The Shaykh also mentioned *"giving preference to the people of the hereafter"* as a necessary etiquette. It means that one engaged with worldly means returns to visit the friends of Allah ﷻ often and takes from them what will strengthen him against the confusion caused by worldly means. Their fragrant breezes wafter over him and their blessings appear on him. Perhaps one's love and recognition of them would be a reason that he is supported in some matter or protected from falling into sin.

The Shaykh also mentioned, *"giving consoling charity to the poverty-stricken."* That is because the slave must be grateful for Allah's blessings when they arrive. When the doors of worldly means are opened for you, remember those for whom its doors remain shut. Know that Allah tests the rich by the poor like he tests the poor by the rich. **"And We made some of you a trial for others; will you be patient? And your Nurturing Lord is All-Seeing."**[172]

The poor are in fact a blessing upon the wealthy. Through the poor, the rich find those who will remove their burdens from them for the home of the hereafter. If the wealthy find someone who will take their wealth from them, it is as if Allah Himself is accepting it from them – and Allah is the Self-Sufficient, All-Rich and Praiseworthy. If He had not created the poor how could your charity ever be accepted? Who could you find to take your gift?

That is why the Messenger ﷺ said, *"Whoever spends in charity from a pure source of wealth – and Allah does not accept except the pure – it as if he placed it in the palm of Al-Rahman, who takes excellent care of it, like one of you might nurture your baby horse or camel. (Allah continues to look after it) until a morsel*

---

[172] Quran 25:20

of food (given in charity) is returned to you like the mountain of Uhud." It is also from the signs of the approach of the Day of Judgement that men will not find someone to accept their charity.

Finally, the Shaykh mentioned the importance of *"sticking to performing the five prayers in congregation."* That is because the seeker of Allah who involves himself with worldly means foregoes the seclusion that would have allowed him to completely devote himself to Allah ﷻ and achieve distinction in continual worship and abidance of good works. So, let him not also miss the five prayers in congregation. His abidance by them becomes a means to revive his light and insight. The Messenger ﷺ has said, *"More blessed is prayer in congregation than prayer performed individually by twenty five levels."* And in another *hadith*, *"by twenty seven times."*

If it was stipulated for us slaves to pray these prayers in our shops or homes, the masjids would become derelict and abandoned. Those very same masjids about which *Al-Haqq* ﷻ states, **"(It is) in houses that Allah has permitted to be raised and wherein His Name is remembered. He is therein glorified, morning and evening."**[173]

During prayer in congregation, hearts unite, support each other and associate. There is also seeing the spectacle of the believers gathering together. The Messenger ﷺ said, *"The hand of Allah is with the congregation."*

When the congregation comes together, the blessings upon their hearts are stretched out to all present, as are their lights to whoever witnesses them. Their coming together

---

173   Quran 24:36

and their order is like an army whose being united and joined closely together is a reason for its victory. Prayer in congregation is one of the two interpretations of the words of the Glorious **"Truly Allah loves those who fight in His way in ranks, as if they were a solid structure."**[174]

In Addition

It is also binding upon you, O believer, that you lower your gaze from the moment you set out to work until you return home. Allow yourself to remember His words, **"Tell the believing men to lower their eyes and guard their private parts. That is purer for them."**[175] One should recognise that one's sight is a blessing from Allah ﷻ. Let him not be of those who are ungrateful to the blessings of Allah ﷻ. It is a trust from Allah ﷻ so let him not betray it. Remember the words of the Glorified, **"He knows the treachery of eyes and that which chests conceal."**[176] And His words, **"Does he not know that Allah sees?"**[177] If you desire to see (the forbidden) then know that He sees you.

One should know that if one lowers one's gaze, Allah ﷻ will open one's power of insight as a reward accordingly. Whoever constrains himself in outer sight, Allah expands for him his inner sight. It has been stated by one of the righteous, *"No one lowers his gaze from the forbidden except Allah brings about a light in his heart. He finds in it sweetness and delight."*

174	Quran 61:4
175	Quran 24:30
176	Quran 40:19
177	Quran 96:14

12. Back on the Path

Know that managing Allah's affairs is considered as opposition to His Lordship by those of insight. That is because when He sends down a commandment binding to you, you desire it to be removed. Or if He denies a matter for you, you desire its attainment. Or you become anxious over a matter when you know full well that He is your Guarantor concerning it and that He is the Facilitator of it.

This would all be disputation of His Lordship and transgressing the limits of slave-hood. Remember the words of the Glorious **"Has man not seen that We created him from a drop, and behold, he is a manifest adversary?"**[178] This verse condemns the one who forgets his origin yet contends with his Creator. Who is heedless of the reality of his creation yet argues with his Originator.

How can it be proper for one created from a sperm-drop to argue with Allah ﷻ over His decrees or oppose Him when He overrules or consents to a matter? So be wary – may Allah's mercy be upon you – of trying to manage Allah's affairs. Know that such managing is from the most severe veils over the heart that blocks the acquirement of deeper knowledge.

One's indulging in managing Allah's affairs for the sake of the animal-self (*nafs*) only arises from having love for the animal-self. If you become annihilated of your animal-self (*fana'*) and witness only Allah (*baqa'*), it would make you

---
[178] Quran 36:77

free of managing for yourself and relying on yourself.

How miserable is a slave who is ignorant of the actions of Allah ﷻ and heedless of His excellent care and guardianship!? Have you not heard His words, be He glorified, "**Say, 'Allah suffices...'**"?[179] Where is sufficiency and contentment with Allah ﷻ when a slave continually tries to organise His affairs? If one is content with the managing of Allah ﷻ, it would rid him of trying to manage alongside Him.

A Signpost

Know that self-direction occurs mostly upon those who seek Allah ﷻ and those taking a path to Him (*sulook*) before their faith becomes firmly rooted and they are established (in certainty). The people of heedlessness and sin have already responded to Satan in regard to great sins, disobedience and in the following of desires. So Satan has no need to invite them to self-direction. If he was to call them to it, it would not be the strongest weapon in his arsenal.

Satan rather focuses on the obedient and dedicated with his schemes of self-direction because of his inability to affect them with anything else. Many a slave who committed to setting time aside for Allah's remembrance (*wird*) neglected it, or was unable to be mindfully present with Allah during it, because of the worry of self-direction and preoccupation with setting aright his affairs. Many a slave, blessed with spiritual blessings, was found to be weak by Satan, so Satan fell upon him with the intrigues of self-

---

179 Quran 29:52

direction to desecrate the productivity of his time with Allah ﷻ. For Satan is envious and an envious one is most jealous when your time is spent productively and your condition is improved.

The whispers of self-direction occur upon each person according to his circumstances. Whoever is preoccupied with the concern for acquiring his daily livelihood, either today or for the morrow, then his cure is in recognising that Allah ﷻ guarantees his sustenance, **"There is no creature that crawls upon the earth but that its provision lies with Allah."**[180] Extrapolation on the matter of sustenance shall come in a dedicated chapter, if Allah, Most High, wills.

As for the one preoccupied with repelling the harm from an enemy he finds no power against, he would do well to remember that the forelock of the one he fears is in the hands of *Al-Haqq*, the Glorious. The enemy can do nothing except what *Al-Haqq* facilitates for him to do. Let him remember the words of the Glorious **"And whosoever trusts in Allah, He suffices him."**[181] And He states, **"Does Allah not suffice His slave? Yet they would frighten you with those apart from Him."**[182] And He states, **"Those, to whom the people said, 'Truly the people have gathered against you, so fear them', but it increased them in faith, and they said, 'Allah suffices us, an excellent Guardian is He!' So they returned with Blessing and Bounty from Allah, untouched by evil. And they pursued the contentment of Allah, and Allah is Possessed of Tremendous Bounty."**[183] And listen with the hearing of your heart to the words of Allah, the Glorified,

---

180	Quran 11:6
181	Quran 65:3
182	Quran 39:36
183	Quran 3:173-174

"So We revealed to the mother of Moses, 'Nurse him. But if you fear for him, then cast him into the river, and fear not, nor grieve'."[184]

Know that *Al-Haqq* is most worthy that protection be sought from Him. He gives refuge for He states, be He glorified, "**(He who is the One) who protects but is not protected against.**"[185] He is most worthy that He be sought for safety for He is the One who safeguards. He states, "**But Allah is the Best Protector, and He is the Most Merciful of the merciful.**"[186]

As for the one who is concerned because of debts he finds difficulty in repaying and the creditor is of little patience, then know that the One who eases affairs for you out of His kindness is the One who grants you all things in the first place. He will make it easy for you to fulfil your obligations out of His kindness. "**Is the reward of goodness anything but goodness?**"[187] How shameful is a slave who is satisfied and at ease when things are under his control yet full of anxiousness and worry when they are in the hands of *Al-Haqq* who safeguards them for him?

If your self-direction and concern is due to your family being left behind after you die, then He is the one who looks after them, in both your presence and absence while you are still alive. Listen to what the Messenger of Allah said, "*O Allah, you are the Companion in travel and the Caretaker of the family left behind.*" So He in whom you have your hopes in regarding what lies before you of death is the One in whom you hope in regarding what you leave

---

184	Quran 28:7
185	Quran 23:88
186	Quran 12:64
187	Quran 55:60

behind. One of the righteous said:

> *The One to whom my face turns towards*
> *He is the One I appointed over my family*
>
> *Not for a moment is He unaware of their condition*
> *And His kindness is grander than my kindness*

Indeed, Allah is more merciful to them than you are. Do not worry over a person who is under someone else's guardianship.

If your self-direction and concern are over a sickness that you fear will lengthen its stay, then know that trials and sicknesses are only for a set time. Just as an animal is not slaughtered except when the time is right, likewise a calamity will end when its time is up. Remember the words of the Glorified "**When their term comes, they shall not delay it by a single hour, nor shall they advance it.**"[188]

There is a narration of a Shaykh's son. The Shaykh passed away and his son's livelihood became difficult. His father had friends spread about in Iraq. He wondered which of his father's friends he should visit to seek their help. He settled on the one with the highest political position. When he arrived, his father's friend honoured him, made good his stay, and said to the boy, *"O my master, son of my master, what has brought you here?"*

He replied, *"My worldly means have dried up. I hoped you could speak to the Sultan of this land to grant me some position in one or other of his districts so I may earn a livelihood."*

The Shaykh became silent for a moment before

---

[188] Quran 7:34

raising his head and saying, *"Everything happens at its right time, which I cannot change. Besides, who am I compared to you when you have been given authority over the people of Iraq!?"*

The boy left the Shaykh angrily, unable to decipher the Shaykh's words. At the same time, the Sultan was seeking someone to tutor his son and it was said to the same young man, *"O son of so-and-so Shaykh! Come and teach the Sultan's son.'* So he taught the son of the Sultan and then consequently remained in his company for forty years. When the Sultan died, the prince appointed the son of the Shaykh to administer the affairs of the people of Iraq!

If your concern is over a wife or mother you have lost, who lived harmoniously with you, who used to help and support you in your affairs, then know that the One who brought her to you has riches that never cease and His kindness is never exhausted. He is capable of granting you, out of His favour, one who is better and wiser than the one you have lost. So do not place yourself among the ignorant.

The different types of self-direction are as numerous as their cures. But to enumerate them all and their treatments is unfeasible because of their sheer number and their having no limit. But if Allah ﷻ favours you with understanding the affair of self-direction, you will know how to proceed.

A Signpost

Know that self-direction only occurs within one's animal-self (*nafs*), when it is veiled from reality. If the heart is preserved from the animal-self's touch and its whispers, the knockings of self-direction will not affect it.

I heard our shaykh, Abu'l Abbas, may Allah be pleased with him, saying *"When Allah, be He glorified, created land upon liquid, it moved so He stabilised it with the mountains. He says, '**and (He) firmly fixed in it (the earth), mountains.**'[189] Likewise, when He created the animal-self (nafs), it moved (agitated towards disobedience) so He stabilised it with the mind."*

Any slave who is rich in intelligence and blessed with light (*nur*) will have tranquillity sent down upon him from his Nurturing Lord. His animal-self (*nafs*) will be subdued from agitations, he will trust in the King of worldly means and so be at peace. The *nafs* would be calm and submissive to the rulings of Allah, firm in the face of His decrees, ready to receive His support and His lights and far removed from managing and contesting His judgements. The *nafs* would be at ease with its Master, finding comfort in the fact that He sees it. **"Does it not suffice that your Nurturing Lord is Witness over all things?"**[190] The *nafs* would then be worthy of **"O you *nafs* at peace! Return to your Nurturing Lord, pleased and pleasing. Enter among My slaves. Enter My Paradise."**[191] This verse alludes to the great characteristics and lofty virtues of this *nafs* at peace.

The First

The *nafs* is of three types. The *nafs* that overpowers one towards evil (*nafs al-amarah*), the *nafs* that criticises itself and attempts reform (*nafs al-lawwamah*) and the *nafs* at peace (*nafs al-mutma'innah*). Al-Haqq did not speak directly to any of them, except the *nafs* at peace. He states regarding

---

189	Quran 79:32
190	Quran 41:53
191	Quran 89:27-30

the *nafs al-amarah*, "**Surely the *nafs* commands to evil.**"[192] He states regarding the *nafs al-lawwamah*, "**And I swear by the self-blaming soul.**"[193] Yet, He preferred the *nafs al-mutma'innah* above the others with his direct speech, "**O you *nafs* at peace!**"

The Second

He addressed the *nafs* by a title (i.e. *mutma'innah* – *nafs* at peace). Alluding to someone in such a way honours and esteems them in the Arabic language, according to the knowledgeable in the matter.

The Third

He praises the *nafs* by describing it as being at peace. This is a recognition of the *nafs'* submission and reliance upon Him.[194]

The Fourth

He described this *nafs* as *mutma'innah* (at peace). *Mutma'in* also means low-lying earth (in Arabic). So when the *nafs* lowers itself with humility and is enfeebled, that is when its Master praises it and parades its glory. This is in accordance with the words of the Prophet ﷺ, "*Whoever humbles himself to Allah, Allah honours him.*"

The Fifth

In His words "**Return to your Nurturing Lord, pleased and pleasing**" is an indication that a *nafs* that is

---

192   Quran 12:53
193   Quran 75:2
194   Since it is only through submission and reliance upon Allah that one finds peace.

in the states of *amarah* or *lawwamah* will not be allowed an honourable return to Allah ﷻ. That honour is reserved for the *nafs al-mutma'innah*. Due to its being in a state of tranquillity (and humility) it is said to it, "**Return to your Nurturing Lord, pleased and pleasing**." As if to say – *We have allowed you to enter Our Presence and eternity in Our Paradise*. This motivates the slave to strive so that his *nafs* may reach the station of *mutma'innah*. But none reach it except by surrendering to Allah ﷻ and abandoning managing Allah's affairs.

The Sixth

He said "**Return to your Nurturing Lord**" and did not say – Return to *the* Nurturing Lord or return to *Allah*. This alludes to the *nafs'* return to Allah as being linked to His kindness and His nurturing. It is not a return linked to His power and supremity.[195] Thus He shows friendliness, gentleness, honour and love to this *nafs*.

The Seventh

He states that this *nafs* is "**pleased**." That is to say, it is pleased with Allah in this world by being pleased with His rulings and decrees. It is pleased in the Hereafter with His generosity and bestowals. This directs the slave to understand that there is no (honourable) return to Allah ﷻ except by being at peace with Him and pleased with Him, not otherwise. There is also an indication here, that the slave will not be pleasing to Allah in the Hereafter unless he is pleased with Allah in this world.

The gist of this verse gives the impression that the slave is first pleased with Allah ﷻ and as a result of that,

---
195 i.e. it is linked to Allah's *Jamal* (Beauty) not His *Jalal* (Majesty).

Allah ﷻ is then pleased with the slave. However, another verse points to the opposite, that Allah ﷻ is first pleased with the slave and as a result, the slave is then pleased with Allah ﷻ. Know that each verse has its truth and there is no contradiction between them. The second verse in question is "**Allah is pleased with them, and they are pleased with Him.**"[196]

The second verse alludes to the order of causation, that Allah is first pleased with the slave and then allows the slave to be pleased with Him. Reality requires this. If He was not initially pleased with them, never could they attain (the honour of) being pleased with Him. Whereas the former verse points to the fact that whoever is pleased with Allah ﷻ in this world, Allah ﷻ is pleased with them in the next world. A fact that is clear with no ambiguity.

The Eighth

He states that this *nafs* is "**pleasing.**" This is tremendous praise to this *nafs al-mutma'innah*, it is the most honourable accolade and description. Have you not heard the Glorious's words "**Allah has promised the believing men and believing women Gardens with rivers running below, to abide therein, and goodly dwellings in the Gardens of Eden. But the pleasure of Allah is greater**"?[197] That is to say, Allah's being pleased with them while they are in Paradise is even greater than all the other blessings they enjoy therein!

The Ninth

He states, "**Enter among My slaves. Enter My**

| 196 | Quran 5:119 |
| 197 | Quran 9:72 |

Paradise." This is a monumental glad-tiding for the *nafs al-mutma'innah*, as it is called and invited to join His slaves – but which slaves are these? These are slaves of distinction and victory, not ordinary slaves that are just subdued by authority and power. They are the slaves about which He states, **"As for My slaves, truly you (O Satan) have no authority over them."**[198] Also, those about whom Satan said, **"I shall cause them to err all together, except Your sincere slaves among them."**[199] Not the slaves about which He generally refers to when He states, **"There is none in the heavens and on the earth, but that it comes unto the Compassionate as a slave."**[200]

This *nafs'* joy over His saying **"Enter among My slaves"** is greater than its joy with **"Enter My Paradise."** That is because the former indicates closeness to Him, while the latter refers to His Paradise.

The Tenth

He states, **"Enter My Paradise."** In this is an indication that it is the characteristics of the *nafs al-mutma'innah* (i.e. its being at peace and in submission) that qualify it to enter with His slaves into His Paradise, the paradise of obedience in this world and the known Paradise in the Hereafter. And Allah knows best.

A Point of Benefit

The verses **"O you *nafs* at peace! Return to your Nurturing Lord, pleased and pleasing"** contain two descriptions, each of which indicates the abandonment of

---

198	Quran 17:65
199	Quran 15:40
200	Quran 19:93

self-direction. Allah ﷻ describes the *nafs*, which has all the virtues we have just mentioned, as being tranquil and in contentment. These qualities do not exist except with abandoning managing His affairs. For the *nafs* is not in a state of peace until it forsakes worry over managing alongside Allah ﷻ and trusts instead in His excellent planning. When the *nafs* is pleased with Allah ﷻ, it surrenders to Him, obeys His command and is subdued to His decree. Hence it becomes at peace through Allah's Nurturing Lordship and gains serenity with its reliance on His Divinity. The blessings this *nafs* has received of intelligence make it firm and it is not in a state of agitation. It does not incline but to thank Allah for His decrees, knowing full well it is in good hands in whatever He allows and whatever He overrules.

A Point of Benefit

Know that the secret in the creation of self-direction and your having choice in the matter, is to make manifest the power of the Overpowering One (*Al-Qahhar*). He, be He glorified, willed to make Himself known to His slaves by His overpowering and so created the ability for them to have self-direction and choice. Then, he spread veils over them so they would resort to self-direction and choice alongside His decrees. If the slaves were in a state of witnessing and observing His power, never could they be able to self-direct or have a choice in His decrees, just like it is not possible for the heavenly angels.

So when the slaves pondered, self-directed and preferred their choosing, He directed His dominating power to destroy what their self-direction and their preferences had built up. The very foundations of their self-direction shook and its buildings came crumbling down. Finally, when the slaves realised His dominance and His purposes, they recognised that He is the Overpowering One, Who compels His slaves. He did not create free choice within you so that you have a choice in His decrees, but so that His choosing can overpower your choosing and you realise that you have no choice in His affairs. Likewise, He did not grant you the ability to manage so that you manage His affairs, but He did so that He plans and you plan, and only His plan comes into fruition, while yours falls apart.

That is why when one of the righteous was asked, *"How did you gain intimate knowledge of Allah?"* He replied, *"By the breaking of my resolve."*

13. A New Road

We had promised to dedicate a chapter to the topic of self-direction regarding one's livelihood, it being the main reason worry affects one's heart. Know that the preservation of the heart from the self-direction of one's livelihood is a great favour. None are granted preservation from it except the firm in faith who believe in Allah's excellent managing for themselves. Their hearts are at peace and they are found to be sincere because of their trust in Him. One of the Shaykhs has said, *"Preserve well for me this matter of livelihood and you will have no difficulty in attaining all other (virtuous) states."*

Another Shaykh mentioned, *"The greatest worry is acquiring one's needs."* The Shaykh refers to the fact that Allah ﷻ created the human being needy of nutrients for his health and for energy to be distributed around his body. What one eats is worn down by the stomach, which draws out goodness from the food so that it can be used to create parts of the body anew with the help of the energy obtained. If *Al-Haqq* ﷻ willed, He would have made the human being so he does not require such material sustenance or need to resort to the wonder of digesting it. Yet *Al-Haqq* ﷻ willed to display the need for nourishment in living beings and their being compelled to seek it so that, in contrast, His self-sufficiency and richness from all of that be recognised.

The Glorified states, "**Say, 'Shall I take as a protector anyone other than Allah, the Originator of the heavens**

and the earth, who feeds and is not fed?"[201] He is praised in this verse with two characteristics. The first is that He is not fed. This applies to nothing else, as every slave needs His kindness and eats from His sustenance and graciousness.

The second is that He is not fed because He is glorified and sanctified above needing nourishment. He is the Self-Subsistent. The Self-Subsistent can have no need. *Al-Haqq* singled out living creatures with need for sustenance as opposed to other creations because He bestowed living creatures with something of His characteristics (such as life). If they were left without need, they would make claims about themselves (of divinity and self-sufficiency) or claims would be made about them. *Al-Haqq* willed, and He is All-Wise, All-Informed, to compel living creatures to food, drink, clothing, and other things so that by the repetition of seeking the means for their needs any claims of divinity would be extinguished.

From another point of view, *Al-Haqq* willed to make the human species, and others, recognise their neediness and be known for their weakness. Have you not considered the words of the Glorified "**O mankind! You are needful of Allah; and He is the Self-Sufficient, the Praised**"?[202] He made man's neediness for Allah as a means that leads to His closeness and eternity by His side.

Perhaps here you will understand the words of the Messenger, "*Whomsoever knows his self, knows his Nurturing Lord.*" That is, whoever recognises his own needs, humility and poverty, recognises his Lord by His honour, His power, His generosity, His kindness and His other perfect qualities.

---

201 Quran 6:14
202 Quran 35:15

This applies particularly to the human being, for *Al-Haqq* ﷻ continually sends to man's aid the means to fulfil his needs. Needs which He has made numerous so that man is always obliged to rectify his livelihood and his hereafter.

Understand the words of the Glorious "**Indeed We have created man (to live) in constant struggle.**"[203] That is, man struggles for his worldly affairs and his hereafter. But it is for honouring the human being that Allah ﷻ continually requires them to fulfil their needs. Do you not see that other living species have no need for garments with their wool, fur and hair? That they do not need to establish a home for shelter with their stables and nests?

He also made human beings needy because He willed to test them. He made them needy for numerous things to observe whether they will enter into the forbidden by the use of their minds and planning for themselves. Or will they resort to Allah's allocating and decree?

He also willed, be He glorified, to make Himself loved to his slaves. When He placed the means of poverty in them and then fulfilled their needs, the slaves found happiness in themselves and relief in their hearts. It renewed their love for their Nurturing Lord. The Messenger ﷺ said, *"Love Allah for what He nourishes you with from His favours."* With each blessing that comes anew, so is their love renewed according to it.

He also willed, be He glorified, that gratitude be shown. He placed poverty in His slaves and fulfilled their needs so they could be thankful to Him. That they may know His kindness and benevolence. The Glorified states, "**Eat of**

---

203 Quran 90:4

the provision of your Nurturing Lord and give thanks to Him."[204]

He also willed, be He glorified, to open the door of intimate conversation with His slaves. When they recognised their need for sustenance and blessings, they directed their worries to Him to ease their pains. Hence, they were honoured with private conversation with Him and awarded His favours. If their poverty had not driven them to this intimate conversation, the general masses would not have realised such an honour was available to them. If the slaves had no needs, this door of intimate conversation would have been closed and opened only by the lovers of Allah ﷻ. So need became the key to intimate discourse with Him. Intimate discourse is a monumental honour and a position of immense prestige! Have you not seen that *Al-Haqq* describes Moses, peace be upon him (with this honour), **"So he watered [their flocks] for them. Then he turned toward the shade and said, 'My Nurturing Lord! Truly I am in need of any good that You have sent down upon me'"**?[205]

Ali, may Allah be pleased with him, said, *"By Allah, he (Moses) did not seek anything but some bread he might eat. The colour of vegetation he had eaten was visible from his stomach due to its thinness and transparentness and his lack of nourishment."* See – may Allah have mercy on you – how Moses ﷺ asked for some bread from his Nurturing Lord because he thought that was all he could lay hold of at the time. The believer should act similarly and ask Allah ﷻ for what is small and what is great.

---

204   Quran 34:15
205   Quran 28:24

One of the righteous said, *"Truly, I ask Allah in my prayers for even the salt of my dough."* Nor should you restrict yourself, O believer, to ask for even less than that from your needs. For if one does not ask for the little, he has not acted deservedly to receive greater than that. Besides, the request, even if it be something small, opens the sublime door of intimate conversing with Allah ﷻ. Shaykh Abu'l Hassan, may Allah be pleased with him said, *"Do not let the concern of your prayer (dua) be the fulfilment of some need. For you would then be veiled from your Nurturing Lord. Let your concern be the intimate conversation with your Guardian."*

In the verse **"So he watered [their flocks] for them. Then he turned toward the shade and said, 'My Nurturing Lord! Truly I am in need of any good that You have sent down upon me'"** there are numerous benefits.

The First Benefit

The believer asks from his Nurturing Lord what is small and what is large, like we have just mentioned.

The Second Benefit

The Prophet Moses ﷺ called upon Allah ﷻ with His attribute of being the Nurturing Lord. This is most fitting in this context. For the Nurturing Lord is who raises you with His kindness and nourishes you with His bestowals. So he sought compassion from his Master by calling on Him with His attribute of nurturing. The blessings of His nurturing are never severed and the benefits of it are never suppressed.

The Third Benefit

Moses ﷺ said, **"Truly I am in need of any good**

that You have sent down upon me." He did not just say – *Truly I am in need of good* – which does not contain the added meaning that Allah ﷻ has already sent down His sustenance and He is not unaware of Moses's plight.

Hence, the verse came with the wording "**...any good that You have sent down upon me**" to show Moses' trust in Allah ﷻ. He knew that Allah ﷻ had not forgotten him. It was as if Moses ﷺ said – *My Nurturing Lord! I know that you are not unaware of my condition nor the condition of anything else You have created. You have already sent down my sustenance. Bring to me whatever You have sent down upon me however You wish and upon whatever You wish! Let it be enclosed in Your kindness and coupled with Your blessings.*

This etiquette of asking has two advantages. One is that it entails asking from Allah ﷻ. The other is that it contains the knowledge that *Al-Haqq* ﷻ has already sent down His sustenance but has hidden its moment of arrival, its cause and mediums. He has done so, so that distress may come upon the slave. With this distress comes the response and help from Allah ﷻ. "**He (is Allah), Who answers the one in distress when he calls upon Him.**"[206] If He had specified the means, the time and medium of His sustenance, the slave would not become distressed, since distress requires uncertainty. So glorified be the All-Wise Lord, All-Powerful, All-Knowing!

The Fourth Benefit

The verse makes clear that asking from Allah ﷻ does not contradict the station of slave-hood to Allah ﷻ. Moses ﷺ had attained perfection in the station of slave-hood and still asked from Allah ﷻ, showing that indeed, the station of slave-hood does not mean one does not ask from Him.

One might ask, if the station of slave-hood does not negate asking from Allah ﷻ, then how is it that the Friend (Abraham), upon him be peace, did not ask from Allah ﷻ when he was thrown by catapult into the large fire? When Gabriel, upon him be peace, called out to Abraham, *"Do you have any need?"*

Abraham ﷺ replied, *"From you, I have no need. But from Allah, then indeed."*

Gabriel ﷺ said, *"Ask Him!"*

Abraham ﷺ replied, *"His knowledge of my situation suffices me from having to ask Him."* He sufficed with the knowledge of Allah ﷻ and did not ask from Him. How is this consistent with Moses' asking from Him?

The reply is that the Prophets, peace and blessings of Allah be upon them, act in every situation in a fitting manner, based on what they understand is desired from them from Allah ﷻ. So, Abraham ﷺ understood that Allah's design through him in that situation was to not ask from Allah ﷻ and suffice with His knowledge. This is what was required from him by his Nurturing Lord. For *Al-Haqq* wished to display the rank of his inner-heart (*sirr*) and His care for him to the heavenly assembly of angels. They are the angels referred to in the verse **"'I am placing a representative upon the earth', they said, 'Will You place therein one who will work corruption therein, and shed blood, while we hymn Your praise and Sanctify You?' He said, 'Truly I know what you know not'."**[207] *Al-Haqq* willed to display the secret

---
[207] Quran 2:30

of His words **"Truly I know what you know not"** the day Abraham ﷺ was flung by the catapult. It was as if He was saying – *O you who said* **"Will You place therein one who will work corruption therein..."**, *how do you see Abraham, my dear friend now? You looked into the actions prevailing on earth from the likes Nimrod and other people of corruption and arrogance. Yet you did not look into the righteousness and right guidance therein from the likes of Abraham and those who follow him from the lovers of Allah.*

As for Moses ﷺ, he recognised that the desire of Allah ﷻ from him at that moment was to display his poverty and reveal the difficulty of his situation to Allah.[208] He only followed what was required from him at the moment. **"Everyone has a direction toward which he turns."**[209] Each is upon evidence, guidance, and has the approval and endorsement of Allah ﷻ.

The Fifth Benefit

Look at how Moses ﷺ requested sustenance from his Nurturing Lord. He did not frankly or plainly mention what he needed. He just acknowledged his poverty and deprivation before Allah ﷻ. He also testified to Allah's richness. For when he confessed that he was poverty-stricken and needy, he acknowledged his Nurturing Lord as wealthy and self-sufficient. *"Whosoever knows his self, knows his Nurturing Lord."* This is one of the mats upon which one sits when in intimate conversation with Allah, and the mats are many.

---

208   His plight and prayer have been a source of solace for those that read his story in the Quran for centuries and will continue to do so till the Day of Judgement.
209   Quran 2:148

At times He will make you sit on the mat of poverty and you will call out, *"O Rich and Self-Sufficient One (Ya Ghani)!"* At times upon the mat of humbleness and lowliness so you call out, *"O Most Exalted One (Ya Aziz)!"* At times, upon the mat of weakness and impotence so you call out, *"O Most Powerful One (Ya Qawiy)!"* So too with the rest of His names.

When Moses acknowledged his poverty to Allah (when he said **"Truly I am in need"**), he alluded to asking from Allah, even though he did not ask directly what it was he needed. Putting forth a request may sometimes be through the slave mentioning his poverty and his need. Or putting forth a request may sometimes be by mentioning the virtues of the Master and His oneness, like it is mentioned in the *hadith, "The most excellent of my prayers (duas) and the prayers of the Prophets before me, was on the Mountain of Arafah – There is no god but Allah, He is Alone and no partner has He."* Here the Prophet made the praise for Allah a prayer in itself, for just by praising the All-Rich Master by mentioning His perfections is seeking His bounty and gifts. As the poet said:

*A generous one is not changed by the coming of day
From his virtue and good manner, neither by the night*

*If he was to be praised on any given day
His desire to help you becomes your right*

Allah, the Glorious, states the words of Jonah, upon him be peace, **"Then he cried out in the darkness, 'There is no god but You! Glory be to You! Truly I have been among the wrongdoers'."**[210] Then He states, be He glorified,

---

[210] Quran 21:87

about Himself, **"So We answered him, and saved him from grief. Thus do We save the believers."**[211] Jonah, upon him be peace, did not ask Allah specifically of his need. But when he praised his Nurturing Lord and confessed to Him, displaying his poverty before Him, *Al-Haqq* treated it as a request (and saved him from the whale).

The Sixth Benefit

This benefit deserves to be mentioned as the first. Moses performed an act of kindness for the two daughters of Shuayb. He did not intend to seek any benefit from them nor did he ask them for any payment. After he had led their sheep and watered them, he directed himself to his Nurturing Lord and asked from Him, not from the women. He only asked from his Guardian, He who bestows upon whoever asks of Him. Truly, the Sufi fulfils his obligations to others but does not ask for his rights in return. In this regard, we have the following lines:

Do not busy yourself with blaming any cohort
You will only waste your time, and your time is short

How can you criticise others when you believe
That all matters are allowed by Divine decrees?

Yes, perhaps they have been of Allah's rights heedless
But so have you, have you forgotten your wickedness?

Honour their rights over you and show some fortitude
Pull their rights from yourself, be they any magnitude

If you do so then you are under watchful custody
Of He whose knowledge overflows abundantly.

---

211   Quran 21:88

Moses ﷺ let others have their full share of his help but sought nothing in return. So he received from Allah the most perfect reward. *Al-Haqq* ﷻ hastened His support to him in this world in addition to what He stored for him in the Hereafter by marrying him to one of the two daughters. He made Moses ﷺ the son in law of His prophet Shuayb ﷺ and a close friend to him until the moment of his own prophethood arrived. O slave of Allah, do not make dealings except with Allah and you will profit greatly. He will honour you with what He honoured His pious slaves.

The Seventh Benefit

Look to the words of the Glorified, "**So he watered (their flocks) for them. Then he turned toward the shade…**" This is evidence that a believer can prefer shade over staying under the hot sun, cool water over hot water, and the easier path over the difficult and rough one. It would not take one out of the station of abstinence *(zuhd)* of this world. Do you not see that *Al-Haqq* ﷻ states Moses "**turned toward the shade**"? That is, he set out for it and arrived at it.

If you rebutted by mentioning the account of one of the righteous who was keeping his drinking vessel in the sunlight and was asked by a passing man about that and he replied, "*When I placed it there, no sunlight was reaching it and now I am embarrassed (before Allah) to act in the way of my selfish interests,*" then know – may Allah have mercy upon you – that this is the state of a slave who demands complete adherence to the truth from his animal-self *(nafs)* and prevents it from its desires lest they distract him from His Master. If he was to ascend to the station he aspires to, he would have moved his water out of the sunlight. For by moving the water into the shade he would be intending the preservation of his body's rights which *Al-Haqq* has commanded him to preserve, not out of the intention to fulfil his desires. He would be only fulfilling the rights of his Nurturing Lord in himself.

The Glorious states, "**Allah desires ease for you, and He does not desire hardship for you.**"[212] And He states, "**Allah desires to lighten [your burden] for you, for man was created weak.**"[213] That is why the scholars of religious law (*fuqaha*) say that if someone vowed to walk to Mecca barefoot, he should put on shoes and not walk barefoot. This is because the *shariah's* purpose is not to inconvenience the slaves. Nor did the *shariah* come to prevent them from enjoyments. How could it possibly do so when delights were created for them?

Al-Rabee' ibn Ziyad once said to Ali, may Allah be pleased with him, "*Help me with my brother Asim.*"

Ali replied, "*What is the matter with him?*"

He answered, "*He has wrapped himself in cloths and desires to be a recluse.*"

Ali said, "*I must attend to him.*" Ali found him wrapped in two cloths and with dishevelled hair and beard. Ali frowned at him and said, "*Woe to you! Are you not ashamed before your family? Will you not have mercy for your child? Do you think that Allah has allowed you the good things of this world and then dislikes any of them reaching you? No, you have little status with Allah. Have you not heard the words of Allah in His book, '**The earth has He laid down for creatures. Therein are fruit and date palms bearing sheaths, husked grains, and fragrant***

---

212   Quran 2:185
213   Quran 4:28

herbs. So which of your Nurturing Lord's blessings do you two (jinn and men) deny? He created man from dried clay, like earthen vessels, and He created jinn from smokeless fire. So which of your Nurturing Lord's blessings do you two deny? Nurturing Lord of the two easts and Nurturing Lord of the two wests. So which of your Nurturing Lord's blessings do you two deny? He mixed the two seas, such that they meet one another. Between them lies a barrier that they transgress not. So which of your Nurturing Lord's blessings do you two deny? From them come forth pearls and coral stones.'[214] *Do you think that Allah has permitted all this for His slaves and then wants them to thank Him for these blessings by belittling these blessings!?"*

Asim replied, *"Then why do we see you having such coarseness in food and clothing?"*

Ali replied, *"Woe to you! Allah has imposed on leaders of the truth to consider themselves as the poorest of their people."*

It is clear from the words of Ali, may Allah be pleased with him, that *Al-Haqq* did not forbid His slaves from engaging with (permissible) delights. He, be He glorified, only requested gratitude from them when they enjoy them. He states, **"Eat of the provision of your Nurturing Lord and give thanks to Him."**[215] And He states, **"O you who believe! Eat of the good things (*tayyibaat*) We have provided you and give thanks to Allah."**[216] And He states, **"O Messengers! Eat of the good things (*tayyibaat*) and work righteousness."**[217] Never did He say, *"Do not eat..."* He only states to eat and work righteousness.

214	Quran 55:10-22
215	Quran 34:15
216	Quran 2:172
217	Quran 23:51

You might say – the good things (*tayyibaat*) referred to in the previous verses only refers to permissible (*halal*) things and not delightful things. Because the permissible is what is good in the view of the religious law.

Know that it is possible that what is meant by **"the good things"** is the permissible (*halal*) things. For the permissible is certainly good in the sense it does not result in any sin, blame or veiling from reality. But it is also possible that what is meant by **"the good things"** is delightful foods. The secret in delightful things being allowed, and in the command to eat them, is the consumer finds its deliciousness a means to renew their eagerness to show gratitude. He is motivated to acts of worship and to abstain from the forbidden.

Shaykh Abu'l Hassan said, "*My shaykh said to me – My son, cool your water. If the slave drinks cold water and says, 'The Praise belongs to Allah (alhamdulillah)', every part of his body will agree with and take part in the thanking of Allah.*"

Shaykh Abu'l Hassan then said, "*As for the one who was found keeping his drinking vessel in the sunlight and said, 'When I placed it there, no sunlight was reaching it and now I am embarrassed (before Allah) to act in the way of my selfish interests' – then he had been overcome by an (exclusive) spiritual state and is not to be imitated.*"

14. Taking a Turn

We have concluded our discussion on why living creatures, especially humans, are in constant need of sustenance and support. We will now turn our attention to *Al-Haqq's* guaranteeing this sustenance that preserves their lives. These two species, the human and *jinn*, have been created so that Allah ﷻ can command them and demand from them their servitude, worship and obedience.

The First Verse Regarding Provision

The Glorified states, **"I did not create jinn and mankind, save to worship Me. I desire no provision from them; nor do I desire that they should feed Me. Truly Allah is the Provider, the Possessor of Strength, the Firm."**[218]

The Glorified makes clear that He only created these two species for His worship, that is so He could command them to worship. Just like one of you might say – I have bought you, O slave, so that you may serve me. That is, so that I order you in my service and you comply. However, the slave may be opposed to your orders and you did not buy him for that. It was only so he could fulfil your tasks and needs.

The Mu'tazilites[219] interpret this verse strictly to the letter and say *Al-Haqq* created His slaves for obedience

---

218   Quran 51:56-58
219   A now mostly defunct school of Islamic theology. Their enthusiasm for Greek philosophy led them to many deviant ideas through their attempts to unify Greek philosophy with Islamic creed.

while disbelief and sin are created by the slaves. We have already disproved this theory.

When the reason behind creation is clarified, the slave understands and is directed to his purpose. Thus, the slaves that save themselves from ignorance of Allah's purposes in them would not be diverted from the path of right guidance and would not be neglectful of their responsibilities.

It has been said that four angels converse with each other every day. The first exclaims, *"If only this creation was not created!"* The second responds, *"Since they are created, if only they knew why they were created!"* The third then states, *"Since they do not know why they were created, if only they acted according to what they do know!"* Finally, the fourth says, *"Since they do not act with what they know, if only they would seek repentance for what they do!"*

Al-Haqq has made it clear He did not create His slaves to be free to do whatever they desired. He only created them to worship Him and affirm His oneness. You do not buy a slave so that he can serve himself, only so he can be a servant. This verse, **"I did not create jinn and mankind, save to worship Me,"** is evidence against every slave who works for, and gives priority to his interests over the rights of his Nurturing Lord and prioritises his desires over obedience to his Master.

Similarly, it is said that Ibrahim ibn Adham heard a voice calling out to him from his horse's saddle strap as he was out hunting, it being the reason for his repentance to Allah, *"O Ibrahim, was it for this you were created? Is this what you have been ordered to do?"* Then he heard it a second time saying, *"O Ibrahim, you were not created for this nor were you ordered to do this!"*

The scholar *(faqih)* is he who understands the reason behind his creation and acts accordingly. This is true knowledge and understanding that whomsoever it is given to is given immense favour. In this regard Imam Malik, may Allah be pleased with him, said "Fiqh *(deep understanding or Islamic law) is not due to memorising many narrations. Fiqh is but a light that Allah places in the heart."*

I heard our shaykh, Abu'l Abbas ﷺ say, *"The scholar* (faqih) *is one who has removed the veils covering the sight of his heart."*

So one who understands the reason behind creation, that Allah ﷻ only brought one into being to obey Him and created one to serve Him, is led to abstinence from this world and preference for the next world. While disregarding the purpose of one's creation leads to fulfilling one's desires and being too busy to fulfil the rights of one's Master. The ponderer of one's final destination prepares for it.

A Signpost

One of the righteous said, *"If it was said to me, tomorrow you will die, I would not find any extra good deeds to do (because I am doing them all already)."*

While to another, his mother said to him, *"My son, why do you not eat bread?"*

He replied, *"In the time to chew the bread and eat the crumbs, I can recite fifty verses (from the Quran)."*

Such are people whose intelligences have distracted them from this world. They await the onset of horrors and terrors of a promised day when they shall meet the Compeller (*Al-Jabbar*) of the heavens and earth. That has distracted them from attending to the delights of this world and inclination to its amusements. One of those with intimate knowledge (*arifeen*) has said, *"I came to one of the shaykhs in Morocco for seeking knowledge. I began to collect water for ablution but the shaykh made to collect water himself despite my efforts. I insisted that I collect for him but he refused and was adamant about collecting water himself. He held on tightly to the end of the rope (to keep the bucket from falling back down the well). In his house, there was an olive tree by the well extending over the house. I said to him 'My master, why don't you tie the end of the rope to this tree?' He replied 'What, is there a tree here!? I have lived here for sixty years and did not realise there was a tree here!'"*

Open your eyes – may Allah have mercy upon you – to this story and others like it. You will realise that Allah ﷻ has slaves who are so preoccupied with Him, they are distracted from all else. But nothing distracts them from Him. They are bewildered by Allah's greatness and astounded in awe of Him. Love for Him has settled in their heart of hearts. May Allah make us among them and never remove us from them!

In a similar story, there was a friend of Allah ﷻ who lived in a masjid, situated on some highlands. One of his students who served him asked if he could take a branch of fruit from one of the two date trees in the masjid. He was allowed permission and asked, *"My master, from which of the two trees should I take it from? From the yellow one or the red one?"* The shaykh replied, *"My son, I have lived in this masjid for 40 years. I do not know which is the yellow one and which is the red one!"*

It has also been recounted that the children of one of the pious passed through his house. He asked, *"Who are they? Whose children are they?"* It was said to him, *"They are yours!"* He did not recognise them until he was reminded again about them because of his preoccupation with Allah ﷻ.

Another of the pious shaykhs would say about his children when he saw them, *"These are orphans even if their father is alive."* But to elaborate on this beam of light would take us out of the purpose of this book.

* * * * *

When Allah, the Most High states, **"I did not create jinn and mankind, save to worship Me,"** He knew that they have natural instincts they need to satisfy and these would disrupt the purity of their slave-hood. So, He guaranteed their sustenance so they would devote time to His service and not be preoccupied with earning their sustenance instead of His worship. He states, **"I desire no provision from them."**[220] That is to say – *I do not want them to provide for themselves for I have guaranteed that through the excellence of My assurance and guardianship.*

"Nor do I desire that they should feed Me."[221] That is to say – *I am the Possessor of Strength and Self-Sufficient One*

---

220   Quran 51:57
221   Ibid

who is not fed. That is why He followed the verse by stating, **"Truly Allah is the Provider, the Possessor of Strength, the Firm."**[222] That is to say – *I do not want them to provide for themselves for I am their Provider. I do not want them to feed Me because I am the Possessor of Strength.* For whoever has strength does not need to feed or be fed. The verse contains assurances to His slaves that He will provide for them when He states, **"Truly Allah is the Provider."**

It is binding on the believers to declare His exclusivity in sustaining and not attribute anything that belongs to Him to His creation. Nor should they ascribe His provision to secondary means and causes. Neither should they ascribe their sustenance to their own efforts. It has been narrated that the Prophet ﷺ said after it had rained in the night, *"Do you know what your Nurturing Lord has said?"*

The Companions replied, *"No, O Messenger of Allah."*

He said, *"Your Nurturing Lord has said that from amongst My slaves, one has become a believer in Me and another a disbeliever in Me. As for the one who said that it has rained on us by the bounty of Allah and His mercy, he is a believer in Me, a disbeliever in the stars. While the one who said it has rained because of the setting of such and such star or because of the star so and so, he is a disbeliever in Me, a believer in the stars."*

This *hadith* contains a great benefit for the believers and deep wisdom for the certain of faith. It also teaches the proper etiquette with the Nurturing Lord of all the worlds.

Perhaps this *hadith* will also prohibit you, O believer, from dealing with astrology and its associated sciences and stop you from claiming that it has any effect. Know

---

222   Quran 51:58

that Allah ﷻ has already decreed your affairs, no doubt His decrees will run on till they are accomplished. He has already set forth His commands concerning you, no doubt they will become apparent. What is the point of trying to spy on the unseen world (*ghayb*) of the All-Knowing of the unseen? He has prohibited us from spying on His slaves when He states, "**And do not spy upon one another.**"²²³ How can we then possibly spy on His unseen world? The poet did well to say:

> *Inform, on my behalf, that 'lucky' star*
> *That I'm a disbeliever in what stars decree*
>
> *I know all that is and all that was*
> *Comes from the Overruler necessarily*

A Benefit

Know that the word form in Arabic used for 'provider' (*razzaq*) in "**Truly Allah is the Provider**" denotes emphasis and exaggeration. So *razzaq* is more intensive in meaning than *raziq* (both mean provider or sustainer). This emphasis on Allah's providing could be due to the variety of creations that He provides for, or it could be due to the different types of sustenance He provides, or it could mean both together.

A Benefit

Based on the science of rhetoric (*balagha*), know that to indicate praise with a noun is more definite than to do so with a verb. To say *"Zaid is a good-doer"* is more emphatic than to say *"Zaid does good"* or *"Zaid has done good."* This is because a noun alludes to deep-rootedness

---

223 Quran 49:12

and to permanence, while a verb is used to denote renewal and temporality. Hence, the Glorified's stating **"Allah is the Provider"** is more intense in meaning than if He were to say – *Allah is the One who provides*. If He had used the phrase *'Allah is the One who provides'*, it would only confirm that He provides, not that He exclusively provides. When He states **"Truly Allah is the Provider"** it also points to Him being the only provider. It is as if He is saying – *there is no provider except Allah* .

The Second Verse Regarding Provision

He states, **"Allah it is Who created you, then provided for you; then He causes you to die; then He gives you life."**[224] This verse contains the meaning that creation and provision are interlinked. That is, just as you have conceded to Allah that He is the Creator and you have not claimed to be a creator alongside Him, concede to Him also that He is the Provider and do not claim to be a provider alongside Him. Just as you know Allah to be exclusive in creating and bringing forth, likewise, He is exclusive in providing and extending provision.

He linked creation and provision so that it would be an argument against His slaves and prohibit them from claiming His provision comes from other than Him. Or that His kindness occurs from His creation and not from Him. Also just as He, be He glorified, creates without intermediary or means, likewise, He is the provider without His sustenance requiring an intermediary or existence of a cause.

---

224   Quran 30:40

Another Benefit

The Glorious indicates with His words "**Allah it is Who created you, then provided for you**" that the matter of His providing has already concluded and the affair has been wrapped up. His decree regarding provision is not a matter renewed with time. Nor is it a consequence of the passage of time. Only the creation and appearance of provision is renewed but it is fixed and determined.

Sustenance is of two types. That which was decreed in pre-eternity and that which appears to the slave after he comes into being. The verse includes both aspects. If the provision referred to is what was decreed in pre-eternity, the '**then**' (*thumma*) in the verse refers to the sequence of events. If the provision referred to is sustenance when it comes into existence, then it is for you to take heed and contemplate over it.

The purpose of the verse is to affirm the divinity of Allah ﷻ. It is as if He says – *O you who worships other than Allah,* "**Who created you, then provided for you; then He causes you to die; then He gives you life**," *do you find these attributes in other than Him? Or is it possible they could belong to any of His creations? Whoever exclusively has these qualities must be recognised with divinity and be singled out as the only Nurturing Lord.* That is why He states in the latter part of this verse, "**Is there anyone among those you ascribe as partners who does anything of that? Glory be to Him and exalted is He above the partners they ascribe.**"[225]

The Third Verse Regarding Provision

He states, "**And bid your family to prayer and**

---
225   Quran: 30:40

be steadfast therein. We ask no provision of you; We provide for you. And the end belongs to (the people of) righteousness."[226] The verse contains many beneficial points.

The First Benefit

You must recognise that even though this verse is directed to the Prophet ﷺ, its ruling is also binding on his nation. So it is said to every slave, "**And bid your family to prayer and be steadfast therein. We ask no provision of you; We provide for you. And the end belongs to (the people of) righteousness.**" If you have understood, O slave of Allah ﷻ, then know that Allah ﷻ commanded you to command your family to perform prayer (*salat*). Just as you must keep the bonds of kinship with them through worldly means and prefer them in it, you must charge them with obedience to Allah ﷻ and prevent them from His disobedience. Just as your family has priority in your worldly devotion, likewise they have priority in your devotion to them for the Hereafter. They are your flock, as the Messenger ﷺ has said, "*Each of you is a shepherd responsible for his flock.*" Allah, the Glorified, states in another verse, "**And warn your tribe, your nearest kin.**"[227] Just as He states, "**And bid your family to prayer.**"

The Second Benefit

Look to the Glorified's words. He commanded the Messenger ﷺ in the verse to command his family to prayer even before commanding the Messenger ﷺ to be steadfast in prayer. The focus of the verse is in commanding family to pray. The rest of the verse only follows from this main

---

226   Quran: 20:132
227   Quran: 26:214

point even though the Messenger ﷺ was also commanded to pray. Since the slave knows with no doubt that he has been commanded to pray individually, *Al-Haqq* ﷻ willed to direct His slaves to what they might perhaps be negligent of. So, He commanded His Messenger ﷺ to that end so they hear and follow, hasten towards it, and perform it diligently.

A Notice

Know that it is obligatory on you to command your family to pray. Whether it be a wife, mother, daughter or other than them. You should show anger at them if they leave prayer. You have no argument with Allah ﷻ if you say – I commanded them but they did not listen. For if they knew it was burdensome on you when they leave prayer, just like it is troublesome for you if they ruin some food or are negligent in one of your needs, they would not have neglected prayer. Rather they became accustomed to you demanding your worldly desires from them and not demanding the rights of your Master. Hence, they neglected prayer. Whoever completes all his prayers while having a family that did not pray and neither did he command them to, will be gathered on the Day of Judgement among the throngs who missed their prayers.

If you were to ask – I commanded them but they did not pray, I advised them but they did not pay heed, I even punished them and still they did not pray, what else can I do? The response is that in such a case you must separate yourself wherever you can by divorce or the like. For those you can not distance yourself from, you should turn away from them (be emotionally distant). Disassociate yourself for Allah's sake, for detachment for Allah's sake necessitates being connected with Him.

The Third Benefit

The Glorified states, "**...and be steadfast therein (in prayer)**." In this is an indication that prayer is taxing on the animal-self and burdensome upon it. That is because prayer comes at times of comfort or preoccupation (with work etc). Prayer demands they leave all of that and stand before Allah ﷻ while being empty of everything except Him.

Do you not see that the pre-dawn prayer *(fajr)* arrives at the time sleep is most delightful? *Al-Haqq* ﷻ thus demands they abandon their delight for His right. That they abandon their wishes for His wish. That is why in the call to the pre-dawn prayer it is specifically said, "*The prayer is better than sleep!*" As for the mid-day prayer *(zuhr)*, it arrives at the time of siesta and return from the toil of labour. The late afternoon prayer *(asr)* comes to them when they are engaged in their places of business and workshops as they guarantee their worldly incomes. The sunset prayer *(maghrib)* arrives as they have dinner to strengthen their bodies. The night prayer *(isha)* comes just as fatigue returns to them from the toil of the labour they were occupied in since the brightness of the morning. That is why the Glorified states, "**...and be steadfast therein (in prayer).**"

He also states, "**Be mindful of the prayers,**"[228] and He states, "**prayer at fixed hours is prescribed for the believers,**"[229] and He states, "**And perform the prayer.**"[230]

What will alert you to the fact that establishing prayer contains the burden of slave-hood and is contrary to the animal nature of man, are His words "**Seek help in patience**

---
228 Quran 2:238
229 Quran 4:103
230 Quran 24:56

and prayer, it is indeed difficult except for the humble."[231] He linked both patience and prayer indicating that prayer requires patience. It requires patience in performing it at its required times, patience in abiding by its necessary and recommended elements, and patience in preventing the heart from being distracted.

That is why the Glorified states, "**...and it is indeed difficult except for the humble.**" What is being referred to here as difficult and is singled out, is the prayer not patience. The Arabic word form used for **"difficult"** (*kabeera*) grammatically matches (and so refers to) prayer (*salat*), not patience. If this was not the case He would have said *kabeer* instead (of *kabeera*).[232]

It is also possible though, that He refers to both patience and prayer together as being difficult. For He has combined two things and referred to them as one in other verses. For example, He states, **"But Allah and His Messenger – it is worthier that He be pleased,"** and He states, **"...those who hoard gold and silver and spend it not in the way of Allah,"** and He states, **"And when they see some commerce or diversion, they scatter toward it."**[233] So understand.

The matter of prayer is great and it is of immense

---

231 Quran 2:45
232 In Arabic, adjectives/descriptors must match the nouns they describe in gender. Patience is grammatically masculine while prayer is a feminine word. Since the adjective, 'difficult' ('*kabeera*') comes in its feminine form in this verse, the Imam notes that it refers to prayer and not to patience. That is, "**it (prayer) is indeed difficult except for the humble.**" For if 'it' had referred to patience, 'difficult' would have come in its masculine form ('*kabeer*'). This is of course, one of two opinions as the Imam mentions in the next paragraph.
233 Quran 62:11

importance to Allah ﷻ. Hence He states, "**Truly prayer prevents against indecency and abomination.**"[234] While the Messenger ﷺ replied when asked what is the most excellent of deeds, *"The prayer in its proper times."* The Messenger ﷺ also said, *"The one who prays speaks intimately with his Nurturing Lord."* He ﷺ also said, *"The closest a slave is with his Nurturing Lord is in prostration* (sujood*)."*

We have also observed that the prayer contains more types of worship within it than any other. Within the prayer there is purification, silence, facing the *qibla*, beginning with saying Allah is Most Great, recital of the Quran, standing, bowing, prostrating, glorifications (*tasbih*) in bowing and prostration, beseeching Allah in prostration and other forms also. Prayer is a collection of many forms of worship together.[235] Remembrance itself is worship, recital itself is worship, glorification (*tasbih*) itself is worship, and bowing, prostrating and standing are all by themselves a form of worship. If not for fear of verbosity, we would have extrapolated on the secrets and lights of this fact. Here this gleam suffices and the praise belongs to Allah ﷻ alone.

The Fourth Benefit

The Glorified states, "**We ask no provision of you; We provide for you.**" That is – *We do not ask you to provide for yourself or your family. How could We command and impose on you to provide for yourself when you are not able to do even that? How would it be befitting for Us to command you to Our service*

---

234 Quran 29:45
235 Imam Sa'id Nursi ﷺ goes as far to say, "*the prescribed prayers are a comprehensive, luminous index of all the varieties of worship, and a sacred map pointing to all the shades of worship of all the classes of creatures.*" For example, the fact that eating is prohibited in prayer indicates it also contains a type of fasting. See the Ninth Word, *The Words*, Sa'id Nursi.

and not ensure your sustenance?

Since He knows that His slaves might be disturbed by the seeking of provision amid worship, and be prevented from dedicating time to Him, He addressed His Messenger so that the slaves would hear, "**And bid your family to prayer and be steadfast therein. We ask no provision of you; We provide for you**." That is, *you undertake Our service, We will facilitate for you Our provision.*

Two matters are hence highlighted. One, that Allah ﷻ has guaranteed your provision, so do not be greedy for it. Two, that He has demanded worship from you so do not neglect it. Whoever strives for, and prioritises, what has been promised to him over what has been demanded from him, his ignorance has intensified and his heedlessness has widened. Little attention does he pay to sound advice. The reality of the matter is that the slave should be occupied with what is demanded of him over and above what has been guaranteed for him.

If the Glorified provides for those that deny Him, how could He not provide for those that affirm Him? If He has caused His sustenance to flow upon the people of disbelief, how could His sustenance not flow upon the people of belief?

You have now realised, O slave, that this world is guaranteed for you. That is to say, the provision of this world that will maintain your existence, has been guaranteed for you. While the Hereafter is what has been requested from you. That is to say, your preparation for the Hereafter has been demanded from you as per His words, "**And take provisions, and indeed, the best provision is** piety (*taqwa*)."²³⁶

How can intelligence or wisdom be validated if it worries over what has been promised and abandons worry over what has been demanded? One of the pious said, "*Indeed Allah has guaranteed this world for us and demanded the Hereafter from us. If only He had guaranteed the Hereafter for us and demanded this world from us!*"

Also, the occurrence of His words "**We provide for you**" in the form they appear points to continuance and permanence. If you were to say, "*I am generous to you,*" it does not hold the same meaning as "*I was generous to you.*" For your saying "*I am generous to you*" points to generosity after generosity. While your saying, "*I was generous to you*" points to there being a single instance of generosity without there being continuance or permanence.

So His stating "**We provide for you**" points to provision after provision. That is to say – *Our gifts to you are not halted, nor are Our blessings cut off. Just as We were gracious enough to bestow life to Our slaves, likewise We undertake the continuance of their sustenance.*

Then the Glorious states, "**And the end belongs to (the people of) righteousness.**" As if He, be He Glorified, says – *We know that if you devote yourself to Our service, if you direct yourself to Our obedience, turn away from the means of the world, and abandon getting involved and preoccupied with it, that your provisions will be less than those of the wealthy. Neither would your livelihood be like that of the extravagant. But be patient over that. For indeed, the good ending belongs to the righteous.* Just as He, be He Glorified, states in another verse, "**Strain** not your eyes toward the enjoyments We have granted certain classes of them, as the splendour of the life of this world, that We may test them concerning it. The provision of your Nurturing Lord is better and more lasting."[237]

Regarding the verse **"Whosoever works righteousness, whether male or female, and is a believer, We shall give them a good life,"**[238] you might ask that since He has stated the righteous have a good life in this world, why does He also single-out that they have a good end?

Know that the Glorious addresses His slaves according to their understandings. It is as if He says – *O My slaves! If you look to the people of heedlessness, then for them and the people of sin is the first world, but for the people of faith and righteousness is the final world,* **"and the end belongs to (the people of) righteousness."** He addresses His slaves according to what their minds have grasped, to what they have reference to and, thus, can understand.

It is similar to the saying of *"Allah is Greater (Allahu Akbar)"* even though nothing has a share of greatness that it can even be compared to Him. Rather, it is said due to what people witness from their perspectives of the greatness of His signs. Just as He states, be He Glorified, **"Surely the creation of the heavens and the earth is greater than the creation of mankind."**[239] So it is as if it is said to them – *If you witness the greatness of anything, as you must, then Allah is greater than that and He is greater than everything you perceive to be great.*

Likewise, it is said, *"The prayer is better than sleep."* If it

---
237 Quran 20:131
238 Quran 16:97
239 Quran 40:57

was said instead, "*There is no goodness in sleep,*" people would have rebutted, "*I know that sleep has delight and refreshment!*" So this understanding of theirs was conceded to them and then it was said to them, "*What We have invited you to is better than what you consider to be good. Prayer is better than sleep! The benefits you are inclined to from sleep are only temporary goods. While what We call you to is an eternal transaction, its payment never-ending '...and that which lies with Allah is better and more lasting'.*"[240]

A Lofty Benefit

Know that the verse teaches those who understand the purposes of Allah ﷻ, how to ask for His provision. When means of livelihood dry up, the pious increase in His worship and in good deeds, for this verse guides them to that. Do you not see that the Glorious states, "**And bid your family to prayer and be steadfast therein. We ask no provision of you; We provide for you**"? That is, He promises provision after two commands. The first command is to enjoin prayer upon the family and the second is to remain patient upon prayer. Then He states, "**We provide for you.**"

The people of intimate knowledge of Allah ﷻ understand from this verse that when the means of livelihood become tightened, they are to knock on the door of His provision and deal directly with the Provisioner. They are not to act like the people of heedlessness and blindness (to reality). For when the means of livelihood become difficult upon the people of heedlessness, they increase in their efforts for it and rush to it with their hearts unaware and their minds inattentive. But those who understand the purposes of Allah ﷻ know the proper way to proceed

---

240   Quran 42:36

since they have heard Allah ﷻ stating **"And enter houses through their (proper) doors."**[241] They recognise that the door of provision is obedience to the Provisioner. How could they ask Him by disobeying Him? How could they invoke Him for His bounty by opposing Him?

The Messenger ﷺ has said, *"What is with Allah is not obtained through His displeasure."* That is to say, do not seek His sustenance except by following His commands. The Glorious demonstrates this fact when He states, **"And whosoever reveres Allah, He will appoint a way out for them, and will provide for them from where they do not imagine."**[242] And the Glorified states, **"...if they hold firm to the path, We shall give them abundant rains."**[243] And other verses too that indicate piety (*taqwa*) is the key to two provisions; the provision of this world and the provision of the Hereafter. As He states, be He Glorified, **"Had the People of the Book believed and been reverent, We would surely have absolved them of their sins, and caused them to enter Gardens of bliss. Had they observed the Torah and the Gospel and that which was sent down unto them from their Nurturing Lord, they would surely have received nourishment from above them and from beneath their feet."**[244] The Glorified explains to you that if they observed the Torah and the Gospel, if they acted by what is in them, they would have nourishment from above them and below them. As if He says – *We would have certainly spread out to them Our provisions and We would have continued to spend on them. But they did not do as We please, so We did not do as they please.*

241	Quran 2:189
242	Quran 65:2-3
243	Quran 72:16
244	Quran 5:65-66

The Fourth Verse Regarding Provision

He states, be He glorified, "**There is no creature that crawls upon the earth but that its provision lies with Allah. And He knows its dwelling place and its repository. All is in a clear Book.**"[245] The verse forthrightly declares *Al-Haqq's* guarantee of sustenance. It cuts off anxieties and doubts that occur in the hearts of the believers. If their hearts become reliant on the means and causes of this world, the armies of faith and trust in Allah ﷻ pounce on those thoughts and defeat them. "**Nay, but We cast truth against falsehood, and it crushes it, and, behold, it vanishes!**"[246]

When He states, "**There is no creature that crawls upon the earth but that its provision lies with Allah,**" it is a guarantee in which He makes known His fondness for His slaves. His providing is not something He has to do. Rather, He enjoined it upon Himself out of kindness and generosity.

He also made His guarantee general. It is as if He says – *O My slave, neither is My guarantee and My sustenance limited to you, rather I am the guarantor of every creature on earth, I am their provider, and I am the One who extends to them their sustenance. So understand the vastness of My guarantee, the richness of My Lordship and that nothing is outside of My embrace. Trust in Me as a guarantor and take Me as a guardian. If you have seen the mention of My care and excellent guarantee for the animals, then know you are nobler than them and it is more fitting of you to trust in My guarantee and to yearn for My bounty.*

Have you not heard Him state, "**We have indeed**

---

245 Quran 11:6
246 Quran 21:18

honoured the Children of Adam"?²⁴⁷ That is – *We have honoured them over other species of living beings. For We have called them to Our service, promised them Our paradise, and invited them to Our presence.*

All creation was in fact created for human beings and human beings were created to be in the presence of Allah ﷻ. What will help you realise the distinction of the human being are the words of our shaykh, Abu'l Abbas ﷺ, *"Allah, the Honoured and Majestic, says, 'O son of Adam! I created all things for you and created you for Me. So do not busy yourself with what is for you over Whom you are for!'"* Likewise, are the words of the Glorified, **"The earth has He laid down for the creatures."**²⁴⁸ And His words, **"He made subservient for you whatsoever is in the heavens and whatsoever is on the earth—all together."**²⁴⁹

I also heard our shaykh saying, *"All of existence is a slave subjected (to humans) and you are a slave whose purpose is to be in His presence."* The Glorious states, **"Allah it is Who created the seven heavens, and from the earth the like thereof. The command descends among them, that you may know that Allah is powerful over all things."**²⁵⁰ He clarifies to you, that the heavens and earth are creations for the sake of humans. If you realise the universe is created for you – either to take benefit from or to take wisdom from, which is also a benefit – then you must conclude that if Allah ﷻ provides for what was created for you, how could He not also provide sustenance for you? Have you not heard the words of the Glorious, **"And (We cause to grow) fruit**

247	Quran 17:70
248	Quran 55:10
249	Quran 45:13
250	Quran 65:12

and pastures, as sustenance for you and your flocks"?[251]

While His words, "**And He knows its dwelling place and its repository**" confirm that He is the Guarantor of His provision. It is as if to say – *there is no worry over where His sustenance is stored, nor are its circumstances hidden from Him. Rather, He knows where it is located and He will send it forth to whoever it is destined for.*

The Fifth Verse Regarding Provision

The Glorified states, "**And in heaven is your provision and that which you were promised. So by the Nurturing Lord of heaven and earth, it is indeed true—as sure as the fact that you speak.**"[252] This verse is the one that especially washes away doubts from the hearts of the believers and causes rays of certainty to shine in their hearts. It places an excess of certitude within them because of the benefits it contains. It mentions His provision, where it is located, an oath that guarantees it and a parable that leaves no doubt. Let us mention these benefits one by one.

The First Benefit

Know, since the Glorified knows about the many anxieties people have over the matter of provision, He repeats the mentioning of it to oppose negative thoughts reoccurring in the mind. Just as you might repeat your argument when you know that doubts persist in the person you are arguing with.

Similarly, the Glorious reiterates the Hereafter in many verses because of the doubts of deniers. He also repeats

---

251   Quran 80:31-32
252   Quran 51:22-23

the point of the Hereafter because people think it far-fetched that they will return to existence after their bones break up, their bodies decay and they become dust or are eaten up by scavengers and vermin. He raises objections in His precious book with numerous arguments. He states, "**And he coins for Us a parable and forgets his own creation, saying, 'Who will revive these bones, decayed as they are?' Say, 'He will revive them Who brought them forth the first time.**"[253] And He states in another verse, "**and that (the second creation) is easier for Him (from the human perspective).**"[254] He also states, "**He Who gives it life is surely the One Who gives life to the dead.**"[255] As well as other verses.

Likewise, He knows the intensity of people's agitation over the matter of provision, so He affirms it in numerous verses. Some of them we have already mentioned and others we have not. Since *Al-Haqq* ﷻ knows the states of the animal-self, He states at one point, "**Truly Allah is the Provider.**"[256] While He states another time, "**Allah it is Who created you, then nourished you.**"[257] At another point He states, "**We provide for you.**"[258] At yet another He states, "**Who is it that will provide for you if He withholds His provision?**"[259] And here He states, "**And in heaven is your provision…**"

If hearts do not know where their provision is, it is difficult for them to find assurance. Also, the guarantee of provision with ambiguity about where it is to come from is

---

253	Quran 36:78-79
254	Quran 30:27
255	Quran 41:39
256	Quran 51:58
257	Quran 30:40
258	Quran 20:132
259	Quran 67:21

not like the guarantee that also reveals where the provision is located. It is as if the Glorious says in this verse – *it was not binding on Us to reveal to you the location of your provision. We have your provision which We deliver to you at its decreed time, We did not need to clarify its location.*

However, because of His kindness, His mercy, His overflowing grace and His favour, He disclosed the location of His provision so that it powerfully induces trust in Him and forcefully removes the doubt within the animal-self.

By identifying the location of His sustenance, He also implies that having hope in the creation should be cast away. They should only seek their provision from the Rightful King. When the yearning from creation and reliance on worldly means occurs in your heart, the Glorious says to you, "**And in heaven is your provision.**" That is – *O you who seeks provision from weak, incapable creations of the earth! Your provision is not with them. Your provision is only with Me and I am the All-Powerful King.*

For this reason, when one of the bedouins heard this verse he immediately slaughtered his she-camel in charity for the sake of Allah saying, *"Allah be Glorified! My sustenance is in the heaven and I seek it upon the earth!?"* So see – may Allah show mercy to you – how that bedouin understood the purpose of Allah from this verse, that His slaves should direct their hopes to Him. That their aspirations should be for what He has with Him. As He states in another verse, "**There is nothing, but that its treasuries lie with Us, and We do not send it down, save in a known measure.**"[260] Here, He directs peoples' aspirations to His door so that hearts may incline to His proximity. So –

---

260   Quran 15:21

may Allah have mercy upon you – be heavenly and elevated not lowly and worldly. Hence one of the poets said:

> *If a hard-hearted man refuses you water*
> *Suffices you contentment in hunger or slaughter*
>
> *Be someone who has his feet upon earth*
> *And the height of his zeal where stars are sought*
>
> *For better the flow of life-giving blood*
> *Than to ask from another and have your face in mud!*

I heard our shaykh, Abu'l Abbas, may Allah be pleased with him, saying, *"By Allah, I only see that honour is attained when one dismisses their aspirations from the creation."* Remember here His words my brother – may Allah have mercy on you – **"Yet to Allah belongs honour and His Messenger and the believers."**[261] The honour with which He honoured the believers includes the believer directing his aspirations to his Guardian and trusting in Him, not anything else besides Him. It includes being ashamed of Allah, that after He clothed you with the robe of faith and adorned you with knowing Him (*irfan*), that heedlessness and negligence should overpower you until you begin inclining towards the creation or seek favours from other than Him. Hence one of the poets said:

> *Distant became my roaming the science of realities*
> *Extinguished was my happiness with gifts from my Creator*
>
> *For at the moment of my illumination in His kingdom*
> *I was seen stretching forth my palm to His creation.*

If your heedless animal-self pushes you to turn away

---

[261] Quran 63:8

from its Guardian and direct your need to the creation, then direct your need to the One to Whom that creation directs their needs. But it is easy for the animal-self to disregard your faith so that it acquires what it desires. It knows it can effectively achieve its desires if you humiliate yourself (by seeking from the creation). As the poet said:

> *My nafs burdened me with humiliation for its honour*
> *How easy for it to disgrace so it be exalted*
>
> *It said go ask for riches from Yahya ibn Akthami*[262]
> *I say you ask from the Enricher of Yahya ibn Akthami!*

It is detestable that a believer unloads his need to other than Allah when he knows full well His oneness and exclusivity in nurturing and Lordship. Even more so when the believer hears the words of Allah, Most High, **"Does Allah not suffice His slave?"**[263] To present a need to other than Allah is detestable from anyone and more so from a believer.

Remember the words of Allah, the Glorified, **"O you who believe! Fulfil your pacts."**[264] Among the pacts that you have entered, is not to raise your needs to other than Him and not to rely on other than Him. This pact is binding on you since the Day of Decrees when you confirmed Him as the One who nurtures you in His Lordship. The day He said, **"'Am I not your Nurturing Lord?' They said, Yes, we bear witness'."**[265] How could you recognise and announce his exclusivity there (in nurturing you) and be ignorant of

---

262 Possibly Yahya ibn Akhtam al-Tamimi (died 242 Hijri). One of the chief judges and scholars during the Abbasid caliphate.
263 Quran 39:36
264 Quran 5:1
265 Quran 7:172

Him here? Would you disregard Him when His kindnesses upon you are consecutive and you are engulfed in His blessings and favours? As the poet says:

> *In my heart, You hold the highest station*
> *No Leila or Juliet has made it a dwelling*
>
> *Before I was, I recognised Your manifestation*
> *Shall I deny You with my beard whitening?*

Removing one's hopes and reliance on the creation is the yardstick by which the Sufis (*fuqara*) are tested and men are revealed. Yes, just as objects are weighed so too are inner states and qualities, **"So set right the weight and fall not short in the balance."**[266] The truthful thus become known by their truthfulness and the pretenders by their hypocrisy. **"Allah will not leave the believers as you are till He separates the bad from the good."**[267]

Allah indeed tests the Sufis (*fuqara*), out of His wisdom, by sending down His favours. He reveals what insincere Sufis hide of desires and lusts. They degrade themselves to the lovers of this world by looking up to them, conforming to them, allowing themselves to be used for the purposes of worldly people, and are driven to their doors. You might see one of them adorning himself like a groom, anxious about setting aright his outer state, ignorant about setting aright his inner state. Indeed, Allah has marked them, revealing their defects, and He makes known the reality of their state. If at one point such a Sufi was considered truthful to Allah and was known as 'slave of the Great' (*abd al-Kabeer*), he now becomes known as 'shaykh of the leader' (*shaykh al-Ameer*) because of the absence of

---
266 Quran 55:9
267 Quran 3:179

sincerity.

Such people are liars against Allah ﷻ as they hinder His slaves from accompanying His friends (*awliya*). For when the general masses witness these imposters, they attribute the same to everyone who associates himself with Allah ﷻ, be he truthful or not. These imposters are then veils over those sincere verifiers of truth. They are dark clouds over the bright suns that are the people of Divinely-supported success. Yes, these imposters may strike the same drums, they may wave the same flags, they may don the same armour, but when the battle ensues, they turn on their heels and flee![268] Their tongues make great claims, yet their hearts are empty of piety (*taqwa*).

Have they not heard the words of the Glorified, "**...that the truthful may be questioned concerning their truthfulness**"?[269] Do you not see that if He will question the truthful about their truthfulness, how could He leave the pretenders without interrogation? Have they not heard the words of the Glorified, "**Perform your deeds. Allah will see your deeds, as will the Messenger and the believers, and you will be brought back to the Knower of the unseen and the seen, and He will inform you of that which you used to do**"?[270] They are in the garb of the truthful, but their deeds are the deeds of those turned away (from Allah). As the poet says:

> *As for their tents, they are as if the very same*
> *But the women here are somehow different*

---

268   i.e. at the time they are tested by Allah to see whether they will rely on creation for their needs or on Him, they fail and the reality of their state becomes known – and Allah knows best what the Imam intended.
269   Quran 33:8
270   Quran 9:105

By the One whose house the Quraish frequent
Raising their hands to its corner from low-lying land

My eyes have not caught sight of any tribe
But I thought my beloved was in its midst.

It has become clear – may Allah have mercy on you – that the abandonment of one's aspirations to benefit from creation, is a jewel adorning the people who take a path to Allah and a mark of the knowledgeable and insightful. In this vein I composed the following lines:

She began to blame me over difficult times
I turned away perhaps she too will turn away

Do not increase in rebuking your days, they are not
The haven in which is sought loyalty or serenity

What does it harm me if I am in them unknown?
The full moon is still the full moon, clouded or clear

Allah knows I have aspirations of virtue
To reject this world and its extravagance

Rather I would honour my face from other men and
Show them the majesty of kings or even more than that

Or shall I present to them my poverty at their feet
When all together they have no capability?

Or shall I ask His provision from His creation?
That would render me but ill-mannered to Him

A complaint of the weak one to another weak one like him
A weakness so poor it as if hangs from a cliff

So seek provision from Allah the One whose hospitality
Touches all His creation by gifts and by kindness

Find refuge in Him, what you desire is with Him
Do not turn away from His door in deviation

The Second Benefit

Returning to the verse, "**And in heaven is your provision**," the Glorified's words possibly mean that your sustenance has been recorded in the Preserved Tablet.[271] If this is indeed the meaning of the verse, then it soothes His slaves, informing them that We have recorded your provision and inscribed it in Our book. We have decreed it by Our favour before you even came to existence. We set it aside before you even came forth. Then what has made you so restless about it? Why is it that you do not find reassurance with Me? Why do you have no confidence in My promise?

Another possible explanation of "**And in heaven is your provision**" is that it refers to water, from which your provision bursts forth. He states, "**And We made every living thing from water**."[272] Hence, Ibn Abbas mentioned the verse refers to water. His words "**And in heaven is your provision**" would then refer to that which is the origin of your provision and water is also in itself provision.

The Third Benefit

Perhaps the aim of *Al-Haqq* by this verse is

---

271 *Al-Lawh Al-Mahfooz*. The heavenly tome in which all of Allah's decrees of what is to occur till the end of time has been recorded and sealed. And Allah knows best.

272 Quran 21:30

to thwart His slaves from making claims of control over worldly means. If Allah, Most High, withheld water from the earth, the means of everyone who takes worldly means would be suspended. Be it a harvester, planter, merchant, tailor, scribe, or other than that. It is as if He says – *It is not your worldly means which provide for you, it is only I who provide for you and it is by My hands that worldly means are facilitated for you. I send down that which makes your worldly means possible (water) and through which your acquirements can be concluded.*

The Fourth Benefit

His combining the matter of provision with the matter of what you are promised in "**And in heaven is your provision and that which you were promised**" is for a lofty purpose. The believers recognise that what *Al-Haqq* ﷻ has promised them will undoubtedly come to pass, they have no power to hasten it or delay it, and nor can they utilise any stratagem to draw it near. It is as if the Glorified says – *Just as you do not doubt that We have what you are promised, likewise, let there be no doubt that your provision is also with Us. Just as you are powerless to hasten what We have promised you before its time, likewise you are powerless to hasten your provision. Our Nurturing Lordship postpones it[273] and Our Divinity specifies its time.*

The Fifth Benefit

He states, "**So by the Nurturing Lord of heaven and earth, it is indeed true—as sure as the fact that you speak.**" This is a great argument against His slaves. It shows that the

---

273   i.e. by delaying our provision our Nurturing Lord nurtures us spiritually. He makes us recognise our weakness, builds our trust in Him when we see His provision finally arrive and directs us to greater worship in such times of trial. And Allah knows best.

Faithful in promise, the One who never breaks His promise, takes an oath for His slaves, assuring them of His promise. This is because He knows that they have doubts within themselves, anxieties and suspicions. When the angels heard this verse they said, *"The children of Adam have perished! They provoked the Majestic One until He took an oath!"* While one of the righteous said on hearing this verse, *"Glorified be Allah! Who compelled the Noble One to take an oath!?"*

Whoever you know has confidence in your words, you do not resort to taking oaths with them. Only when you notice their uneasiness in your promise, do you swear by an oath.

This verse filled one group with delight and put another to shame. As for the people it delighted, they are those whose faith it increased and consolidated their certainty thereby. They triumphed over the whispers of Satan and the doubts of the animal-self. As for people it embarrassed, they are those who realised that *Al-Haqq* knew about their having no confidence in His promise and restlessness regarding it. That He designated them as people of doubt and He resorted to taking an oath to reassure them. Hence they became embarrassed out of shame before Him. This (sentiment) is from the means that cause Allah ﷻ to bestow even deeper understanding upon them.

Many a thing makes a group rejoice and another grieve, depending on their differences in understanding and intimate knowledge. Do you not see that when the words of the Glorified were revealed, **"This day I have perfected for you your religion, and completed My Blessing upon you, and have approved for you as religion, Islam,"**[274] a group of

---

274   Quran 5:3

the Companions rejoiced together but Abu Bakr, may Allah be pleased with him, was grieved? He understood that the verse was the news of the death of the Messenger of Allah ﷺ and so he wept. From this insight, it is understood that when something is perfected, it is feared that it will fall into disrepair, as the poet says:

> *When it is perfected, has drawn near its blemish*
> *Expect its demise, when you see it has flourished*

Know that the matter (of Islam) did not deteriorate so long as the Messenger ﷺ was alive. The Companions did rejoice due to the obvious, good news that the verse contained and did not perceive what Abu Bakr, may Allah be pleased with him, perceived. Abu Bakr ؓ thus demonstrated the secret in the words of the Prophet ﷺ *"Abu Bakr did not gain precedence over you by fasting or prayer. But by something that established itself in his heart."* It was by that thing in his heart that he holds precedence. It was that same thing that allowed him to grasp what others did not grasp.

Similarly, the Glorified states, **"Truly Allah has purchased from the believers their souls and their wealth in exchange for the Garden being theirs. They fight in the way of Allah, slaying and being slain."**[275]

I heard Shaykh Abu Muhammad Al-Marajaani, May Allah be pleased with him, saying, *"A group heard this verse and rejoiced with this bargain, their faces radiating with happiness that Al-Haqq had declared them suitable to purchase from. For He esteemed them highly when He was pleased to trade with them. They rejoiced further with the magnificent price He put forward and that is indeed an abundant reward. But another group became*

---

275   Quran 9:111

pale with shame in front of Allah if He was to buy from them what is already His. They understood that it was because Allah knew of the hidden claims within themselves. If in their inner selves, they had no assertions of ownership over their souls, He would not have said **'Truly Allah has purchased from the believers'**. *So those who rejoiced in the verse have two gardens of Paradise with silver vessels and silver of whatever is therein. As for those who became pale with shame, they have two gardens with golden vessels and gold of whatever is therein."*

If the believers had handed over to Allah what remained in their inner selves of opposition against Him, He would not have offered to trade. That is why He said, **"Truly Allah has purchased from the believers"** and He did not include the Messengers or Prophets in the verse. That is why Shaykh Abu'l Hassan said, *"Souls are of three types. A soul that is not bought because of its vileness, a soul that is bought to honour it, and a soul that is not bought to attest to its freedom. As for the first type, they are the souls of the disbelievers. They are not bought because of their vileness. The second type are the souls of the believers, they are bought to honour them. The third type are the souls of the Prophets and Messengers. They are not bought to attest to their freedom."*[276]

The Sixth Benefit

The Glorified takes an oath with His words **"So by the Nurturing Lord of heaven and earth…"** When He takes an oath by His nurturing Lordship which is responsible for taking care of heaven and earth, it is not fitting that one

---

276   i.e Prophets and Messengers do not see themselves as owning their souls so that they can be sold. Rather they see themselves owned by Allah. Hence, they are free of all attachments other than Allah and are like free men that are not bought or sold in the parable above of a slave market. And Allah knows best.

doubt the reliability of His oath. He is the One responsible for the caretaking of this immense universe, which you are a part of. If you are compared to the universe it is as if you do not exist. His taking an oath by His being Nurturing Lord of the heaven and earth is thus more effective than if He took the oath by His name of All-Hearing, or the All-Knowing, or the Most Merciful or another name. So understand!

The Seventh Benefit

The Glorified states, "**So by the Nurturing Lord of heaven and earth, it is indeed true.**" Truth is the opposite of falsehood and falsehood is what is flawed with no validity to it. Your provision arriving to you is truth just like the Provider is truth. Doubt in provision is doubt in the Provider.

A man once repented from robbing graves and said to one of the righteous, *"I opened many graves and found them all turned away from the Qiblah!"*[277] The shaykh replied to him, *"It was only their accusations against the arrival of their provision that turned their faces away."*

The Eighth Benefit

The Glorified states, "**it is indeed true—as sure as the fact that you speak.**" He emphasises the affirmation of His provision and declares its reality. The verse stresses that it does not befit the believer to doubt in His provision nor should the certain of faith have suspicions over it. Indeed, hearts witness the truth of His provision just as physical eyes witness the one who speaks. In this verse, He changes what is abstract into concrete meaning and gives us a glimpse of the unseen. Thus He cut off the doubts of His slaves in the

---

277   It is part of Islamic burial rites that the deceased is placed with their head facing the Qiblah, i.e. Mecca.

matter of provision. Just as you speak to one another, and you have no doubt that you do because of what your eyes witness, likewise do not doubt Allah ﷻ in the matter of provision.[278] For the light of faith affirms it.

So see – may Allah have mercy upon you – the consideration that *Al-Haqq* ﷻ gave to the matter of sustenance, His repetition of it, His clarifying the place it is located, His simplifying and depicting the matter as something tangible which the observer would not doubt, and His taking an oath over it by His Nurturing Lordship that encompasses heaven and earth.

See also the repetition of the Master of the Law, peace and blessings of Allah be upon him, for he says, *"The Holy Spirit (Gabriel) uttered into my heart that a person does not die until all his provisions have been dispatched to him. So be conscious of Allah and be moderate in seeking (sustenance)."* And he ﷺ said, *"If you trusted upon Allah with due reliance, He would provide for you as He provides for the birds. They set out in the morning hungry and return full."* And he said, upon him be peace, *"Allah takes upon Himself the provision for the student of knowledge."* And there are other *hadiths* too that mention provision.

A Noteworthy Point

Know that by taking worldly means, one does not contravene his trust in Allah ﷻ. As the Messenger ﷺ alluded to, *"So be conscious of Allah and be moderate in seeking (sustenance)."* He allowed the taking of means to seek a living. If it was contradictory to the station of trust in Allah ﷻ why

---

[278] Just as when you observe someone speaking and are certain his words will reach your ears, likewise have faith that Allah's provision will also reach you when you hear His promise.

would he allow it? He did not say – *Do not seek sustenance*. He only said, "*...be moderate in seeking (sustenance).*" It is as if he said – *If you seek sustenance, seek in moderation*. That is have proper and good manner with Allah ﷻ when seeking sustenance and rely on Him. He allowed the seeking of sustenance and seeking sustenance is from worldly means. We have already mentioned his words, upon him be peace, "*The most excellent of what a believer eats is (from the means of) what his right hand has earned.*" And other *hadiths* too indicate the permissibility of taking worldly means, rather they encourage worldly means and mandate them.

The First Benefit of Worldly Means (*asbab*)

Al-Haqq ﷻ knew the weakness in the hearts of His slaves, their shortcomings in witnessing His allotment, and their incapability to have true confidence (in His promise). He allowed them the taking of worldly means so their hearts could lean on them and their states could stabilise. This is from His favour upon them.

The Second Benefit of Worldly Means

By taking worldly means, one can protect his honour by not having to degrade himself through asking (or begging) from others. One also protects the delight of faith which diminishes by asking from the creation. Whatever Allah ﷻ grants you via worldly means, you have no debt of kindness to repay the creation for it. For no one does you a kindness by buying from you or hiring you for some work since they strive for their own fortunes and intend benefit for themselves. So worldly means allow for the taking from others without being indebted to their kindness.

The Third Benefit of Worldly Means

When His slaves become occupied with their worldly means, it keeps them busy so as not to perform sins and not have the leisure to act in disobedience to Him. Do you not see the heedless, when their work is on hold over their holidays and the such, having the leisure time to transgress the laws of Allah ﷻ and they become engrossed in His disobedience? Their preoccupation with worldly means was a mercy from Allah ﷻ upon them.

The Fourth Benefit of Worldly Means

There is a mercy in taking worldly means for those who abandon worldly means. This is a favour from Allah ﷻ on those who dedicate themselves to His obedience. If the people of means did not take means, how could the one desiring worship in solitude be able to remain in his continual worship? Or how could the one desiring abstinence be able to do so (without the support coming to them from those that take worldly means)? *Al-Haqq* ﷻ made those who take means to be as servants to those that dedicate and devote themselves to Him.

The Fifth Benefit of Worldly Means

Al-Haqq ﷻ willed that the believers be united as He said, **"The believers are but brothers."**[279] Taking worldly means is a reason for them to be acquainted and friendly with each other.

No one rejects taking worldly means except an ignorant one or one heedless of Allah ﷻ. Nor has it reached us that the Messenger ﷺ ordered people to abandon their

---

[279] Quran 49:10

worldly means when he invited them to Allah ﷻ. Rather he approved what would please Allah ﷻ from worldly means and invited them to right guidance. The Quran and Sunnah are rife with confirming the legitimacy of worldly means. The poet did well to say:

> *Do you not see that Allah to Mary said*
> *Shake the tree, ripe dates it shall shed?*
>
> *If He willed, the tree would to her lean*
> *But every thing must have its means*

The poet refers to the words of the Glorious, "**And shake toward yourself the trunk of the date palm; fresh, ripe dates shall fall upon you.**"[280] The Messenger ﷺ appeared for battle with two breast plates of armour at the Battle of Uhud and he ate cucumbers with dates saying, *"This repels the harm of this."* There are many such examples of him taking means. Also in his saying, *"If you trusted upon Allah with due reliance, He would provide for you as He provides for the birds. They set out in the morning hungry and return full,"* there is concordance with taking means as the birds' setting out and returning involves taking means. It is like the setting out of humans to their places of work and their returning home in the evening.

The final word on the matter is that taking worldly means is necessary but it is also necessary that you do not see them as having significance. Affirm and take worldly means in so much as Allah ﷻ has established them out of His wisdom. Do not trust in them since you know that power and creation belong only to Allah ﷻ.

15. A Detour

You might wonder what is meant by *"moderate"* in the Prophet's words *"So be conscious of Allah and be moderate in seeking (sustenance)."* Know that being moderate in seeking carries many meanings. We will mention some of what Allah ﷻ has facilitated understanding of out of His overflowing bounty.

Know that seeking sustenance is of two types. One type is the slave who seeks his provision by being engrossed in it and focuses all his aspirations on it. This will distract him from Allah ﷻ. That is because aspiration, when directed towards one thing, turns away from everything besides it. Shaykh Abu Madyan, may Allah be pleased with him said, *"The heart only has one direction it pays attention to. When it directs itself in that direction, it turns away from everything else."* Allah, the Glorious, states, **"Allah has not placed two hearts in the breast of any man."**[281] That is, He has not made the heart so that it can be oriented to two different inclinations at the same time. This is because of the weakness of the human race. They are incapable of directing themselves to two things without shortcomings affecting one of them.

Truly, attending to multiple things at the same time without any shortcomings touching any of them is the characteristic of Divinity. Hence, the Glorious states, **"He it is Who is God in heaven and God on earth."**[282] This verse

---

281 Quran 33:4
282 Quran 43:84

points to how He directs the affairs of the people of earth as well as the people of heaven. His occupation with the people of the earth does not distract Him from His occupation with the inhabitants of the heavens. That is why the Glorified repeats His Divinity twice in the verse. If He did not repeat it, it would not allude to this meaning but would nevertheless be known from the necessity of His Divinity, be He glorified.

It so becomes clear that seeking provision by devoting yourself to it in a way that distracts you from Allah ﷻ, is not being "*moderate in seeking.*" If one does not follow this (extremist) way they would be showing moderation in seeking their sustenance.

A second meaning of "*be moderate in seeking*" is that you ask for provision from Allah ﷻ without specifying the amount, the means or the time. *Al-Haqq* ﷻ will provide what He wills, how He wills, when He wills. This is how one shows good etiquette in seeking. Whoever seeks sustenance and specifies the amount, the means, and the time, then he has attempted to overrule his Nurturing Lord and heedlessness has encompassed his heart.

It has been related from one of the Sufis, "*At one time, I wished to abandon taking means. I wished that I could be given two loaves of bread every day.*" He desired thereby to rest from the fatigue of toiling with worldly means. He continues, "*I was subsequently imprisoned and I would receive two loaves of bread in prison every day. I remained in that situation for a long time until I became exasperated. One day I pondered my condition and it was as if I heard a voice saying, 'You asked Us for two loaves of bread every day but you did not ask for wellbeing. So We gave you what you asked for.' I repented for that and sought forgiveness from Allah. Suddenly there was a thump at the door and I was freed and exited the prison."*

Show proper etiquette, O believer, and so that your affair may run in accordance with His knowledge. Do not ask Allah ﷻ that He takes you out of one situation and places you in another. Otherwise, you would be acting shamelessly with Allah ﷻ. Rather, show patience so as not to seek exiting your circumstance of your own accord. You may be given what you ask for, only to find no peace of mind in it. There is many a man who left one situation and entered another only to find no blessings and no peace of mind. He becomes fatigued and is met with difficulties as a punishment for having a choice alongside Allah ﷻ.

From the words we recorded in another book are *"Your seeking to be free of worldly means when Allah has established you with them is from a hidden, selfish desire. Your seeking to be occupied with worldly means when Allah has established you as being free of them is backsliding from elevated aspiration."*[283]

So understand – may Allah have mercy upon you – that it is the nature of this enemy (Satan), that he comes to you in the situation that Allah ﷻ has established you in. He makes it seem contemptible in your eyes so that you may seek other than what Allah ﷻ has chosen for you. Your heart then becomes confused and your time with Allah is spent unproductively. Satan would come to those who take worldly means and say – *If you leave worldly means and dedicate yourself to worship, lights will shine within you. The hearts of others will glow a little because of you. Look at how so and so has done.* But this slave is not meant to divorce himself from worldly means and would not be able to handle its

---

[283] *Kitab al-Hikam*

demands. His safety lies only in interacting with worldly means. But alas, he abandons worldly means and his faith is shaken terribly, his certainty of belief diminishes, and he proceeds to ask for help from the creation or begins to worry about his provision. Thus he falls into the dark ocean of separation from Allah ﷻ and that was what his enemy had intended all along.

Satan will only come to you in the guise of a sound adviser. If he came in a manner other than that, you would never accept his seductions. That is how he came to Adam and Eve, peace be upon them both, in the guise of a well-wisher – "**And he said, 'Your Nurturing Lord has only forbidden you this tree, lest you should become angels, or among those who abide (forever)'. And he swore unto them, 'Truly I am a sincere adviser to you'.**"[284] We have mentioned his deceit of Adam ﷺ earlier.

He comes too, to those who have turned away from worldly means saying – *For how much longer will you abandon worldly means? Do you not realise that by leaving worldly means aside, it only emboldens your heart to seek what the people have and opens the door to coveting? Nor can you aid others or be charitable or fulfil the rights of your family. Instead of always anticipating what others might gift you, enter into worldly means so others can anticipate your goodness.* And he uses other such sophistry. Perhaps this slave was spending his time productively in the worship of Allah ﷻ, perhaps he was becoming illuminated, finding peace in his seclusion from creation. Yet Satan continued working on him until he returned to occupying himself with worldly means, until he is struck with its turbidity affecting his heart, and is covered in the darkness it entails.

---

284   Quran 7:20-21

Better than he is the one whose path was via worldly means and he remained consistent on that road. For such a one did not start a path and turn his back on it. He did not intend a purpose and then turn away from it. So understand and seek the protection of Allah ﷻ from your enemy, "**And whosoever holds fast to Allah is indeed guided unto a straight path.**"[285]

Satan's goal in all of this is to prevent slaves from having contentment with Allah ﷻ over their circumstance. He desires to extract them from Allah's choice for them so they can prefer their own choosing. But what Allah ﷻ places you in, He will look after you therein. What you enter upon yourself, he leaves you there to your own devices. "**And say, 'My Lord! Grant me an honourable entrance and an honourable exit and give me a supporting authority from Yourself'.**"[286] The "**honourable entrance**" is when you enter, not out of your own accord. Likewise, the "**honourable exit**" is when you exit, not out of your own accord. So understand!

Al-Haqq ﷻ requires from you that you remain where He establishes you until *Al-Haqq* ﷻ Himself oversees your exit from it, just as He undertook your entry into it. The matter is not that you abandon worldly means. The matter is that worldly means abandon you. One of the righteous said, *"I abandoned such and such from the worldly means only to return to it. Then it would leave me and I would not return to it."*

Once I entered into the presence of my Shaykh (Abu'l Abbas Al-Mursi), may Allah be pleased with him. I had a determination to abandon worldly means saying to myself –

---

285 Quran 3:101
286 Quran 17:80

The way to Allah is in being in such a state (of abandoning worldly means). It is not by way of being overly occupied with memorising knowledge (ilm al-zahir) *and mixing with the masses.* But my Shakyh said to me, without me mentioning any of that to him, *"A man who would busy himself with memorising outward knowledge and excelled in it accompanied me once. He tasted something of the delight of this path and so came to me and said, 'O my master, I shall abandon my current circumstance so I can free myself to be in your companionship'. I replied to him, 'This matter does not work like that. Remain as you are. Whatever Allah has decreed for you through our hands, will certainly reach you'."* Then the Shaykh looked directly at me and said, *"Such is the state of the truthful. They do not exit any circumstance until Al-Haqq, Himself, oversees their exit from it."* I left his presence and Allah had cleansed my heart from those thoughts and I found peace of mind in my surrender to Allah ﷻ. Alas, it was as the Messenger of Allah ﷺ said, *"They are a people whom their companion is never made miserable!"*[287]

Being *"moderate in seeking"* may also mean that you ask from Allah ﷻ with your purpose being intimate conversation with Him, not what you ask for. Your request is just a pretext to have intimate discourse with Him. Shaykh Abu'l Hassan ؓ said, *"Do not let your concern in asking from Him be the fulfilment of your need for you will be veiled from your Nurturing Lord. Let your concern be intimate discourse with Him."*

It is said that Moses, upon him be peace, would roam around the Children of Israel saying, *"Who has a message they would let me a carry to my Nurturing Lord?"* That was so he could lengthen in his intimate discourse with Allah ﷻ.

---

[287] Sahih Muslim 2689

Perhaps being *"moderate in seeking"* is that you seek provision but you recognise that what has been decreed for you is in fact seeking you. It is seeking you out and your seeking it does not bring it to you. For although you think you seek it, you are drowning in the ocean of helplessness, submerged in poverty.

Perhaps to be *"moderate in seeking"* is that you do not seek your provision by regarding your human means and blessings but by displaying your slave-hood. Just as Simnoun the Lover ﷺ is said to have recited:

> *And besides You I have no fortune*
> *So however You wish test Me!*

He was then tested by the suppression of urine. He showed patience and bore it with strength until one of his companions came to him and said, *"O teacher, I heard you yesterday asking for cure and well-being from Allah."* But he had done nothing of the sort. Then a second companion came saying the same, then a third, then a fourth. He realised that the desire of *Al-Haqq* from him was that he display his need and poverty before Him. So he asked to be cured by Allah ﷻ. He would then go around the youth of the school saying, *"Pray for this lying uncle of yours..."*

Perhaps to be *"moderate in seeking"* is that you seek from Allah ﷻ only what is sufficient for you, not what will make you negligent (in matters of worship). That you do not aspire for more than you require out of gluttony or greed. It was the Messenger ﷺ that taught us this when he said, *"O Allah, make the sustenance of the family of Muhammad only the bare necessities."*

The one who seeks more than what would meet

one's needs is blameworthy. While the one who just seeks his needs is not blameworthy. That is why it has been reported that the Messenger ﷺ said, *"One is not blamed over seeking his bare necessities."*

But sufficient for you in this matter is what the Messenger ﷺ replied to Thalabah ibn Hatib when Thalabah asked, *"O Messenger of Allah, ask Allah to enrich me."*

The Messenger ﷺ replied, *"O Thalabah, a little that you can be grateful for is better than a lot which you cannot handle."* But he continued to request from the Messenger ﷺ what was his own choosing. The result of him choosing for himself and opposing the choice of the Messenger of Allah ﷺ was that his wealth increased until he was hindered from praying some of his prayers behind the Messenger of Allah ﷺ. His wealth continued to multiply so that he became so preoccupied with it that he missed all the prayers behind the Messenger ﷺ except the Friday prayer. Then his sheep and cattle increased further till he was not able to attend the Friday prayer either. Finally, when the *zakat* collector of the Messenger ﷺ came to him, Thalabah said, *"This is just a poll tax (jizya), I see it as nothing more than a tax."* In the end, he refused to pay the *zakat*. His story is well known and Allah revealed regarding his affair, **"And among them are those who make a pact with Allah (saying), 'If He gives to us from His bounty, we will surely spend in charity, and we will surely be among the righteous'. But when He gave them from His bounty, they were miserly with it and turned away in rejection. So He requited them with hypocrisy in their hearts, till the Day they will meet Him, for having failed in that which they promised Him and for having lied."**[288]

---

[288] Quran 9:75-77

Perhaps to be *"moderate in seeking"* is that your seeking provision does not cast doubts at His allotting, thereby failing in His sanctification.

Or perhaps to be *"moderate in seeking"* is that you seek from Allah what will please Him, not seek your worldly fortunes. Allah, Most High, states, **"For among mankind are those who say, 'Our Nurturing Lord, give to us in this world', but have no share in the Hereafter. But among them are those who say, 'Our Nurturing Lord, give us good in this world and good in the Hereafter, and shield us from the punishment of the Fire!'"**[289]

Or perhaps to be *"moderate in seeking"* is that you seek from Allah but do not hasten for a response. To hasten for a response would not be moderation. The Messenger prohibited such impatience, *"One of you is responded to as long as he does not say, 'I prayed but was not responded to'."*

Moses and Aaron called upon Allah in the face of Pharoah, saying, **"Our Nurturing Lord! Truly You have given Pharaoh and his notables ornament and wealth in the life of this world, our Nurturing Lord, so that they may lead astray from Your way. Our Nurturing Lord! Obliterate their wealth and harden their hearts, so that they will not believe till they see the painful punishment."**[290] The time between this prayer and the moment Allah replied to them with **"Your supplication has been answered. So stand firm..."**[291] and the destruction of Pharoah was forty years.

While Shaykh Abu'l Hassan said, ***"'Your***

---
289 Quran 2:200-201
290 Quran 10:88
291 Quran 10:89

supplication has been answered. So stand firm', means there should be no hastiness over what you have supplicated for." Regarding His subsequent words, "**and follow not the way of those who know not**,"²⁹² the Shaykh said, "*(Those who know not) are those that are hasty for a response (to their supplications)*."

Perhaps being *"moderate in seeking"* is that one seeks provision from Allah ﷻ and is grateful for it if he receives it. If he does not receive what he sought, he marvels at the excellent choice of Allah ﷻ. Many a seeker is not grateful when he is given, nor does he witness Allah's excellence in choosing when he is not given. Such a one is certain that his welfare lies in him being given. From where does this ignorant slave think that he can pass a verdict over the knowledge of Allah? Or that he even knows the secrets of Allah?

It is enough ignorance for a slave that he shows himself arrogant to his Master. When you ask Allah ﷻ, ask Him by committing your affairs to Him, do not be managing alongside Him, or choosing for Him. "**And your Nurturing Lord creates what He wills, and chooses; no choice have they**."²⁹³ Otherwise, the slave would be embroiled in what would complicate his affair.

There are three types of supplications. The first is that which is good without any doubt. So supplicate for them from Allah ﷻ without exception. These include faith and obedience to His command. Then there is what is evil without a doubt. Ask Allah ﷻ for protection from them without exception. These include disbelief and sin.

---

292   Ibid
293   Quran 28:68

Then there are those things that are uncertain such as wealth, fame and power. Ask them from Allah ﷻ saying *"If You know them to be good for me."* That is how I heard it from my Shaykh, may Allah be pleased with him.

Perhaps being *"moderate in seeking"* means that when one is seeking from Allah ﷻ, one relies on His pre-eternal decree. One should not be depending on one's praying.

Or perhaps being *"moderate in seeking"* refers to seeking from Allah ﷻ and at the same time witnessing one's unworthiness. That would then be worthy to deserve the favour of the Nurturing Lord of the worlds. Shaykh Abu'l Hassan ؓ said, *"I do not ask anything from Allah except that I place my errors before me."* He intended by that, may Allah be pleased with him, to not see himself entitled to Allah's favour when supplicating. He desired that his seeking of Allah's bounty occur only by Allah's bounty.

These are then ten or so interpretations of *"be moderate in seeking."* The intention was not to limit them, for the matter is more comprehensive than this. They have only been limited by what has been presented from the unseen realm and what the Master, be He glorified, endowed.

Such are words of the possessor of encompassing lights (i.e. the Prophet Muhammad ﷺ). But none takes from him, except according to their own light. None grasps jewels from his ocean except according to the depth of their immersion. And each understands according to the station in which they have been established, "**...watered by one water, and We have favoured some above others in bounty.**"[294] But what they do not take from him is far greater

---

294   Quran 13:4

than what they take. Hear his words, *"I was given concise and comprehensive speech."* Indeed, he was extremely succinct in expression. If the scholars of Allah ﷻ endeavoured for eternity to expound on the secrets of one of his words, they could neither comprehend it completely nor appreciate its depths fully.

One of the righteous spoke the truth, may Allah be pleased with him, when he said, *"I acted upon this hadith for seventy years and I am still not finished with it. It is his words, 'From the excellence of a person's Islam, is his leaving aside what does not concern him'."* Indeed, if this pious man remained for the age of the earth, he would not be done with the demands of this *hadith* nor from the fascinating knowledge and secrets of understanding imbibed in it![295]

---

295 The reply of Imam Sa'id Nursi ﷺ is a just a single ray from the brilliance of this hadith. When asked why he never enquired into news regarding World War II - while living as that terrible war raged - he answered, *"Life's capital is minimal, yet ther are very many crucial matters (to take care of). Many spheres exist in the world of a human being, like concentric circles; beginning with the sphere of the heart and stomach, then the sphere of the body and home, the sphere of the neighbourhood and city, the sphere of homeland and country, the sphere of the earth and mankind, unto the sphere of living creatures and this world (itself)....yet the greatest, most important and most permanent duty lies in the sphere that is smallest (i.e. the heart)...Yet those larger spheres wield an attraction, and because of this, man occupies himself with useless, fruitless extraneous matters, neglecting his crucial service in the smaller spheres. He futilely sqanders the capital of his life itself. He wastes his precious life engaging in things of no value."* See the Fourth Issue, *The Staff of Moses*, Sa'id Nursi.

16. Back on the Path

Look to the words of the Prophet ﷺ, *"If you trusted upon Allah with due reliance, He would provide for you as He provides for the birds. They set out in the morning hungry and return full."* You will notice that he directs attention upon trusting in Allah ﷻ, he does not renounce worldly means. He affirms worldly means when he says *"They set out in the morning hungry and return full."* For their setting out and returning are the worldly means of the birds.

The *hadith* does however renounce storing wealth. It is as if the Messenger ﷺ says – *If you trusted upon Allah with due reliance you would not store your wealth. Your trust in Him would be sufficient for you and you would not see the need to store away your wealth. He will provide for you as He provides for the birds. Their daily sustenance arrives to them without them storing for the morrow due to their certainty that Allah has kept their provisions safe.*

As for you, O believer, you are more worthy to trust in Him than the birds. The Messenger ﷺ alluded to storing wealth as being due to weakness of certainty. You might ask – is storing wealth looked down upon in all circumstances or does it vary according to the situation? Then know that storing away wealth is of three types: the hoarding of oppressors, the storing away of those taking a middle path and the storing away of the pre-eminent.

The First Type of Storing Wealth

The first type is the hoarding of wealth in error and in arrogance. They are stingy, have a need to boast, and are self-conceited. Heedlessness has become deep-rooted in their hearts, while greed commands their animal-selves. Their gluttony for this world is never satiated, nor do they concern themselves with anything else. It is confirmed they are in poverty, even though they think themselves rich. It is obvious they are humiliated, even though they think themselves honoured. They are never content with enough, never do they slacken from chasing after the world. Worldly means rule and dominate over them while the pious separate themselves from them. **"Such as these are like cattle. Nay, they are even further astray. It is they who are heedless."**[296]

Their hearts are so full (of their desires) that no place remains to be conscious of wisdom or to hear admonition. Rare it is indeed that their deeds are accepted or their inner-states purified. That is because the fear of poverty has settled in their hearts and the Messenger ﷺ has said, *"Whomsoever has had the fear of poverty settle in his heart, rare it is that his deeds are accepted."*

It is binding upon the believer, who has been protected from such preoccupations, saved from such fixations, and purified from such dirtiness, to thank Allah ﷻ. Such a believer should praise Him for distinguishing him out of His bounty and blessing him with His gifts. If you have been saved, then say when you see those unfortunate ones, *"All praise belongs to Allah, who saved me from what He tested them with, and preferred me immensely over a great many He has created."*

---

296 Quran 7:179

Thank Him just as you would when you see someone whose body has been injured. In such a case you would thank Allah ﷻ for preserving you from a similar injury and you recognise your Master's blessings upon you. Likewise, it is necessary and more important to thank Him for protecting you from obsession and greed over worldly means with which He tested others.

But be wary not to look down upon others. Replace any spite you might have for them with mercy for them. Replace your supplications against them with supplications for them. Follow the example of the knower of Allah, Marouf Al-Karkhi ؓ, for he acted in a way that was the essence of goodness.

He and his companions were one day crossing the Tigris river. They caught sight of another boat on which there were foolish, immoral people, singing in amusement. His companions said to Marouf ؓ, *"O our master, pray to Allah against them."*

So he raised his hands and said, *"O Allah, just as you have made them joyful in this world, make them joyful in the next!"*

They said, *"Our master, we asked you to supplicate against them!?"*

He replied, *"If He makes them joyful in the Hereafter it means He has forgiven them and that would not harm you in any way."*

In time, that boat docked and the men were seen leaving one side, separating themselves from the women who left on the other.[297] Their states were

---

297   i.e. they suddenly became conscious of their free-mixing and sin and so separated themselves.

purified, they left the boat repentant to Allah ﷻ, and there arose great worshippers and ascetics from them due to the blessing in the supplication of Marouf ﷺ.

When you see the people of misguidance and sin, know that their state is due to their being judged in Allah's pre-eternal knowledge and is due to the potency of His will.[298] If you do not show compassion, it is feared that what they have been tested with will also afflict you and you may be distanced from Allah ﷻ like them.

Listen to the words of Shaykh Abu'l Hassan ﷺ, *"Honour the believers even if they be immoral sinners. Call them to goodness and forbid them from evil. Disassociate from them out of compassion for them*[299] *not out of disgust for them."* He also said, *"If the light of the sinful believer was uncovered, it would spread over what is between the heaven and earth. So what do you think of the obedient believer?"*

But sufficient for you to esteem the believers, even though they be sinners, are the words of the Nurturing Lord of all the worlds, **"Then We bequeathed the Book to those of Our slaves whom We had chosen. Among them are those who wrong themselves, those who take a middle course, and those who are foremost in good deeds, by Allah's Leave."**[300] Look at how He confirms that they were chosen, even with their wronging of themselves. He did not make their sins a reason to remove them from those He chose

---

298 i.e. their states have been decreed by Allah over them because of their outer and inner sins – and Allah knows best. Nevertheless, there should be compassion for them as fellow human beings, all who struggle in walking the same path.

299 i.e. disassociate from them so that they might recognise the error of their ways. Or possibly, disassociate from them to save them from your own evil – and Allah knows best.

300 Quran 35:32

nor from those who inherited the Book. He chose them for their faith, even if they blemished it with disobedience. So glorified be the One of vast mercy and who is unfathomable in bounty!

Know that in His kingdom, there must necessarily be slaves who have an allotment of His forbearance, a share of His mercy and forgiveness, and are benefactors of intercession. Understand what the Messenger ﷺ said, *"By the One who has my soul in His hands! If you did not sin, Allah would have sent you off and replaced you with a people who do sin so that they could ask Allah for forgiveness and He could forgive them."* He also said, *"My intercession is for those who have committed great sins* (kaba'ir) *from my nation."*

A man once came to Shaykh Abu'l Hassan ؓ and said, *"O my master, yesterday near our house there was such and such depravities going on!"* The man was shocked that such disobedience could have taken place. The Shaykh replied, *"O man! It is as if you wish that Allah not be disobeyed anywhere in His kingdom. Whoever likes there to be no disobedience of Allah in His kingdom, likes that His forgiveness not be shown nor that there be the intercession of His Messenger ﷺ."* And how many a great sinner there was, whose humility because of his transgressions, entailed forgiveness from his Nurturing Lord. So be compassionate to the believers because of their faith, even if you know of their mistakes.

The Second Type of Storing Wealth

The second type is the storing away of those who take the middle path. They are those who store away wealth, not out of arrogance, showing off, or self-importance. Rather, they know that they will be uneasy if they did not save their wealth. They know that if they do not store some wealth away, it would cause restlessness in their faith and shake their certainty. They gather and store because of their shortcomings in attaining the state of those that have complete trust and because they know of their own weakness in attaining the station of certainty.

The Messenger ﷺ has said, *"The strong believer is better in the eyes of Allah than the weak believer, but in all there is good."* The strong believer is the one in whose heart the light of certainty shines. He knows that Allah ﷻ drives His provision to him, whether he is to store it away or not. He knows that if he has not stored up anything, then His Nurturing Lord has stored it up for him. He recognises that those who store their wealth are dependent on what they have stored away. But the people of trust (*tawakkul*), they trust upon Allah ﷻ, nothing else. The strong believer does not rely on worldly means whether they be on hand or not. The weak believer involves himself with worldly means while relying on them and when worldly means leave him, he anticipates and hopes for worldly means to return.

The Third Type of Storing Wealth

They are the pre-eminent in this affair. They are the ones who outstrip others in closeness to Allah ﷻ due to their hearts being purified from everything other than Him. Obstacles on the path do not divert them, nor do worldly attachments distract them, because there is nothing to hold them back.

It is only the attractions of attachments to other than Allah ﷻ that pull one back from taking precedence over others in being close to Him. For whenever someone, who has attachments to other than Allah ﷻ in his heart, desires to journey to Him, those attachments will instead pull him back towards what he is attached to. The attachments return to his mind and become the goal that he seeks. Being in intimate contemplation (*hadrah*) with Allah ﷻ is forbidden to whoever has this characteristic and trait. One of the knowers of Allah ﷻ has said, "*Do you think you can enter into the intimate contemplation with Him when something pulls you in another direction?*"

Understand at this point the words of the Glorified, **"The Day when neither wealth nor children avail, save for him who comes to Allah with a sound heart.**"[301] Indeed, the sound heart is the one that has no attachments other than Allah, Most High.

Understand, too, His words, **"Now you have come to Us individually, just as We created you the first time.**"[302] This verse also has a deeper meaning that is inferred. That is, your spiritual returning (in this world) to Allah ﷻ is not sound except if you come to Him individually, independant of all else besides Him.

Understand too, His words, **"Did He not find you an orphan and shelter you?**"[303] From this verse it is also inferred that He will not shelter you with Him except when your heart is orphaned from all other than Him.

Understand too, the words of the Messenger, upon him be peace, "*Allah is only witr*[304] *(One) and loves the witr.*" That is, He loves the heart which is not stained with trust

---

301	Quran 26:88-89
302	Quran 6:94
303	Quran 93:8
304	*Witr* generally refers to odd numbers.

for worldly means. Such hearts are only for Allah ﷻ, by the leave of Allah ﷻ. Slaves with such hearts have let Allah ﷻ act on their behalf, so He does not abandon them to themselves. Nor does He leave them to their own managing. They are the people of intimate contemplation of Him (*hadrah*) and the addressees of His special favour. The attractions of worldly means do not remove them from Allah ﷻ nor do temporary delights distract them.

O Delightful One in Beauty, of which there is no like
Here is but beauty's shadow which You cast down

I know You privately, but doing so is not attained
Except by seeking You at horizons and prolonged pining

One of the righteous said, "*Even if it was asked of me to contemplate something other than Him, I would not be able to. For there is nothing else equal to Him that I could consider it besides Him.*" Such is the state of a people whom Allah takes care of and embraces with His protection. So what self-directing could they have? Or how is it possible for them to store wealth when they are in continual, intimate contemplation of the Nurturing Lord of the worlds? If they were to store wealth, they would never be reliant on what they save. How is it possible for them to rely on anything besides Him when they witness His oneness (and worldly means having no power)?

Shaykh Abu'l Hassan, may Allah be pleased with him, said, "*Once, my contemplation of Him became too intense for me so, I asked Him to remove this realisation away.*" It was said to the Shaykh, "*Even if you asked Him how Moses, speaker with Allah, asked Him, and how Jesus, spirit* (ruh) *from Allah, asked Him, and how Muhammad, the beloved of Allah, asked Him,*

He would not do so (i.e. take back this spiritual state from you). Rather, ask Him to strengthen you." The Shaykh continued, *"So I asked Him to strengthen me."* For a people for whom such is their state, how could they require storing away wealth? Or how is it possible for them to rely on worldly means?

Rather, it suffices the believer to store up his faith in Allah ﷻ, store up confidence in Him, and store up trust in Him. Those that have intimate knowledge of Allah ﷻ trust in Him so He stores up for them. They seek His protection so He is their Protector. Their only purpose is Him, and that too is by His permission and power. He favours them with gifts, He suffices them against their troubles, and He diverts away from them their distress. They busy themselves with what He has commanded them to do instead of worrying over what He has guaranteed for them (i.e. their provision). That is since they realise He has not appointed them to oversee (the distribution of His provision) and that He would not prevent His bounty from them. Relief falls over them, they find themselves in the paradise of surrender and taste the delight of committing affairs to Him. So, Allah ﷻ raises their ranks and perfects their lights (*nur*).

They are deserving of not having to face the ordeal of being judged (on the Day of Judgement), as the Prophet ﷺ said, *"Seventy thousand from my nation shall enter Paradise without judgement."*

He was asked, *"Who are they, O Messenger of Allah?"*

He replied, *"They are those who neither distribute charms nor seek them. Neither do they observe (so-called) omens. And only in their Nurturing Lord do they trust."* And how could someone who has nothing be judged?[305] Or how could someone who witnesses that they have no deeds be questioned about their deeds?[306]

Only those that make claims (of ownership over their good deeds and wealth) are held to account. Only the heedless are questioned, who witness themselves as possessors or actors alongside Him. Whoever did not store anything other than confidence in Allah ﷻ and trust in Him, Allah ﷻ drives His provisions to him alongside feelings of bliss. He brings about richness in their hearts.

One of the intimate knowers of Allah ﷻ became bankrupt and said to his wife, *"Take out everything from the house and give it to charity."* She did so but kept with her the mortar and pestle saying, *"Perhaps we will need it later and not find another like it."* She had just given everything else to charity when the door was knocked and it was said, *"Here is wheat that was sent for the Shaykh."* The house became full of wheat. When the Shaykh returned, he looked around and said, *"Did you take out everything from the house?"* She replied that she had. The Shaykh replied, *"The matter is not so..."*

She answered, *"I did not leave anything behind except the mortar*

---

305   i.e. they have not stored anything away to be judged over it. They only they sought their necessities and the Prophet ﷺ said, *"One is not blamed over seeking his bare necessities."* So in effect, they have no wealth to be judged over. And Allah ﷻ knows best.

306   i.e. they attribute all their good deeds only to Allah ﷻ, not to themselves. As for any bad deeds they might have, they repent from them and so they also become good deeds in accordance with Allah's words, **"Save for those who repent and believe and perform righteous deeds. For them, Allah will replace their evil deeds with good deeds, and Allah is Forgiving, Merciful"** [Quran 25:70]. Since all their deeds are then good, and all good is from Allah ﷻ, they in effect have no deeds to be judged for. And Allah knows best.

and pestle fearing we may need it."

He replied, *"If you had also given away the mortar and pestle, ground flour would have come to you. But you kept it back so you were given what you will now have to toil over."*

If the pre-eminent, righteous ones do store wealth, it is not for themselves. Rather they act as trustworthy treasurers and honoured slaves. If they take hold of wealth, they do so rightly. If they spend it, they do so rightly. And the one who holds on to wealth rightly only does so when he spends it rightly. They do not witness themselves as possessing anything alongside Allah. They see what is in their hands as trusts from Allah and spend it as representatives for Allah. They have heard the words of the Glorified, **"Believe in Allah and His Messenger and spend from that over which He has appointed you as trustees."**[307] They understand that they have no possessions in the first place along with Allah.

For ownership is just an attribution that is attached to you. It is a favour connected to you by which He sees – while He is the All-Knowing, All-Informed – whether you will settle with the apparent meaning (of ownership) or whether you will pierce into its secrets.

Such were the Prophets of Allah, blessings of Allah be upon them. It was not binding on them to pay the *zakat* charity because they had no possessions alongside Allah so that *zakat* could be necessary on them. *Zakat* is only binding on you over what you own. As for the Prophets, they had in their hands only the trusts of Allah, which they would spend at the right time. They would be prevented

---

307 Quran 57:7

from spending it in its incorrect place.

Zakat is a purification, for those upon whom it is necessary, for any sins they may have accrued. For the Glorified states, "**Take charity from their wealth, cleansing them and purifying them thereby.**"[308] But the Prophets are free from the dirt of sin because of their infallibility. For this reason, Imam Abu Hanifa ﷺ deduced that young children do not have to pay zakat since they are also sinless. Sins are only recognised after the condition of responsibility is met, which is after puberty.

Heed the words of the Messenger ﷺ, "*We, the community of Prophets, are not inherited from. What we leave behind is charity (sadaqah),*" and what we have mentioned and explained will become clear. If those of intimate knowledge of Allah ﷻ, who witness His total oneness, do not see themselves as having any possessions, what do you think of the Prophets and Messengers? The people of monotheism (tawheed) and intimate knowledge have only scooped up from the oceans of the Prophets and Messengers and derive from their lights.

It has been narrated regarding Imam Shafi' and Imam Ahmed ibn Hanbal, may Allah be pleased with them, that they were sitting together when they saw Shaybaan Al-Ra'e ﷺ. Imam Ahmed ﷺ said to Imam Shafi' ﷺ, "*I would like to question this famous man (Shaybaan) of our time.*"

Imam Shafi' ﷺ replied, "*Do not do so (out of respect and awe of Shaybaan).*"

"*I must do so,*" Imam Ahmed ﷺ replied before continuing, "*O Shaybaan. What do you say about the one who forgets to make*

---

[308] Quran 9:103

four prostrations across four units (rakaat) *of prayer?"*

He replied, *"O Ahmed, this is a heart heedless of Allah. He must be punished so that he does not return to the like of it."*

Imam Ahmed ﷺ was taken aback by this response. When he regained his composure he asked a second time, *"What do you say about (the* zakat *charity due from) someone who has forty sheep?"*

Shaybaan ﷺ asked, *"According to your school of thought* (madhab) *or ours?"*

Imam Ahmed ﷺ replied, *"And are there 2 different schools of thought on the matter?"*

Shaybaan ﷺ replied, *"Indeed. As for your school of thought, for every forty sheep, one sheep is to be donated. As for our school of thought, the slave does not own anything alongside his Master (i.e. all the sheep are donated)."*

It is mentioned in one *hadith* that the Prophet ﷺ stored the sustenance for a year. This could be because of the reason we mentioned, that the Prophets only hold on to wealth as a trust until it is the right moment to spend it. It could also be that the Prophet, upon him be peace, stored it for the sake of his family. Another possibility is that he did it so that his nation would know that storing wealth is permissible, for as long as one's reliance is not on what is stored away, it does not negate having trust in Allah ﷻ.

Evidence that the Prophet's storing of wealth was only to demonstrate its permissibility is that for most of the time he did not keep wealth with him. His storing wealth was a reprieve for his nation, mercy on them and gentleness with the weak in faith among them. If he did not store wealth, it would not be possible for the believers to store wealth after him. He did so to clarify the ruling regarding it. He said, "*I only forget, or am made to forget, to establish a law (sunnah).*" Hence he clarified for you, upon him be peace, that forgetting was not his nature nor his quality. Rather, forgetting came upon him to clarify his rulings and those matters that concern his nation (as opposed to himself exclusively). So understand.

As for the *hadith*, "*Allah takes upon Himself the provision for the student of knowledge,*" know that knowledge, in so far as it is repeated in the Honourable Book and Sunnah, refers to only beneficial knowledge which is accompanied by His fear (*mukhafah*) and results in His awe (*khushyah*). The Glorious states, **"Only those of His slaves who have knowledge are in awe of Him."**[309] Here, He illustrates that being in awe of Him is correlated with knowledge. It is thus understood that the scholars are only those that are in awe of Him.

Likewise, (this is the knowledge referred to in) His words, **"Those who were given knowledge will say, 'Surely, this day, disgrace and evil are upon the disbelievers'."**[310] Also, **"...and those firmly rooted in knowledge."**[311] Also, **"...but say, 'My Nurturing Lord! Increase me in knowledge!'"**[312]

Also in the words of the Messenger ﷺ, "*Indeed, the Angels spread out their wings for the student of knowledge.*" Also, "*The scholars are the inheritors of the Prophets.*" Likewise

---

309   Quran 35:28
310   Quran 16:27
311   Quran 3:7
312   Quran 20:114

too, his words, "*Allah takes upon Himself the provision for the student of knowledge.*"

In all these places, only beneficial knowledge is being referred to, knowledge which overpowers desires and lusts and suppresses (eagerness for) this world. This must be the knowledge being referred to because the words of Allah ﷻ and the words of His Messenger ﷺ are far too sublime to refer to anything less. We have clarified this matter in another book.

Help is sought from beneficial knowledge to help you abide by Allah's obedience, compel you to have fear of Him and stop you at the borders of what He has forbidden. It is the intimate knowledge of Allah (*ma'rifa*). Beneficial knowledge comprises intimate knowledge of Allah ﷻ and knowledge of what Allah ﷻ has commanded.

If one's studying was in pursuit of this type of knowledge, then according to the Messenger's words, "*Allah takes upon Himself the provision for the student of knowledge,*" Allah ﷻ would guarantee the student's provision arrives together with his peace of mind, protection of his honour, and safety from veils appearing between him and Allah ﷻ. This is a special guarantee from Allah ﷻ and we have interpreted this guarantee to be special because *Al-Haqq* ﷻ is the Guarantor of the provision of all His slaves, whether they seek this type of knowledge or not. Since Allah ﷻ makes special mention of guaranteeing the provision of such students of knowledge, it denotes a more privileged guarantee.

In this regard, our Shaykh, may Allah be pleased with him, while asking for things from Allah ﷻ would include "*...and provision with peace of mind, that does not lead to any veiling in this world and no questioning or accounting or punishment in the next world, on the foundation of the knowledge of tawheed and Islamic law, sound from desires, lusts and greed...*" He asked for provision with peace of mind and that is the provision that is guaranteed to the student of knowledge.

He then clarified what provision with peace of mind is, it is what does not result in being veiled (from Allah) in this world. Certainly, whatever results in being veiled has no happiness in it. Being veiled entails anxieties spouting in your innermost heart (*sirr*) due to being prevented from intimate contemplation of Him (*hadrah*) and not being acquainted with Him. Peace of mind in provision is not, as people may generally think, provision which comes without toil or labour. For peace of mind or happiness with the heedless masses is connected with the body (i.e. what is material). But for the people who understand, happiness is connected with the heart.

The occurrence of veils being cast over one in the matter of provision may occur because someone begins to attribute power to worldly means and forgets Allah ﷻ. Or it could be because you consume His provision but your intention is not to attain energy to help you in His worship and obedience. The former veil is during the acquirement of it and the latter is when consuming it.

Then our Shaykh said in his supplication for provision, "*and no accounting or questioning or punishment in the next world.*" Questioning will indeed occur over the matter of blessings received, for the Most High states, **"Then, on that Day, you will be called to account for all**

the bounties you enjoyed."[313] Once the Messenger ﷺ ate with some of his Companions and then said, "*By Allah, you will certainly be questioned about the blessings of this day.*"

Our Shaykh, may Allah be pleased with him, would say, "*The questioning is of two types. A questioning that honours and another that condemns. The questioning of the obedient and those under Divine care is one of honouring. The questioning of the heedless of Allah and those that turned away from Him is one of condemnation.*"

So understand – may Allah have mercy upon you – that *Al-Haqq* ﷻ will only question the truthful to publicise the rank of their sincerity to His other slaves. He will broadcast their virtues in the Hereafter by questioning them, even though He is better informed about them – even of the subtlest depths of their hearts. Much like any master would say to their slave – *how did you fare in such and such matter?* The master would already know he perfected it and carried it out expertly, but wants other slaves to know of his high regard and consideration for this one. So understand!

The Shaykh also asked for provision that would result in "*no accounting.*" Being held to account is the result of being questioned. Whoever makes it safely through questioning will make it safely through being held to account. And whoever makes it safely through questioning and being held to account, avoids the punishment. The Shaykh mentioned them all separately even though they are as one, to enumerate the blessings that receiving such a provision entails. Even if only one aspect of this provision could be attained it would be worthy to seek after it.

---

313   Quran 102:8

Then the Shaykh mentioned, may Allah be pleased with him, *"on the foundation of the knowledge of tawheed."* That is – *allow me to witness only You in Your sustaining me, that I see only You as the one who feeds me, no one else. Do not let me attribute Your provision to anything from Your creation.*

Such are the people of Allah ﷻ, they eat only at the table of Allah ﷻ, no matter who appears to give them food. They understand, that nobody besides Allah ﷻ possesses anything. Thus, esteeming creation falls away from their hearts and they direct their love to none other than Allah ﷻ. They do not direct their acts of devotion to other than Him, for they see that it was He who fed them, gave them of His bounty, and honoured them.

Shaykh Abu'l Hassan ﷺ once said, *"Truly we do not love, except Allah, Most High."* That is – we do not direct our love to the creation. A man said to him, *"Your grandfather (the Messenger) contradicted you there my master when he said, 'Hearts are predisposed to love someone who does them good...'"*

He replied, *"Indeed. We are a people that do not see anyone doing us favours, except Allah. So our hearts are predisposed to love Him."*[314]

Whoever sees that the benefactor is *Al-Haqq*, be He glorified, increases in his love to the degree that he receives blessings. The Messenger ﷺ said, *"Love Allah for what He nourishes you with from His favours,"* and we have already mentioned this *hadith*.

---

314 It is worthwhile to note that loving what Allah ﷻ loves is an important element of loving Allah ﷻ. Hence, love for the Messenger, the saints and scholars of Islam, one's family, the Muslims, etc., also falls under love for Allah ﷻ. And Allah knows best.

Whoever sees that it is indeed Allah ﷻ who feeds him, this insight will preserve him from degrading himself in front of the creation. It will also preserve his heart from inclining in love towards anything other than the True King.

Have you not heard the words of Abraham, the friend, upon him be peace, "(Allah is the one) **Who feeds me and gives me drink**"?[315] He testified to Allah being the only One who provides for him. He acknowledged that Allah exclusively holds that position.

The Shaykh mentioned in his supplication for provision, that it be *"on the foundation of the knowledge of* tawheed *and Islamic law."* For whoever compromises on the issue of *tawheed* and on the fact that the kingdom belongs to Allah ﷻ, there being no sovereignty to anything else alongside Him, nor follows Islamic law (*shariah*), falls into the depths of heresy. His state will bring only bad consequences to him.

The reality of the matter of religion is that one is supported by spiritual realities (*haqeeqah*), but one must also restrict their actions to the precepts of the law (*shariah*). Such is the careful and vigilant seeker of truth. One must not accept spiritual realities unconditionally nor limit oneself to just the outward precepts of the law. Limiting oneself to only following the law outwardly is polytheism (*shirk*).[316]

---

315 Quran 26:79

316 The one who does not contemplate inner realities ends up attributing power and effect to worldly means or ends up performing deeds for the sake of creation, thus ascribing partners to Allah. Or attributes his good deeds as originating from himself when they are in fact a blessing and creation of Allah. It can occur subtly without a person even being aware of it. But the one who truly contemplates *tawheed* lives out the meaning of "there is no power or might except through Allah", sees only Allah as the Creator of all things, and seeks only the pleasure of

While submitting to spiritual truths without weighing them first by the Islamic law is destruction. The place of truth is between the two, "**...between refuse and blood, is pure milk, palatable to those who drink.**"[317]

Allah in all his affairs. And Allah knows best.
[317] Quran 16:66

17. Taking a Turn

Know there are certain matters and challenges related to the issue of provision. Our Shaykh, may Allah be pleased with him, has mentioned many of them when he said, *"Take care for me this matter of provision, save yourself from greed and fatigue when seeking it, from the heart's preoccupation with it, from the attachment of worry in acquiring it, from humiliating oneself to the creation because of it, from overthinking and self-direction when attaining it, and from miserliness and greed after gaining it."*

The obstacles connected with provision are not limited in that they can all be presented in detail, so we shall discuss what the Shaykh, may Allah be pleased with him, mentioned.

Know that the slave is in three states regarding provision. A state before Allah ﷻ provides for the slave, it is the state of striving. A state after provision has been acquired, it is the state of having acquired provision. And a state after having spent or consumed it. These are then the three states.

As for the obstacles that occur before acquiring provision, they are greed for it, fatiguing oneself when seeking it, the preoccupation of the heart over it, having worry over it, humiliating oneself to others because of it and overthinking and self-directing when acquiring it.

What is meant by greed for it is a subsistent desire in

one's animal-self to acquire provision and dedicating oneself to that end. Such greed arises from losing confidence (in Allah's promise) and weakness in certainty of faith. These two arise when one loses light (*nur*). The loss of light occurs with the presence of veils. If the heart is filled with the lights of seeing reality (*mushaahada*) and submerged in the gifts of Allah, the hammering of greed would not knock upon it.

If the light from certainty of faith extended itself upon one's heart it would reveal to one that Divine decree indeed sends forth one's sustenance and having greed for it would not be possible. The slave would recognise that Allah has already set aside sustenance that must reach him.

As for *"fatigue when seeking it,"* it could be physical exertion and Allah's protection is sought from that. When fatigue overwhelms the seeker of sustenance, it keeps him preoccupied from fulfilling Allah's commandments. While gaining sustenance with ease supports one to dedicate time to the service of Allah and His obedience.

But if the fatigue is the fatigue of the heart and not physical toil, then it is more paramount that Allah's protection be sought from it. In such a case, the heart is exhausted by what it loads upon itself in seeking sustenance and by its thoughts regarding it. The heart becomes burdened by all that. There is no way out, no peace for the heart, except by placing its trust in Allah.

He who places his trust in Allah and lays down his burdens, Allah, be He glorified, carries them for him. As He states, **"And whosoever trusts in Allah, He suffices him."**[318]

---

318   Quran 65:3

Then the Shaykh warns about in the matter of provision, "*the heart's preoccupation with it, from the attachment of worry in acquiring it.*" Preoccupation of the heart with the matter of provision indeed severs one (from Allah). Shaykh Abu'l Hassan, may Allah be pleased with him, said, "*Two things predominately veil the creation from Allah: worrying over provision and fear of the creation.*" Worrying over provision is the more formidable of the veils. Many people free themselves from having fear over the creation but very few free themselves from worrying about their provision. Especially since evidence of poverty is undeniable in your existence and you are in constant need to strengthen your body and gain your strength.

Worrying over provision is also having eagerness for it, focusing on it and being engrossed in it, until there remains no room for anything else. This is a state that entails being severed (from Allah) and it peels away the lights of being connected (with Him). This state announces that its bearer's heart is in desolation from the light of certainty of faith and that his heart is bankrupt of power and strength. It heralds that such a one humiliates himself to the creation for the sake of provision.

Know that whoever has weakness in his certainty (of Allah's promise) and his lot in life was to have little intelligence, humiliation is binding on him. This is due to his yearning for the creation and his having no confidence in the Real King of creation. That is due to his not contemplating the previous blessings that Allah ﷻ had decreed for him and not attributing truth to Allah's promise. So he humiliates himself to the creation by flattering them and being servile to them. He resorts to them persistently with attachment. This is punishment for being heedless of Allah ﷻ, "**And** surely the punishment of the Hereafter is more severe and more lasting."[319]

Such a person would be honourable if only he remained true to his faith and to his certainty in Allah's promise. **"Yet unto Allah belongs honour and to His Messenger and the believers."**[320] The honour of the believer is through his Nurturing Lord. The believer does not pride himself by other than Him since he knows **"Truly honour belongs to Allah altogether."**[321] He is the Dignified One (*Al-Aziz*), there is no dignified one next to Him. He is the Bestower of Honour (*Al-Muiz*), there is no bestower next to Him.

The worthy believers are honoured by their confidence in Him and given victory by their trust in Him. They do not lose heart due to the sincerity of their faith in their Nurturing Lord and His apportioning. They are not grieved due to their reliance upon Him and His favours, for they hear the words of Allah, the Glorified, **"Do not falter and do not grieve, for you will have the upper hand if you are believers."**[322]

The honour of the believer is through forsaking his yearning to seek from the creation and by having confidence in the Real King. His faith prohibits him from directing his need to other than his Nurturing Lord, or to devote to other than Him, the hope of his heart. Hence the poet said:

319	Quran 20:127
320	Quran 63:8
321	Quran 4:139
322	Quran 3:139

Forbidden upon the one who claims Allah as his Nurturer
To walk a path to seek his fortunes elsewhere

Stand with Al-Haqq, my friend, firm-footed
On that land I die with rapture! There I live likewise!

And say to the kings of earth to strive with all it has
That kingdom is not bought nor gifted from hand to hand

Whomsoever Allah liberates from bondage to greed and honours with piety, then much favour has been bestowed on him and Allah's blessing upon him has been completed. Indeed, Allah has clothed you in many robes, O believer. There is the robe of faith, the robe of intimate knowledge of Him, the robe of obedience, the robe of His Prophet's *Sunnah*, etc...Do not dirty them because of your yearning to seek from the creation and your leaning on other than the Nurturing Lord of the worlds.

Shaykh Abu'l Hassan said, *"I saw the Prophet in a dream and he said to me, 'O Ali, purify your garment from dirt, you shall be blessed with Allah's support with every breath.'*

I said, 'O Messenger of Allah, what is my garment?'

He replied, 'Know that Allah has clothed you in the robe of faith, the robe of intimate knowledge of Him (ma'rifah), *the robe of Allah's oneness* (tawheed), *and the robe of (Allah's) love.'*

*It was then I understood the words of the Glorified, '**And your garments purify!**'"*[323]

Know – may Allah have mercy upon you – that the seeker on the path to the Hereafter is more beautified than a bride with her jewels when he discards placing his

---
[323] Quran 74:4

hopes in the creation and turns his yearning away from them. The seekers are more in need of this than bodies are in need of water. Whoever is gifted a robe from the King and preserves and protects it, is worthy of it remaining with him and not being stripped from him. Whoever desecrates the robe bestowed on him only confirms he is not worthy of it remaining with him. So, do not defile your faith, dear brother, by seeking and yearning from the creation. Certainly, do not place your reliance on anything other than the Nurturing Lord of all the worlds.

If you take your honour from Allah ﷻ, your honour will continue as long as the One you took honour in continues. If you take honour from other than Him, then your honour cannot remain. For, in that case, the one you took honour in will pass away. One of the eminent ones composed these lines to himself:

> *Let your honour only be through your Lord*
> *For it is there well guarded and guaranteed*
>
> *But if you take honour in who will die*
> *Then your honour is already dead*

Once a man came crying to one of the knowers of Allah (*arifeen*) who asked him, *"What is the matter?"*

"My teacher has died," he replied.

The shaykh said to him, *"And why have you made your teacher one who dies when it is said to you – If you seek honour by someone other than Allah, then you will lose him and if you seek support from other than Allah, you will be deprived of him?* **'Now observe your god, to whom you remained devoted: we shall surely burn it and scatter its ashes in the sea!"** *Your only god is*

Allah, besides Whom there is no other god. He encompasses all things in knowledge'."[324]

Be Abrahamic, O slave of Allah. Your father Abraham, may the peace and blessings of Allah be upon him, said, **"I love not things that set (i.e. pass away)."**[325] Whatever is besides Allah ﷻ is passing away. The fact that all creation passes away is known by observation or by recognising its perishable nature.

The Glorified said, **"(it is) the creed of your father Abraham."**[326] It is binding upon the believer to follow the creed of Abraham ﷺ. From the tenets of his creed is removing one's eagerness and hopes from the creation. When he was flung by catapult, Gabriel ﷺ appeared to him and said, *"Do you have any need?"*

He ﷺ replied, *"From you, I have no need. But from Allah, then indeed."*

Gabriel ﷺ said, *"Ask Him!"*

But Abraham ﷺ only replied, *"His knowledge of my situation suffices me from having to ask Him."*

So see how Abraham, blessings of Allah be upon him, removed his eagerness and hope away from the creation and directed it only to the True King. He did not seek help from Gabriel ﷺ nor did he even think to ask Allah ﷻ explicitly. Rather, he saw that Al-Haqq ﷻ was closer to him than Gabriel ﷺ and closer than if he was to ask Him. Hence, (because of his truthfulness) he was later

---

324   Quran 20:97-98
325   Quran 6:76
326   Quran 22:78

saved from Nimrod and his tyranny, Allah ﷻ blessed him with His kindness and bounty, and distinguished him by drawing him near.

Also from the creed of Abraham ﷺ is opposition to everything that might distract from Allah ﷻ and turning one's aspirations to Allah ﷻ with love for he said, "**For they are all enemies to me, save the Nurturing Lord of the worlds.**"[327] It means, if you require direction understanding it, that you give up your hopes in people.

Shaykh Abu'l Hassan ﷺ has said, *"I gave up hope that I could benefit myself, so how can I not give up hope of others benefitting me? I held hopes in Allah for others, how can I not have high hopes in Him for myself?"*

This is true alchemy and this is the true elixir, whoever attains it has attained riches after which there is no poverty. He attains honour after which there is no disgrace and he spends with no depletion of his wealth. It is the chemistry of the people who understand Allah's purposes.

Shaykh Abu'l Hassan ﷺ said, *"A man accompanied me once and became burdensome upon me. So I indulged him one day and said, 'Son, what is your need and why have you accompanied me?'*

He replied, 'My master, I have been told that you teach alchemy so I accompanied you to learn it from you.'

'You are right and so is the one who informed you. But I don't think you will be able to learn it.'

He rebutted, 'No, but I can!'

---

327   Quran 26:77

I said to him, '(The secret to alchemy is that) I contemplated the creation and found it to be one of two types. Either enemies or beloved ones. As for enemies, I know they cannot prick me with a thorn if Allah does not so desire it. So I diverted my attention away from them. Then I contemplated the beloved ones and saw that they cannot benefit me in any way if Allah does not so desire it. So I lost any despair I might have had because of them. I attached myself only to Allah, Most High, and the thought came to me – You will not reach the reality of this matter until you remove your despair in Us over not receiving something We did not decree for you, like you have removed your despair in other than Us'."

The Shaykh said another time when he was asked about alchemy, "*Remove the greed from your heart and remove any despair over not receiving something that your Nurturing Lord has not decreed for you.*"

It is not a great number of deeds or continual performance of supplications (*wird*) that indicate that a slave deeply understands. Rather, what is indicative of his light is his sufficiency with his Nurturing Lord, his confining himself to Him in his heart, his protection from being enslaved to greed and his being adorned with the jewel of piety. With these are deeds made worthy and states purified. Allah, the Glorified states, "**Surely We made whatsoever is on the earth an adornment for it, that We may try them as to which of them is most virtuous in deed.**"[328]

Worthy deeds are only those undertaken while understanding Allah's purposes. Understanding is devotion to Allah ﷻ, sufficiency in Him, reliance upon Him, raising one's needs to Him and consistency in His service. All of this is a fruit of understanding Allah's purposes. Examine

---

328   Quran 18:7

yourself for piety more than you examine it for the presence of other things and purify yourself from yearning from the creation. If a greedy one, who seeks from creation, was washed with seven oceans it would not purify him, except by despairing in the creation and removing his aspirations from them.

Ali ibn Abi Talib, may Allah be pleased with him, came to Basra and entered its masjid. He found therein storytellers telling tales and expelled them until he came to Hassan Al-Basri ﷺ and said to him, *"Young man, I shall ask you about a matter. If you answer it correctly I will let you stay here, otherwise I will expel you like I expelled your companions."* Ali ﷺ saw in him dignity and serenity.

Hassan ﷺ replied, *"Ask whatever you wish."*

"What is the foundation of the religion?"

"Piety (wara')," he replied.

"What is the corrupter of the religion?"

"Greed."

Ali ﷺ said, *"Remain sitting, for the likes of you shall speak to men."*

I heard our Shaykh, may Allah be pleased with him, saying, *"In my early days I was in one of the coastal towns of Alexandria. I came across a man who knew me and I bought something I needed off him for half a dirham. I said to myself – Perhaps he will not take any money from me. Then a voice called out to me – Soundness in the religion is by abandoning greed for the creation."* I also heard our Shaykh ﷺ saying, *"The greedy one is never satisfied. Do you not see that all the letters that make up the word are hollow?*[329]*"*

So be vigilant, O seeker, to rid yourself of aspirations for the creation and do not disgrace yourself in the matter of provision. Allah's distribution precedes even your existence, it has been assured before you even appeared in this world. Listen to what one of the Shaykhs has said, *"Take heed! What has been decreed for the jaw to chew, it will certainly chew! So eat it honourably and not with disgrace!"*

Know that whoever knows Allah ﷻ, trusts in His assurance and care. The understanding of a slave is not perfected until he depends on what is in the hands of Allah ﷻ more than what is in his own hands. Until he relies on the guarantee of the Creator of creation more than that of the creation. It is enough ignorance not to be otherwise.

One of the intimate knowers of Allah (*arif*) would see a man sticking to the masjid, never leaving it. He was amazed by his persistence and wondered to himself, how does the man eat? One day this *arif* asked the man, *"From where do you eat?"*

He replied, *"I have a Jewish companion he promised to give me two loaves of bread every day and he brings them to me."*

The *arif* said to himself - Ah, now I see. He turned to the man saying, *"O poor one, you talk to me of your reliance on the promise of a Jew but you did not mention the promise of Al-Haqq who is the Faithful of Promise, who never breaks His promise! He has said,* **'There is no creature that crawls upon the**

---

[329] i.e. the Arabic letters that make up the word 'greed' (Arabic: ط م ع) all have hollow elements that are not filled – a metaphor for the letters themselves never being satisfied.

earth but that its provision lies with Allah'."³³⁰ The man became ashamed and left hurriedly.

Another righteous man prayed some days behind an *imam*.³³¹ One day the *imam* said to him, being amazed by the righteous man's adherence to the masjid and his turning away from worldly means, *"From where do you eat?"*

The righteous man replied, *"Wait a moment until I repeat my prayers (that I prayed behind you). For I do not pray behind someone who doubts in Allah!"*

There are many other such stories. It was once said to Ali ibn Abi Talib, may Allah be pleased with him, *"If a man was placed in a house and that house was covered in clay from where would his sustenance come?"*

He replied, *"His sustenance would come from the same place where his death comes."* Look at how brilliant this argument is and how clear of a proof it is!³³²

Returning to the words of the Shaykh ﷺ, the next obstacle he warned about was *"from overthinking and self-directing when attaining it."* As for overthinking, it is that you call to mind your need for sustenance to strengthen your body. While self-directing is that you say – *I shall attain my provision from such and such means, no by this and that means!* You increase and repeat those thoughts excessively upon your heart until you do not know what you have prayed if you are praying. Or what you have recited if you

---
330 Quran 11:6
331 A man who leads the daily prayers in congregation.
332 Death too is a creation of Allah just as life or sustenace is. **"Blessed is He...Who created death and life..."** [Quran 67:1-2]. Each have their worldly means that are created by Allah which ultimately reach the slave, no matter what obstacles are in their way.

are reciting. Your worship, from whatever you perform, becomes troubled and you are prohibited from its lights and forbidden from attaining its secrets.

If this happens to you, then cut down its foundations with the axe of trust in Allah ﷻ before devastating it completely with the power of certainty in Him. Remember that Allah ﷻ has taken upon Himself your affairs before you even existed. If you want good counsel, then do not take it upon yourself to be responsible for managing your own self. Your managing your affairs will only harm them as it will necessitate the responsibility falling back on to you. It will prevent the reach of His kindness reaching you.

Al-Haqq ﷻ does not let the believer have the traits of self-direction and opposition to His decrees. If such thoughts do occur to them, they are not firmly established. For the light of faith does not allow for that, "**and it is incumbent upon Us to help the believers.**"[333] "**Nay, but We cast truth against falsehood, and it crushes it, and, behold, falsehood vanishes.**"[334]

Then the Shaykh mentioned, "*and from miserliness and greed after gaining it.*" These are two obstacles that occur after gaining wealth and they derive themselves from weakness in certainty and lack of confidence (in Allah's promise) – in such circumstances miserliness and avarice exist. *Al-Haqq* ﷻ has condemned miserliness and avarice in His book where He states, "**And whosoever is shielded from the avarice of his soul, it is they who shall prosper.**"[335] It is understood from this verse that the bearer of miserliness and avarice does not prosper, that is, he has no success. For

---

333 Quran 30:47
334 Quran 21:18
335 Quran 59:9

to prosper is to have success.

The Most High also describes the hypocrites as **"greedy for good things. Such as these have not believed; so Allah made their deeds come to naught."**[336] He also states, **"And among them are those who make a pact with Allah (saying), 'If He gives us from His Bounty, we will surely spend in charity, and we will surely be among the righteous'. But when He gave them from His Bounty, they were miserly with it, turning away in rejection."**[337] He also states, **"And whosoever is miserly is only miserly toward himself."**[338] Miserliness can be of three types:

The first is that you be miserly with what you have and not spend on your obligations to Allah.

The second is that you be miserly over helping the slaves of Allah when it is not obligatory.

The third is that your miserliness is over yourself so that your self is spent for Allah.

The First Miserliness

It is to be miserly to the extent of not paying the *zakat* even though it has been made obligatory. Or not to pay for a responsibility binding on one, such as spending on poor parents, the poor, or young children, or on the expenditure of wives. In short, it is every responsibility that Allah has made binding on you and your deficiency in it makes you worthy of blame and punishment. In this regard are the words of the Glorified, **"(As for) those who hoard gold**

---

336 Quran 33:19
337 Quran 9:75-76
338 Quran 47:38

and silver and spend it not in the way of Allah, give them glad tidings of a painful punishment."[339] The scholars have mentioned that hoarding referred to in the verse is that on which the *zakat* has not been paid. If you have paid the *zakat* it would not be considered hoarding, the threat of the verse would not apply to you, nor would you be blamed.

The Second Miserliness

It is miserliness in spending over what is not obligatory. Like one who pays the *zakat* on his wealth but not a cent more. Even though one fulfils his obligations, he should not constrict himself to that. For limiting oneself to only the obligatory and leaving voluntary good deeds (*nawafil*) is only the condition of the weak (in religion). So the believer who is concerned with amending his standing with Allah cannot abandon having good dealings with Him when he gets the chance. Otherwise, his state is not different from one who prays the obligatory prayers and abandons the supererogatory ones.

But what suffices for you, O slave, are the words of the Glorified as relayed by His Messenger, *"The near ones do not come close by anything like they do by performing what I have obligated upon them. My slave continues to grow closer to Me with voluntary deeds until I love him. When I love Him, I am for him hearing, seeing, speaking, heart and mind, hand and support."*

The Glorified makes it clear that it is the repetition and establishing of voluntary, good deeds that bring about love from Allah. None of the voluntary deeds are made obligatory on you whether they be from prayer, charity, *hajj*

---

339   Quran 9:34

or other than that.

The example of one who only limits himself to the compulsory prayers and the one who also performs the voluntary prayers in addition to them and the example of one who constricts himself to *zakat* and the one who adds voluntary charity to it, is like the example of two slaves upon whom their master has imposed a tax of two dirhams each.

One of the slaves comes to his master every day with just two dirhams, nothing more. He brings no gift that might gain his master's favour. The other slave also brings two dirhams to his master every day but adds to it some exquisite gift or exotic fruit. No doubt, this second slave is more valued in the eyes of the master, has a greater portion of the master's love, and is closer to him in position.

The slave limiting himself to two dirhams did not strive for the master's love. He only gave to avoid the master's punishment. While the other slave walked the path of love for his master and made himself susceptible to it. He is worthy of winning proximity to his master.

Al-Haqq has obligated responsibilities on His slaves because He knows of their weaknesses and the lazy nature of the animal-self. So He obligated what He obligated because if He had left the choice to them they would not perform those good deeds, except for a few. "**Yet how few are they!**"[340] So He obligated certain deeds on them and if they perform what He obligated, they enter His Paradise. He drove them into Paradise with the chains of obligation, "*Your Nurturing Lord marvels at a people driven into Paradise by*

---

340   Quran 38:24

chains."[341]

A Notice

Know – may Allah have mercy on you – that we considered all the obligatory actions and saw that *Al-Haqq* ﷻ made voluntary actions in the same form as obligatory actions. This is so that voluntary actions can rectify any obligatory ones if some defect were to occur in what was obligated. This has been mentioned in a *hadith*, that He looks at the obligatory prayers of His slave and if there is something left wanting in them, they are perfected by the slave's voluntary prayers.

Understand this – may Allah have mercy upon you – and do not limit yourself to what Allah ﷻ has obligated upon you. Let there arise in you a compelling love that makes you devoted to voluntary dealings with Allah ﷻ. If the slaves were not to find in their balance of good deeds anything other than the reward for their obligatory actions and avoidance of the forbidden, then such goodness and bounties would have passed them that cannot be enumerated nor won again. Glorified be He who opened the door of extra deeds for His slaves and prepared for them the means of closeness to Him.

Know that *Al-Haqq* ﷻ knows that among His slaves there are the weak and the strong. So He imposed the obligations and clarified the forbidden. The weak confined themselves to the obligations and just avoided what was made forbidden. They had no power of love or presence of passion that might carry them to extra, good dealings with Him. His example is of the slave who, if the master had

---

341   Sahih Bukhari 3010

not imposed a tax on him, would not offer anything to the master.

Hence, the Glorified appointed times for worship and assigned duties of servitude. He made the times of worship known whether by the rising (of the sun), its setting, its reaching its zenith or by the shadows of objects becoming twice their length[342] in the matter of prayer. He made the passing of a year as a measure to pay *zakat* over produce, resources and livestock. He stipulated the time of harvest also concerning farming "**and pay the due thereof on the day of its harvest.**"[343] He appointed the ten days of (the month of) *Dhul-Hijjah* for *Hajj* and the month of Ramadan for fasting. He assigned duties and specified their times and still allowed souls the opportunity to seek their worldly fortunes and strive amongst worldly means.

However, it is the people of Allah ﷻ that understand His purposes. They are the ones who did not partition time. They made their entire lives a road that leads to Allah ﷻ. They realised that the entirety of time belongs to Him, so they do not spend anything of it for other than Him. Hence Shaykh Abu'l Hassan ﷺ said, "*Take only one litany (wird)! It is the abandoning of desires and diving into love for Allah.*" Love only employs the lover in what is agreeable to the beloved. The people of Allah ﷻ know that each breath is entrusted to them from *Al-Haqq* ﷻ. They recognise that they have been requested to safeguard each breath and so direct their concern to that end.

Just as Allah's Lordship is eternal, likewise the rights of His Lordship are always binding upon you. His Lordship

---

342 This heralds the beginning of the *Asr* prayer in the *Hanafi madhab*.
343 Quran 6:141

is not for specified times so the rights of His Lordship should also not be limited to specified times. Shaykh Abu'l Hassan ﷺ says, *"There is upon you, at every moment, something of slave-hood due to Al-Haqq as required by His Lordship."* We draw back the reins of these words here so as not to trespass beyond the purpose of this book.

The Third Miserliness

(The third is that your miserliness is over yourself so that your self can be spent for your Lord). It is preferring others over yourself and is most excellent of the three. One is commanded to do other deeds for the sake of attaining this.

One may prefer Allah ﷻ in those things He has made obligatory but not prefer Him over the voluntary. In such a case, he has not preferred Allah ﷻ over himself and has been selfish in spending from his 'self'.

Unselfishness and sacrificing from one's self are from the etiquettes of the truthful and from the affairs of those of certainty who recognise Allah ﷻ and spend their own selves for His sake. They know that the slave owns nothing next to his Master.

If being selfless over one's life is the most perfect of these states, then greed for it is the most repugnant of them. From this is understood the words of our Shaykh, *"and from miserliness and greed after gaining it."* We take only a cursory glance at this point for it is not the purpose of this book.

The Third Type of Obstacle in the Matter of Provision

We had earlier mentioned that there are three types

of obstacles that one faces in the matter of provision. It includes those that occur before attaining it and those that occur during attaining it. We have already mentioned the words of our Shaykh regarding that and expounded on it.

There are also other obstacles that occur after attaining and consuming provision. These include remorse and regret (over spending or losing wealth) and continual desire for it. You must purify yourself from such sentiments also. Hear the words of the Glorified, **"That you not despair over what has passed you by, nor exult in that which He has given you."**[344] The Prophet ﷺ also said when the child of one of his daughters passed away, *"Inform her that for Allah is what He takes and for Allah is what He gives."*

One should save themselves from remorse when losing anything, losing anything other than Allah ﷻ that is, for he would otherwise only be announcing his own ignorance and aloofness from Allah ﷻ. For if he found Allah ﷻ, he would not lose anything else. For whoever finds Allah ﷻ does not find anything besides Him that he may lose it.

Let the slave know that what has passed him by was not meant for him in the first place. Nor has he lost part of his sustenance. If it was his sustenance, it would not have left him for someone else. Rather, it was only loaned to him for a time. The Creditor took back what He loaned. He repossessed what He entrusted.

One of the righteous had a cousin who was betrothed to him from a young age. When they became older, it became apparent he could not marry her (because they had both

---

344   Quran 57:23

been breastfed by the same woman). The girl then married somebody else. Some men of deep knowledge came to him and said, *"It would be appropriate for you to go and apologize to her new husband if you were aspiring to marry her when she was to be his wife since pre-eternity."*

These words of Allah are enough a warning for the believer to not have remorse over what is lost, **"And among mankind some worship Allah upon a brink: if good befalls him, he is content thereby, but if a trial befalls him, he is turned over upon his face, losing this world and the Hereafter."**[345] Allah, the Glorified, rebukes those who are contented when things fall in their hands. See how He says **"if good befalls him, he is content thereby."** That is, they find reassurance in material goodness. Only if he realised, when he was busy being reassured with something other than Allah, most High, that his reassurance is only through Allah, alone.

In a similar state is the one who grieves over some material loss, **"but if a trial befalls him, he is turned over upon his face."** That is, his mind is baffled, his animal-self is dazed and his heart is sunk in heedlessness. This is due to his having no knowledge of Allah, Most High.

If he had knowledge of Allah, he would have sufficed with Allah's existence over all other existences. He would be rich with Him, despite any loss. Whoever loses Allah does not find anything. How can one lose anything when he finds the One in whose hand is the kingdoms of all things? How can one lose anything, who finds the Originator of everything? How can one lose anything, who finds the One, whose shadows of His Names and Attributes

---

345   Quran 22:11

are manifest in all things?

For the people of intimate knowledge of Allah ﷻ, things other than Him do not fit the mould of being found or lost. His oneness is so instilled in them that they do not consider anything else besides Him. They consider no loss other than if they were to lose Him since only one who gains something can lose it (and they see themselves as owning nothing). If the veil of self-delusion was wrenched away, one would witness the passing away of all observable things. The light of certainty would radiate over all existence.

If you have understood this, O slave, then you must not grieve over the loss of anything. Nor should you rely on the possession of anything. If something is gained and relied upon or lost and grieved over, then it is obvious that one's slave-hood is for that very thing, what delighted with its being possessed and pained with its loss. Understand at this juncture the words of the Prophet ﷺ, *"May he be miserable, that slave of the world. May he be miserable, that slave of the dirham. May he be miserable, that slave of extravagant garments. May he be made miserable further. If he is pricked by a thorn, let him not find the means to remove it."*

O believer, do not give anything authority over your heart except love and devotion for Allah ﷻ. You are too noble to enslave yourself to anything other than Him. The Master has created you honourable, be not a contemptible slave. Those that have intimate knowledge of Allah ﷻ refuse to rely on what they possess or have aspirations over what they have lost, in order to preserve their state of slave-hood with Allah ﷻ and to attest to their freedom from all else other than Him.

I heard our Shaykh, Abu'l Abbas ﷺ saying, *"One who is in a spiritual state is of two possible types. Either he is in the spiritual state for the sake of the spiritual state or he is in the spiritual state for the sake of the One who changes states."*

The one who is in a spiritual state for the sake of the spiritual state becomes the slave of that state. He is delighted when he gains that spiritual pleasure and grieved when he loses it. As for the slave who is in a spiritual state for the sake of the One who changes states, then he is the slave of Allah, not the slave of spiritual states. He does not despair when spiritual states leave him or rejoice when he attains them.

As for Allah's words, **"And among mankind some worship Allah upon a brink,"** it refers to worshipping Allah ﷻ in one circumstance only. If that circumstance was to pass, so would his obedience and his concordance with Allah ﷻ be severed. The verse holds the meaning of – *If they understood Me, they would have worshipped Me in each and every state and circumstance.* Just as He is your Nurturing Lord in all conditions, be His slave in all conditions.

As for His words **"if good befalls him, he is content thereby,"** they allude to one attaining goodness that suits his animal-self, but it is good only in his opinion. It may be evil for him in reality.

As for **"but if a trial befalls him,"** it alludes to the loss of that goodness in which he found contentment and reassurance. Allah ﷻ labelled it a trial, for in loss the faith of the believers is examined and the reality of the inner states of men comes to the fore.

How many men have supposed they were enriched

by Allah ﷻ, but in reality their faith was in worldly means and in the diversity of their acquisitions? How many a man supposes his intimacy is with Allah, but in fact it is with his spiritual state? Evidence of that is he loses his closeness with Allah the moment he loses his spiritual state. If his intimacy was truly for his Nurturing Lord, his intimacy would have remained as long as his Lord remains and persisted as long as his Lord persists.

Finally, He states "**(he is) losing this world and the Hereafter**." Such a one loses this world since he loses what he hoped to gain from it. He loses the Hereafter since he did not work for it. That is – *he lost what it was that he desired and did not seek Us so that We could be for him*. So understand!

18. Promenade

We now mention some parables of managing alongside Allah, Most High and of those that fall into it. As well as parables related to provision and *Al-Haqq's* guarantee of it. Indeed, reality is clarified by parables.

A Parable

The parable of one who plans alongside Allah ﷻ is like a man who builds a house on the coast of a furious ocean. Every time he struggles with its construction, powerful waves bear down upon it and the building falls on all sides. Likewise, he who manages affairs alongside Allah ﷻ constructs buildings out of his plans and hopes while the decrees of Allah ﷻ leave them decimated in wreckage. Hence it is said – *one plans and manages and all the while fate laughs*. While the poet said:

> *On what day will the building be completed*
> *If you build it up and someone else pulls it down?*

A Parable

The parable of one who manages with Allah ﷻ is like a man who comes to a pile of heaped up sand and proceeds to build upon it. A violent wind comes and scatters the sand so his house is destroyed. As the poet said:

> *Their contracts were by sand eventually effaced*
> *And likewise buildings are not founded on sand*

A Parable

The parable of one who manages alongside Allah ﷻ is like a child travelling with his father. They set out at night and the father, out of concern for the child, keeps an eye on the child without the child noticing. The child does not see the father because of the darkness between them. The child becomes troubled and begins to worry about who will take care of him. But when the moon appeared and he saw how close his father was, his heart was soothed and his fear abated. By witnessing the closeness of his father he sufficed with his father's managing for him over his own managing for himself.

Such is the one who manages over himself, alongside Allah ﷻ. Such a person is only in the darkness of estrangement from Allah ﷻ so sees not His nearness. If the moon of Allah's ultimate Oneness (*tawheed*) was to ascend, or the sun of intimate knowledge of Him (*ma'rifah*), he would have witnessed the proximity of *Al-Haqq* ﷻ and been ashamed to manage affairs alongside Him. He would have sufficed with the managing of Allah ﷻ for himself over his managing for himself.

A Parable

Self-direction is a tree, watered by a river of negative thoughts about Allah ﷻ. Its fruit is estrangement and being cut off from Allah ﷻ. If the slave made good his thoughts about his Nurturing Lord, that tree of self-direction would have withered away. It would live no longer in his heart once its nutrients have dried up. But the fruit of self-direction is only estrangement from Allah ﷻ since whoever manages over himself relies solely on his own intelligence and marvels at his own planning and schemes. His punishment is that he becomes the target of a grander plan and Allah's favours and bounties are prevented from reaching him.

A Parable

The parable of he who manages alongside Allah ﷻ is like that of a slave sent by his master to a distant locality to fabricate a garment. The slave enters the town and asks – *Where shall I live? Who shall I marry?* He busies himself with that and diverts his concern so he can managing those affairs. He neglects what the master commanded him to do until the master calls him back. The master punishes him by distancing him and revoking his elevated standing because he preferred his own fortune over the rights of his master.

You are the same, O believer. *Al-Haqq* dispatched you to this land and commanded you to His service. He undertook your care through management from Himself. If you are to then busy yourself with self-direction instead of observing the rights of your Master, you have strayed from the guided path and follow the road to destruction.

A Parable

The parable of one who manages alongside Allah ﷻ and the one who does not is like the parable of two slaves to a king. One of them is absorbed in fulfilling the commands of his master and does not concern himself with his clothing or food. His endeavour is only the service of his master. It has preoccupied him from attending to his personal needs. The other slave is always found to be washing his clothes, organising his mount or embellishing his appearance, no matter how the master asks him to do otherwise. No doubt, the first slave is more beloved to the master than the second, who is more concerned with his desires and needs than the rights of his master.

A slave is bought only for his master, he is not bought to serve himself. Likewise, you will not see the insightful slave except that he is occupied with the rights of Allah and the observance of His commands, so much so that he does not worry about his personal needs and desires. When the slave becomes like this, *Al-Haqq* ensures all his affairs for him and dispatches to him abundant gifts because of the slave's sincerity and trust. **"And whosoever trusts in Allah, He suffices him."**[346]

As for the ignorant one, you will not find him except reaching out towards worldly means. You will see him seeking out things that ingratiate his desires and lust. He relies on his self-direction and is so left to his own devices. He is banished from the serenity of true confidence and trust in Allah.

A Parable

The parable of managing alongside Allah is like a shadow stretching out as long as the sun does not reach its zenith. Once the sun reaches its peak, that shadow disappears and nothing remains except the little outline of shadow that remains when objects are directly facing (beneath) the sun. Such too is the sun of intimate knowledge of Allah (*ma'rifah*). If hearts turn their attention directly (to Allah), self-direction is completely effaced except for a little of the form of self-direction of the slave so that he can use it to fulfil his obligations to Allah.

---

346 Quran 65:3

A Parable

The parable of one who self-directs his affairs alongside Allah ﷻ is like a man who sells a house and a slave. After the transaction has been completed and signed, the seller comes to the buyer and says – *Do not build anything upon the house nor destroy such and such part of it or do such and such with it.* Or the buyer comes to the house himself to do from that what he wills. It would be said to him – *You have sold the house you can not do whatever you like freely over what you have sold! There is no right for you to dispute the managing of something after you have sold it!*

The Glorified states, **"Truly Allah has purchased from the believers their souls and their wealth."**[347] Therefore, it is binding upon the believer to deliver his soul to Allah ﷻ and not attribute his soul to himself. Indeed, Allah ﷻ created it and indeed, He bought it. From the requirements of surrendering your soul is to abandon the managing of what you have handed over, as we have discussed.

A Parable

The parable of the matter of provision of the slave in this world is like a master who says to his slave – *Stay in this house to perform such and such service of mine.* No doubt, the master would not command that from the slave without feeding him, clothing him and undertaking the responsibility for the slave's needs. The master would not abandon and neglect the slave of his care.

Likewise, Allah ﷻ has ordered the slave to act obediently in this world and in harmony with Him. He has

---

347 Quran 9:111

guaranteed the apportioning of His provisions. So, let the slave undertake His service, for the Master has undertaken upon Himself to deliver His grace. He states, be He glorified, **"And bid your family to prayer and be steadfast therein. We ask no provision of you; We provide for you. And the end belongs to (the people of) righteousness."**[348] Its discussion has already preceded.

A Parable

The parable of the slave and Allah ﷻ in this world is like a child with its mother. The mother would not leave the child out of her care and guardianship. Likewise, is the believer with Allah ﷻ. *Al-Haqq* watches over him with His excellent guardianship, drives blessings towards him and repels away distress. The Messenger ﷺ once saw a woman with her child and said, *"Would you think that she would throw her child into fire?"*

They replied, *"No, O Messenger of Allah."*

He said, *"Allah is more compassionate to His believing slave than she is to her child."*

A Parable

The parable of the condition of the slave in this world is like that of a slave to whom his master says, *"Go to such and such land but be careful because you will need to cross a desolate wasteland to reach it. And make your preparations and take equipment with you on your way."* When the master has allowed this, the slave knows that it is permissible for him to eat what will give him strength so that he can strive to attain those preparations and the necessary equipment.

---

348   Quran 20:132

Such is the slave. *Al-Haqq* ﷻ created him in this land and commanded him to take provisions from it for his final destination. He states, "**And make provision, for indeed the best provision is reverence (*taqwa*)."**[349] It is hence understood that since He commanded his slaves to take provisions for the Hereafter, He has allowed them to take from this world that which will help them take their provisions, prepare themselves, and equip themselves for their final destination.

A Parable

The parable of the slave and Allah ﷻ is like a master who has a garden. He commands his slave to cultivate and care for it. If that slave was to do all that his master asked him, then it is not for the master to blame the slave or prevent him from eating something from that garden. If the slave ate from the garden, then he also worked in it. However, the slave must only eat what will help him in his service, he should not eat out of enjoyment and greed.

A Parable

The parable of the slave and Allah ﷻ is of a man who plants many crops and builds a great house. It is said to him – *For whom have you done all this?* He replies – *For a child I hope will be mine in the future.* He made preparations for everything the child would need before the child existed out of his love for him. Do you think that, after the father has made such preparations for the child before the child's existence, he would prevent the child from it after the child came into existence?

Similarly, *Al-Haqq* has prepared kindnesses for

---
349   Quran 2:197

the slave before He established him in this world for His kindness necessarily precedes your existence, if you have so far understood. Do you not see that His gifts to you have preceded your existence and His favours appeared before your appearance in this world? He bestows in pre-eternity before the slave existed and before the slave had any work or occupation. What He set aside for you in pre-eternity and stored for you, He did not do so to prevent you from it here. Would He make preparations for you before your existence and prevent you from it after your existence?

A Parable

The parable of the slave and Allah ﷻ is that of a labourer that a king brings to his home and commands him with some task. The king would not bring that labourer and employ him in his home and leave him without provision, for the king is too noble to do otherwise.

Likewise is the slave with Allah ﷻ. This world is the house of Allah ﷻ and the labourer is you. Your work is obedience and payment is Paradise. He would not order you to His work without driving to you what will sustain you in it.

A Parable

The parable of the slave and Allah ﷻ is like a guest who lodges with a noble king in his home. That guest would not worry about his food or drink for if he did it would be an accusation against the king and thinking badly of him.

The words of Shaykh Abu Madyan, may Allah be pleased with him, have already been mentioned, *"The world belongs to Allah. We tarry here only as His guests."* Further, the

Glorified would not command us to honour the guest, on the tongue of His Prophet ﷺ, and then abandon it Himself.

The one who throws accusations at the king over receiving food and drink is contemptible in the eyes of the king. If he had no doubts about Allah ﷻ, he would not accuse Allah of not taking care of his affairs.

A Parable

The parable of the slave and Allah ﷻ is like a king who commands a slave to base himself in such and such land to fight the king's enemies. He commands him to expend his courage and be relentless in fighting. Thus it is understood that since the king has commanded this, he has allowed the slave to eat from that land and its treasuries to maintain his war against the enemy.

Likewise, *Al-Haqq* ﷻ has commanded His slaves to fight Satan when He states, "**And strive for Allah as He should be striven for.**"[350] Also, "**Truly Satan is an enemy unto you; so take him as an enemy.**"[351]

When Allah ﷻ has commanded them with fighting against Satan, it is permissible for them to eat from His favours to strengthen themselves for it. If you abandoned food and drink, you could not fulfil His obedience nor move in His service. So the command of the king to fight includes eating from the king's riches, that is those things that have been predetermined for you as a trust and ensure your well-being.

---

350   Quran 22:78
351   Quran 35:6

A Parable

The parable of the slave and Allah ﷻ is like a tree that was planted to seek its growth and fruit. Would the tree think, if we suppose it can think, that its sower would plant it and then not water it? How could it be, when the sower desires its fruit and its growth?

You are like that O slave, a tree of Allah ﷻ that He planted. He is the One who waters you at every moment and is responsible for your sustenance. Do not throw accusations at Him of planting the tree of your existence and then prohibiting its water. For He would never do so.

A Parable

The parable of the slave with Allah ﷻ is like a king who builds a house, beautifies it, embellishes it, undertakes growing its foliage and finishes it with all sorts of desirable goods. The king wishes to move his slave into this home. Do you think that if this is the king's concern, he would not store provisions for them and facilitate their journey? Would he prevent them to eat from his favours and bounties here when he has prepared a much grander and more excellent lodging for them there?

Likewise, Allah ﷻ has established His slaves in this world but prepared Paradise for them. He has not prepared for them the Hereafter and then prevented them from what would sustain them in this world. Hence, He states, "**Eat of the provision of your Lord and give thanks to Him.**"[352] And He states, "**O messengers! Eat of the good things and work righteousness.**"[353] And He states, "**O you who believe! Eat**

---

352   Quran 34:15
353   Quran 23:51

of the good things We have provided you."[354]

If He has postponed the eternal paradise for you and gifted it to you, He would not prevent you from this perishing world. If He prevents you from it, then it is only what He has not apportioned to you. What has not been assigned to you is not yours to claim. Perhaps that prohibition is due to wisdom He grasps, there being in its prohibition a benefit for you and the excellent administering of your affairs. Much like water is diverted from a tree so that it is not ruined by continual watering.

A Parable

The parable of one concerned with his worldly life, heedless of taking provisions for his Hereafter, is like a person attacked by a lion. The lion is about to devour him when suddenly the man preoccupies himself with repelling a fly that lands on him, instead of worrying about the lion. This slave would certainly be considered a fool, deprived of intelligence. If he was characterised by intelligence he would have occupied himself with preventing the lion from attacking him instead of swatting the fly.

Such is the one who concerns himself with his worldly life and is ignorant of his preparations for the hereafter. This is evidence enough of his stupidity. If he was intelligent and astute he would prepare for himself the home of the Hereafter which he is responsible for and what was assigned to him to strive for. He would not busy himself with worrying about his provision. His concern for it in comparison to the Hereafter is like the fly compared to a sudden ambush by a ferocious lion.

---

[354] Quran 2:172

A Parable

The parable of the slave and Allah ﷻ is like a young child with his father. The child bears no worry and fears no loss because he knows that his father is taking care of him. The child has great confidence in his provision and his reliance on his father removes any anxiety.

This is how the believing slave is with Allah ﷻ. He does not bear worries nor do anxieties return to his heart over the affair of provision because he realises that *Al-Haqq* ﷻ would not abandon him. He knows that Allah ﷻ would not prevent him from His bounties or cut him off from His kindness and generosity.

A Parable

The parable of the slave with Allah ﷻ is like a slave who has a rich master, known for his great fortune and kindness to his slaves. The master is known never to withhold, always bestowing gifts freely. Hence, the slave has confidence in His bounty and always expects his kindness. He recognises his master's great wealth and that saves him from fatigue and worry.

This is exactly what caused the repentance of Shaqeeq Al-Bakhli ﷺ. He narrates, *"At a time of famine, I came across a young slave who was happy and cheerful, he seemed to have no knowledge of the difficulties people were going through. I said to him, 'O young one, do you not know that the people are suffering?'*

He replied, 'And what does that matter to me when my master has a farm reserved for us. Every day he sends us from it what we need.'

I said to myself – If this master has a farm reserved for them, then my Master has the treasuries of the heavens and earth. It is more worthy I have confidence in Him than this slave has with his master." This was the cause for his turning to Allah ﷻ.

A Parable

The parable of a slave who utilises worldly means is like a slave to whom his master says – *Stick to my service and I will send you my gifts.*

The slave who takes worldly means and his reliance is on Allah ﷻ is like a man who sits underneath a waterspout when it rains. He thanks Allah ﷻ, alone, and does not attribute the bestowal of water to the waterspout. He just knows that if he did not sit there, he would not find any water.

Likewise, worldly means are the waterspouts of Allah's favours. Whoever takes worldly means and his aspiration is only towards Allah ﷻ, not with the worldly means he interacts with, will not be harmed by that and being distanced from Allah ﷻ would not be feared for him.

As for those whose reliance stops with the worldly means, who are heedless of their Master, then they are like a herd of cattle. Their owner passes in front of them but they pay no attention to him, even though he pays for their upkeep and employs the farmhand that cares for them. But when the farmhand passes by they give him much attention and move close to him because of their being accustomed to their food coming from him. The heedless person is like this. When he receives kindnesses from people he attributes it to them when in reality it does not originate from them. He is akin to cattle and in fact, cattle are in a better state them him.

"Such as these are like cattle. Nay, they are even further astray. It is they who are heedless."[355]

A Parable

The parable of one who relies on worldly means compared to the one who transcends them is like that of two men that enter a public bath. One is intelligent, the other is dull and foolish. When the water stops flowing, the intelligent one knows there is a canal and waterway that directs and pushes the water out. He inspects them to remove what has blocked the water or see to whatever else needs to be done.

As for the other man, he comes up to the water pipe saying – *O water pipe! Pour forth for us some water! What is wrong that you have stopped your water?* It would be said about him – *He is indeed crazy! Does a water pipe hear or do anything!? It is only the spot where the water appears not the cause of the water to flow!*

A Parable

The parable of a slave who hoards wealth is like the slave of a king. The king places him in his garden so the slave can look after it. It is acceptable that the slave eats from it to strengthen himself so he can sow and farm. But it is not acceptable that he gathers and stores away food from the garden because there will always be fruits in the garden and his master is rich. If he hoards without permission from his master, out of greed and throwing accusations at his master (that his master will neglect him), then he has acted treacherously.

---

355   Quran 7:179

Such is the slave who does not hoard. He is like a slave in the garden of a master or in his house, knowing full well that his master will not forget or neglect him. Rather, he knows his master will grant him goodness and reward in return. He suffices in his master from having to hoard and in his master's richness from needing anything else. Such a slave is worthy of the master's friendliness and in being supported by the master's gifts.

A Parable

The parable of the one who gathers wealth in good faith, as a trust, is like the slave of a king. The slave does not consider himself as owning anything alongside the king. He does not rely on what he has stored in his possession nor does he spend it, he has no choice in the matter except for what his master chooses for him to do. When the slave understands that his master intends for him to hold on to wealth, he holds on to it. He holds on to it for the sake of his master, not for his own sake. When the right time to spend it arrives, he spends it recognising that is what the master desires. He is not to be blamed for not spending because he held on to the wealth for his master, not for himself.

Likewise are the people of intimate knowledge of Allah ﷻ. If they spend, it is for Allah ﷻ and if they keep, it too is for Allah ﷻ. They desire thereby to seek His good pleasure, they seek nothing else but Him alone by their spending and keeping. They are trustworthy treasurers, distinguished slaves and generous, liberated people. For *Al-Haqq* ﷻ has freed them from bondage to worldly means. They do not incline to worldly means with love nor do they devote themselves to worldly means with ardour. The love for Allah ﷻ and yearning for Him that has settled in their hearts, as well as His greatness and majesty that has filled their chests, prevents them from regarding worldly means.

Nor is the one who holds onto wealth for the sake of Allah ﷻ any less than the one who spends it for His sake. For when things are in their hands it is like they are still in the treasuries of Allah ﷻ. They realise that Allah ﷻ owns them together with what they own. Whoever does not master their keeping wealth for the sake of Allah ﷻ does not master spending it for His sake. So understand!

19. Intimate Conversation

We mention here an intimate conversation between *Al-Haqq* and his slave on the tongue of observed reality in the matter of provision and self-direction.

O slave. Listen well while you witness. More blessings will arrive to you. Listen with the hearing of your heart for I am not far from you.

O slave. I was managing your affairs before you were doing so for yourself. So be for yourself by not being for it. I took charge of you before you appeared into existence and still my care for you has not changed.

O slave. I am Alone in creating and fashioning and I am Alone in commanding and managing. You did not participate in My creating and fashioning so likewise, do not participate in My command and My managing. I direct the affairs of My kingdom and I need no supporter in doing so. I am Alone in commanding and I have no need of intermediaries.

O slave. Do not dispute about what you hope for with the One who was administering your affairs before your creation. Do not repay with obstinacy the One who accustomed you to His excellent care for you.

O slave. I accustomed you to my excellent care for you so accustom me to seeing the abandoning of self-direction from you.

O slave. Is there doubt after experiencing? Is there

confusion after demonstration? Is there misguidance after guidance has been manifested? Will not your knowledge that there is no director of affairs other than Me gather you to My side? Will not all the previous goodness that has been bestowed on you prevent you from opposing Me?

O slave. Look to your existence compared to the rest of My creation. You will see that you disappear into nothing in comparison to it. Will you not consider the administering of the prominent and vast of My creations? You have surrendered to Me the managing and direction of their affairs. You are also of My kingdom so do not oppose My Nurturing Lordship nor defy My Divinity with your own managing.

O slave. Is it not enough for you that I be enough for you? Does not My previous kindnesses on you demand your serenity and peace of mind with Me?

O slave. When have I made you needy of yourself so that you plan and depend on yourself? When have I entrusted anything in My kingdom to other than Me that I entrust it now upon you?

O slave. I have made preparations for you out of My generosity before I even manifested My existence to you. I made My power apparent in everything so how do you reject Me?

O slave. How often did you fail someone you managed and planned for? How often was the one you supported, disappointed?

O slave. Do not let your seeking of what I have already reserved for you distract you from My service. Let your good opinion of Me prevent you from casting accusations at My Nurturing Lordship.

O slave. It is not fitting to accuse a charitable One. Nor to dispute with a powerful One. Nor to oppose a conquering One. Nor to object to a wise One. Nor to carry worry with a kind One.

O slave. The one who disregards his will for My Will obtains success. The one who trusts in Me has been guided to ease in his affair. The one who keeps true to his poverty to Me wins the treasure of sufficiency. The slave who relies on Me, whenever he moves, necessitates My giving him victory. Whoever holds onto Me as a means has clung to the most powerful of means. I have taken it upon Myself to repay the people of self-direction with inner disquiet and confusion. I destroy what they build and unfasten what they tie together. I leave them to their own devices. I prohibit them from the refreshment of contentment and the bliss of trusting in Me. If they had understood My ways they would certainly be contented with My managing instead of their managing for themselves. They would suffice with My care for them instead of their care for themselves. In which case I would travel with them on the road of contentment, proceed with them on the path of guidance and strive with them on the way filled with light. My care for them would protect them from everything they might fear and would bring to them everything they hope for – and that is easy for Me.

O slave. We desire from you that you desire Us and not desire anything with Us. We chose for you that you choose Us and that you do not choose anything alongside Us. It pleases Us if you work to please Us and it does not please Us if you work to please anyone besides Us.

O slave. If I have decreed for you, then it is because I desire to show My benevolence upon you. If I have decreed against you, I have placed hidden kindnesses within it for you.

O slave. Do not repay My blessings upon you by disputing with Me. Do not exchange My kindness upon you by gifting you with intelligence, through which you have been distinguished, by opposing Me.

O slave. Just as you have surrendered the management of My earth and My heavens to Me and My exclusivity of command and decree in them, surrender to Me your existence for you belong to Me. Do not manage alongside Me for you are under My care. Take Me as a trustee and have confidence in Me as a guarantor and I shall bestow on you endless gifts and grant you sublime glory.

O slave. Indeed, I decreed in pre-eternity that the light of submission to me and the darkness of opposition to Me are not to be combined in the heart of My slave. When one of them exists, it removes the other. So choose one of them for yourself. Take heed! We have honoured you above your having to occupy yourself with yourself. Do not belittle yourself, O one We have elevated. Certainly, do not humiliate yourself by turning to other creations, O one We have honoured. Woe to you, you are more honoured to Us than preoccupying yourself to other than Us. For My presence did I create you, to that did I invite you and by the enticement of My care for you did I attract you. If you then become preoccupied with your animal-self, I veil you. If you follow its desires, I exile you. If you abandon it, I bring you near. If you love Me by turning away from all else, then I love you.

O slave. Does it not suffice you – if you would suffice yourself – and would it not guide you – if you would be guided – that it is I who create, who fashions, who bestows and who gifts? Will that not stop you from opposing what I have decreed and from dissenting over what I apportion?

O slave. He has not believed in Me, who disputes with Me. He has not declared My Oneness who manages My affairs alongside Me. He is not happy with me who complains about what I have sent down to My creation. He has not preferred Me who chooses other than Me. He has not obeyed My command who does not surrender to My dominating power. He does not know Me who does not commit his affairs to Me. And indeed, he is ignorant of Me who does not trust upon Me.

O slave. It is enough folly for you to be reassured by what is in your hands and not find peace over what is in My hand. It is enough ignorance that when I chose you for Me that you prefer other than Me. Woe to you, do not combine slave-hood with your own preferences. Do not combine darkness with light. Do not combine your inclination to Me with your inclination to worldly means. Either I am for you or you are for yourself. So choose one of the two with consideration. Make sure to not exchange guidance for loss!

O slave. If you explicitly asked me to manage your affairs you would be ignorant and ill-mannered. So what is the case when you manage for yourself? If you chose alongside Me, you would have acted unjustly, so what is the case when you choose for Me?

O slave. If I had permitted you to direct your affairs, it would be necessary for you to be too ashamed to even attempt to do so. Then how is the case when I have commanded you to not direct your affairs, O one consumed with worry over himself? If you burdened Us with your affairs, you would find relief. Woe to you, the burden of managing affairs cannot be carried except by My Nurturing Lordship. The weakness of humanity cannot bear it. Woe to you, you are carried, so do not carry! We desire your relief so do not weary yourself. It is not befitting that you oppose the will of the One who directed your affairs when you were in the innards of your mothers and who gave you what you willed after you came into existence.

O slave. I commanded you to My service and guaranteed you My apportioning of provision. But you ignored what I commanded and doubted what I guaranteed. I did not suffice with guaranteeing you your provision but I also decreed it and set it aside for you. And I did not suffice with decreeing your provision but I addressed and illustrated the matter for slaves who understand, "**And in heaven is your provision and that which you were promised. So by the Nurturing Lord of heaven and earth, it is indeed true—as sure as the fact that you speak**."[356] *Truly, those with intimate knowledge of Me have sufficed with just My qualities. Those with certain knowledge trust in just My generosity. For if I had not promised their provision, they would not lose their certainty of My aid and support. If I had not guaranteed their provision, they would still have confidence in My kindness. If I provide for the one who is heedless of Me and rebels against Me, how could I not provide for the one who obeys Me and devotes himself to Me? Woe to you, the sower of a tree waters it and he who makes something sustains it. The creator of a thing is sufficient as its gurantor and benefactor. And yet, from Me did all things appear and so upon Me is its continuance of provision. From Me did all creation come about and upon Me is its continuation of sustenance. Woe to you, do you invite someone to your house except the one you wish to feed? Do you attribute one to your name except for the one you wish to honour?*

O slave. Make your concern for Me instead of your concern over My provisions. Do not burden yourself over what I have carried off your shoulders! Concern yourself with the responsibility I have not removed from you. Have I entered you into My house to prevent you My generosity? Have I created you for Myself just to prohibit you from My bestowals? When I have requested you to fulfil My rights, would I stop the flow of My provisions to you? Would I require you to work in My service but not decree for you a portion of sustenance? I have apportioned provisions for you, none of which will remain behind with Me. I have prepared My favours for you and have manifested My mercy in you. I was not content for you to enter this world until I stored away Paradise for you. And I was not content to grant you Paradise until I offered you the spectacle of seeing Me! If such are My actions, how is their doubt over My generosity?

O slave. There is certainly a receiver for each of My blessings. There is certainly one to accept each of My bounties. I am Self-Sufficient and have no use for such things – this is proven by certain evidence. Even if you were to ask Me to prevent My provisions from reaching you, I would not agree to your request. Even if you were to ask me to deprive you of My bounty, I would not deprive you of them. Then how is the case when you continually and constantly ask of Me? So be ashamed to doubt Me. And if you cannot show shame, then at least understand Me. I certainly give endlessly to those who understand Me.

O slave. Make Me the one who chooses for you and do not choose for Me. Direct your heart with sincerity to Me. If you do so, I will show you wonders from My kindness and marvels from My generosity. I will delight your heart by opening it to Me. I have certainly made apparent the right way to the exacting people of knowledge. I have made evident the landmarks of guidance to those that deserve Divine support. Those of certain faith have then surrendered to Me truthfully. The believers trust in Me by clear proofs. They realised that I am better for them than they are for themselves. And that My management for them is more advantageous than their own self-direction. Hence they have submissively yielded to My nurturing Lordship. They have cast their own selves to Me, trusting in My plan. I exchanged that with placing relief in their selves, light in their intellects, intimate knowledge in their hearts and realisation of My nearness in their heart of hearts. And that is just in this world. When they come before Me, I shall honour their ranks, elevate their stations and hoist up high the flags of majesty for them. For them in My Paradise is what no eye has seen, what no ear has heard, and what has never occurred to the mind of any man.

O slave. As for the future, I have not asked you to pay its due of My service, so do not ask Me for what I have allocated to you in it of your provision. For if I have enjoined responsibilities upon you, then I shall provide for you. If I have engaged you in service, I shall feed you. Know that I will not forget you, even though you may forget Me. Know that I remember you before you even remember Me. Know that My sustenance to you is persistent even if you disobey Me. If I am such when you turn away from Me, then how do you think I am when you come close to Me? You have not understood nor valued Me when you do not submit to My conquering power. Nor have you revered Me as I ought to be if you do not comply to My command. Do not turn away from Me, for you will not find one to take My place! Nor rely on other than Me for none will suffice you against Me. I am your Creator by My power and I extend to you My favours. Just as there is no creator other than Me, there is no provider other than Me. Do I create and hand over the reins to others when I am the Kind and Gracious Bestower? Shall I then prevent My slaves from My goodness? So, O slave, have confidence in Me for I am the Nurturing Lord of all. Abandon your other goals alongside Me and I shall deliver you to the true goal! Remember My previous kindnesses upon you and do not forget the rights of true loyalty and love.

We hoped to end this book with a final prayer that suits its topic of discussion.

O Allah, indeed, we ask You to send blessings upon Muhammad and upon the family of Muhammad like you sent blessings on Abraham and the family of Abraham, (send prayers upon them) among all worlds. Indeed you are the Praiseworthy, the Majestic.

O Allah, make us from those who surrender and submit to You. From those who continue to stand before You. Remove us from managing with You or over You. Make us from those who commit their affairs to You.

O Allah, You were there for us before we were even for ourselves. Be for us after our existence like You were for us before our existence. Clothe us with the garments of Your kindness. Receive us with Your tenderness and compassion. Remove the darkness of self-direction from our hearts and illuminate the depths of our hearts with the light of dependence upon You. Make us witness the excellence of Your choosing so that what You have decreed for us and chosen for us is more loved to us than our own choices for ourselves.

O Allah, do not occupy us with what You have guaranteed for us instead of what You have commanded us to do, nor with those things You have chosen for us instead of what you have asked from us.

O Allah, indeed, You have invited us to submit to You and be steadfast in our obedience to You, but we are incapable of fulfilling that unless You enable us. We are weak unless You strengthen us. How can we possibly achieve anything except if You facilitate it for us? How can we reach anywhere unless You take us there? How can we be capable of anything unless You aid us? So grant us success, O Allah, to fulfil what You have commanded us and support us to avoid what You have prohibited us.

O Allah, enter us into the gardens of entrusting affairs to You and into the Paradise of submitting to You and delight us by it and in it but make our inner-hearts be with You and not with the heart's bliss, delights, adornments and attractions.

O Allah, illuminate us with the light of surrendering to You and growing close to You and make our inner-hearts delighted thereby and thereby perfect our lights.

O Allah, indeed, You managed the affairs of all things before all things even existed. We know that only what You will occurs, but this knowledge is not beneficial for us except when You will it to be. O Allah, will for us the goodness of this knowledge, desire for us Your bounty, intend for us Your care and concern, surround us with Your guardianship, clothe us from the garments of Your friends and beloved ones, and enter us into Your protection, You are capable of all things and powerful over all things.

O Allah, we know that Your decision is not opposed, Your decree is not contradicted, that we are incapable of resisting Your judgement and deflecting what You bring about. We ask you for kindness in what You have decreed and help in what You choose to bring about. Make us from among those You guard and protect, O Nurturing Lord of all the worlds!

O Allah, You have indeed apportioned for us Your provision. You will no doubt dispatch it to us. O Allah, make it reach us with happiness, ease and preservation from fatigue, let it arrive in a manner while we are protected from veils and enveloped with lights of attachment to You. Make us witness its arrival directly from You so that we be thankful to You. Let us attribute it to You and not to any creation in all the worlds.

O Allah, indeed provision is in Your hand, the provision of this world and the Hereafter. O Allah, sustain us from it whatever You choose and what You know our benefit to be in. O Allah, strengthen us with the benefits of your sustenance.

O Allah, make us from those who choose You. Do not make us from those who choose for You. Make us from those who entrust affairs to You, not from those who challenge and oppose You.

O Allah, we are poverty-stricken and in need of You, so bestow Your charity upon us. We are incapable of obedience, so empower us. Bestow on us the ability to act in Your obedience and incapability to act in Your disobedience. Grant us submission to Your Nurturing Lordship, patience upon Your Divine decrees, honour us by being connected with You, and relief in our hearts by trusting upon You. Make us from among those that enter the courtyards of contentment and sip from the fountain of submission and who pluck the fruits of intimate knowledge. Clothe us with the robes of honour, grant us the gift of Your nearness, open for us the door to Your presence and bonds of Your love, make us steadfast in Your service, make us from those who truly realise You, followers of Your Messenger, his inheritors, those who take from him, who enact his way and value it, who are worthy deputies of him and seal the endings of our lives with goodness from You, O Nurturing Lord of all the worlds. Ameen.

"Praise be to Allah, Nurturing Lord of the worlds, the Compassionate, the Merciful, Master of the Day of Judgment. Thee alone we worship and from Thee we seek help. Guide us upon the straight path, the path of those whom Thou hast blessed, not of those who incur wrath, nor of those who are astray."

And send peace and blessings upon Muhammad and upon the family of Muhammad.

Titles by Dhikr.

The Illumination on Abandoning Self-Direction,
Al-Tanwir fi Isqat Al-Tadbir.
Ibn Ata'illah Al-Sakandari

Sayidah A'isha: Wife to the Prophet,
Mother to A Nation. A Short Biography.
Dr Muhammad Said Ramadan Al-Bouti

The Reviver of the Second Millenium:
Imam Al-Rabbani.
Shaykh Osman Nuri Topbas

Forthcoming, God Willing:
The Prayer of those Brought Close,
Salat Al-Muqarrabeen
Al-Hassan ibn Salih ibn Aidrous
Al Bahr Al Jafari Al Alawi

dhikr.com.au

www.ingramcontent.com/pod-product-compliance
Lightning Source LLC
Chambersburg PA
CBHW022039290426
44109CB00014B/908